The Glamorgan Centre for
Art & Design Technology

031752

The exhibition is held under the
Patronage of the President of the Swiss Confederation

Flavio Cotti

Theater of Reason / Theater of Desire
The Art of Alexandre Benois and Léon Bakst

Catalogue by
John Bowlt

with contributions by
Richard Buckle
Elizabeth Durst
Alexander Schouvaloff
Alexandre Vassiliev

Thyssen-Bornemisza Foundation

Grafic Design
Marcello Francone

Editorial Coordination
Franco Ambrosio

Editing
Emma Cavazzini

Layout
Mariella Tabacco

Cover illustrations
Léon Bakst
Design for Scene 4:
The Awakening, 1921
(Cat. 52)

Alexandre Benois
Backdrop for the Moor's Room,
Scene 3, 1956
(Cat. 20)

With the generous support of

 CORNÈR BANCA
LUGANO

Distributed outside the United States and Canada
by Thames and Hudson Ltd., 30 Bloomsbury
Street, London WC1B 3QP, United Kingdom

Printed in Italy
In June 1998
by Skira, Geneva - Milan

Theater of Reason / Theater of Desire
The Art of Alexandre Benois and Léon Bakst

Thyssen-Bornemisza Foundation
Villa Favorita, 6976 Castagnola
June 5 - November 1, 1998

Catalogue

by John Bowlt

with contributions by
Richard Buckle, Elizabeth Durst,
Alexander Schouvaloff,
Alexandre Vassiliev

Coordination
Maria de Peverelli

Photography
State Bakhrushin Theater
Museum, Moscow
State Museum of Theater
and Music, St. Petersburg
State Tretiakov Gallery, Moscow
The E.O. Hoppé Trust, Curatorial
Assistance, Pasadena (California)
Metropolitan Museum
of Art, New York
Giuseppe Pennisi, Lugano
Michael Smith, San Antonio
(Texas)
Aneta Zebala, Los Angeles

Exhibition

Curator
John Bowlt

Exhibition Coordinator
Maria de Peverelli

Registrar
Denise Morax

Conservation
Emil Bosshard

Texts for the panels
James Bradburne

Exhibition design
James Bradburne
Maria de Peverelli
with the collaboration of
Takashi Shimura

Installation
Adriano Pierobon
Gianni Mascherin

Installation of Room XIII
Alexandre Vassiliev

Insurance
WILLIS CORROON FINE ART ♦♦♦

Transport
Masterpiece International,
New York
Mat Securitas, Zürich
Momart, London

Press Office
Mara Vitali Comunicazioni,
Milano
Thyssen-Bornemisza Foundation,
Lugano

Lenders

Thyssen-Bornemisza Collection,
Lugano
State Bakhrushin Theater
Museum, Moscow
State Museum of Theater
and Music, St. Petersburg
State Tretiakov Gallery, Moscow
University of Southern California,
Doheny Library, Los Angeles
The E.O. Hoppé Trust, Curatorial
Assistance, Pasadena (California)
Getty Research Institute,
Los Angeles
Institute of Modern Russian
Culture, Los Angeles
Istituto Universitario Orientale,
Napoli
Nina e Nikita D. Lobanov-
Rostovsky, London
The Metropolitan Museum
of Art, New York
Alex Rabinovich, New York
C. and A.L. de Saint-Rat, Oxford
(Ohio)
Alexander Schouvaloff, London
Robert Tobin, San Antonio
(Texas)
Alexandre Vassiliev, Paris
Los Angeles County Museum
of Art

I always liked Bakst and Benois and have collected their works over a long period of time. What fascinated me were their colors and their excellent craftsmanship.
I hope the visitors to this exhibition will be fascinated as well by their way of representing the magic of theater.

Hans Heinrich Thyssen-Bornemisza

Once again, Cornèr Bank has set another date on its artistic agenda, enthusiastically supporting the idea of exhibiting highly refined works which are precious testimonials of the history of art and theater at the beginning of the twentieth century.
Two great leading figures of the famous Ballets Russes, Benois and Bakst, were fundamental in providing an impulse to the transformation of theatrical representation through their costumes and stage sets.
Some of their masterpieces, which are part of the Thyssen-Bornemisza collection, had already caught the attention of Cornèr Bank, which, in 1987, produced a prestigious volume entitled Sets and Costume Designs. It is no coincidence, then, that we have given our full support to this first public exhibition, in this part of Europe, of such works of art, including loans from museums as well as from private collections.
On behalf of Cornèr Bank, I thank the Baron and Baroness Thyssen-Bornemisza, the other lenders of the pieces, the Thyssen-Bornemisza Foundation and all of those who have played a role in the making of this splendid event, which will contribute to spreading knowledge of works of art in local collections as well as in collections abroad from such an original and interesting area.
I truly hope that an ever wider public will be able to admire and enjoy the works exhibited.

Luigi Dell'Acqua
General Manager of Cornèr Bank

*My first encounter with the works of Léon Bakst and Alexandre Benois in the Thyssen-
Bornemisza Collection goes back to 1986, when, during my stay at Daylesford House,
Baron Thyssen-Bornemisza's English residence, I had the opportunity to examine
the sketches which will be shown here to the public for the first time.
In the following year the book* Set and Costume Designs for Ballet and Theatre
in the Thyssen-Bornemisza Collection *by Alexander Schouvaloff was published;
he was director of the Theater Museum in London at that time. This publication marked
the beginning of a period of collaboration with the Cornèr Bank of Lugano,
which also became an enthusiastic supporter of this exhibition.
Figures created by Bakst, like the vindictive sultan or the Sultan Samarcande,
or the sketch for the set of the second scene of the "Princess Swan" by Benois made a lasting
impression on me, and instilled a long-standing desire to organize an exhibit based on this
group of works. My encounter with John Bowlt of the Institute of Modern Russian Culture
at the University of Southern California was a godsend. His interest in and enthusiasm
for the project, together with his in-depth knowledge of the subject, were not only encouraging,
but more importantly, a source of continual discovery. The world of the Ballets Russes
opened before my eyes; its magic enchanted me. Without him, it would never have been
possible to produce this exhibition or this catalogue.
Unpublished documents, photographs, costumes, postcards and posters from the period
have been selected by John Bowlt to go together with the sketches by the two artists,
in order to emphasize differences while at the same time presenting, through the creations
of two of its greatest interpreters, the work of Diaghilev. This ingenious impresario carried
the ballet to the empyrean heights of the fine arts through the fusion of movement, music
and stage design, —characteristics which have marked it for the entire twentieth century.
The unconditioned support from Baron and Baroness Thyssen-Bornemisza, who have made
available works which are usually part of the interior decoration at the Villa Favorita,
as well as all the others lenders, has been just as important.
I extend my most heartfelt thanks to them.
Meeting James Bradburne, the museologist who was entrusted with the "interpretation"
of this show, was also fundamental. Our ability to understand more about the world
of the theater and of the personalities of Bakst and Benois, and to be transported into their
world, is largely due to his text for the descriptive panels of the exhibit. It was a real pleasure
to work with him.*

*I also thank the two authors of the articles in the catalogue, Richard Buckle
and Alexander Schouvaloff, for agreeing to work with us.
Alexandre Vassiliev is a direct descendent of the world of the Ballet Russes: he is Russian,
but has lived in Paris for several years. A set designer and collector of costumes,
he has reinterpreted the sets for two scenes which are considered Bakst's
and Benois' masterpieces,* Schéhérazade *and* Petrushka, *especially for this exhibit.
It is impossible not to mention the continual support from the publishing house Skira
in Milan, and all of my assistants here in Lugano: Emil Bosshard, Denise Morax, Christine
Bader Nicoli, Loredana Battalora, Adriano Pierobon and Gianni Mascherin.
The enthusiasm of the Cornèr Bank, and of Dr. Paolo Cornaro, Dr. Luigi Dell'Acqua
and Anna Russo in particular, has been fundamental to the production of this exhibit.
My thanks to them for having believed in this project, and for having let themselves
be seduced – like all of us – by the magic of the work of Bakst and Benois and their way
of conceiving of the world of ballet.*

Maria de Peverelli
Gallery Director of the Thyssen-Bornemisza Foundation

Table of Contents

Acknowledgements

"Theater of Reason / Theater of Desire.
The Art of Alexandre Benois and Léon Bakst"
is the fruit of a collective effort and many
individuals and institutions have given
their encouragement. However, without the
ready support of the Thyssen-Bornemisza
Foundation and Collection, to which many
of the works belong, this Exhibition would
not have been possible and primary thanks,
therefore, must go to Baron Hans Heinrich
Thyssen-Bornemisza.
Among those who helped the Exhibition with
loans of works or wise counsel, particular
mention should be made of the following:
John Ahouse, Natalia Aleksandrova, Natalia
Avtonomova, Nancy Van Norman Baer,
Lia Barshchevsky, Elena Basner, Disma Benois
De Cecco, Richard Buckle, Paola Cortella,
Jim Dimitroff, Elizabeth Durst, Irina
Evstigneeva, Tim Geiger, Linda Hardberger,
Helen Kizler, Susan Kechekian, Tatiana Klim,
Mark Konecny, Iosif Lempert, Nina and Nikita
Lobanov-Rostovsky, Natalia Metelitsa, Nicoletta
Misler, Erik Näslund, Evgeniia Petrova,
Alik Rabinovich, Sandra Rosenbaum, Catherine
and André L. de Saint-Rat, Alexander
Schouvaloff, Hilary K. Snow, Alexandre
Vassiliev, Dimitri Vicheney, Lidiia Yovleva,
Ekaterina Yudina, and Aneta Zebala;
Aurora Publishers, St. Petersburg; Costume
Institute and the Department of Prints and
Drawings, The Metropolitan Museum of Art,
New York; Dansmuseet, Stockholm; Doheny
Library, University of Southern California,
Los Angeles; Doris Stein Research and Design
Center for Costumes and Textiles, Los Angeles
County Museum of Art; Galart, Moscow; J. Paul
Getty Research Institute, Los Angeles; Harry
Ransom Center, University of Texas at Austin;
Hazlitt, Gooden and Fox, London; The E.O.
Hoppé Trust, Curatorial Assistance, Pasadena,
California; Institute of Modern Russian Culture,
Los Angeles; Iskusstvo, Moscow; Istituto
Universitario Orientale, Naples; Marion Koogler
McNay Museum, San Antonio, Texas; State
Bakhrushin Theater Museum, Moscow; State
Museum of Theater and Music, St. Petersburg;
and State Tretiakov Gallery, Moscow.
"Theater of Reason / Theater of Desire"
is devoted to the art of Alexandre Benois
and Léon Bakst both within and beyond their
careers as stage designers; it is not, therefore,
just another survey of Sergei Diaghilev
and the Ballets Russes. While constituting
the focal point of the exhibition, the relevant
works in the Thyssen-Bornemisza Collection
have been supplemented by a number of pieces
drawn from other museums and private
collections. Inevitably, important loans are
missing, in part because 1998 coincides with
the centennial celebration of the founding
of the World of Art society and the 90th
anniversary of the first season of the Ballets
Russes, both enterprises being closely linked
to the artistic development of Benois and Bakst.
Naturally, these jubilees have prompted the
organization of concurrent exhibitions in
Moscow, St. Petersburg, Helsinki and elsewhere,
exhibitions that incorporate works of direct
relevance to "Theater of Reason / Theater
of Desire". However, if Bakst's portraits
of Benois (1898) and Sergei Diaghilev (1906)
or Benois' more familiar pictures of Versailles
are missing, there are also paintings and
documents that are being displayed here for
the first time and that will shed new light
on the complex careers of these two stellar
members of Russia's modern movement.

Notes to the Reader

Transliteration

The English language transliteration of the Russian modifies the Library of Congress system, so that the Russian soft and hard signs have either been omitted or rendered by an "i" (e.g., Grigoriev). This system is also used throughout the footnotes and the bibliographical data where references involve Russian language sources. This catalog will be read by people who appreciate the visual and performing arts, but who may not know Russian. Consequently, the more sophisticated academic transliteration systems that, to the layman, may render a recognizable name (e.g., Chekhov) unrecognizable (e.g., Cexov), have been avoided. Many Russian artists and writers spent part of their lives in Europe or the United States and often their names received various, even contradictory, transliterations from the original Russian into the language of their adopted home. For the sake of uniformity, however, names have been transliterated in accordance with the above system, except when a variant has long been established and recognized, e.g., Alexandre Benois (which is used in the main text), not Aleksandr Benua (which is, however, used in the transliteration of the titles of Russian sources).

Times and Places

Dates referring to events in Russia before January 1918 are in the Old Style. Consequently, if they are in the 19th century, then they are twelve days behind the Western calendar, whereas if they are between 1900 and 1918 they are thirteen days behind. The city of St. Petersburg was renamed Petrograd in 1914, Leningrad in 1924, and then St. Petersburg again in 1992. However, both the names Petrograd and St. Petersburg continued to be used freely in common parlance and in publications until 1924. As a general rule, however, Petrograd has been retained here as the official name of St. Petersburg for the period 1914-1924. Titles of books, catalogs, journals, and newspapers are italicized; titles of articles, manuscripts, and exhibitions are in quotation marks, but names of societies and institutions are not.

Abbreviations

Cat. = *List if Works (1-72)*
D = *Documents Section (D1-D92)*
Fig. = *Figure Illustration (Fig. 1-79)*
LRC = *John E. Bowlt,* Sobranie Nikity i Niny Lobanovykh-Rostovskikh. Khudozhniki russkogo teatra 1880-1930. Katalog-rezone, *Iskusstvo, Moscow 1994 (This is the catalogue raisonné of the Lobanov-Rostovsky collection of Russian stage design)*
RGALI = Rossiiskii Gosudarstvennyi arkhiv literatury i iskusstva *(Russian State Archive of Literature and Art), Moscow*
TBC = *Alexander Schouvaloff,* The Thyssen-Bornemisza Collection. Set and Costume Designs for Ballet and Theatre, *Sotheby's Publications, London 1987*

1. Photograph of Alexandre
Benois in his study,
St. Petersburg, ca. 1914.
Photograph courtesy of Natalia
Aleksandrova, Moscow

Sense and Sensuality

"Theater of Reason, Theater of Desire: The Art of
Alexandre Benois and Léon Bakst" is devoted to the work
of two of Russia's foremost artists of the 20th century,
Alexandre Benois (Aleksandr Nikolaevich Benua, 1870-
1960; Figs. 1, 2, 3, 4, 5) and Léon Bakst (Lev
Samoilovich Bakst, 1866-1924; Figs. 6, 7, 8, 9, 10, 11,
57, 65)[1] Benois and Bakst are remembered for many
achievements – their sets and costumes for Sergei
Diaghilev's Ballets Russes and other theater companies
(Figs. 12, 13), their book designs, portraits and landscapes and, in Benois' case, at least, critical essays on a
wide variety of cultural subjects. The two artists had
much in common: they owed their early development to
the cultural ambience of St. Petersburg, they were central members of the World of Art
group, contributing regularly to its publications and exhibitions (D34-D36), they made
each other's portraits (Fig. 14), they collaborated on the Contemporary Art enterprise
(Cat. 6; Figs. 15, 16), and, of course, they were partly responsible for the "artistic bac-
chanalia"[2] that the first seasons of the Ballets Russes presented to their Paris audiences
(Figs. 17, 18, 19) – Benois with *Le Pavillon d'Armide* and *Petrushka* (Cat. 7-16,18-31;
D48, D76, D83, D91, D92) and Bakst with *Cléopatre* and *Schéhérazade* (Cat. 45; D61,
D66, D67).

    The posthumous careers of Benois and Bakst also intertwine, for their names contin-
ue to grace the same books and catalogs concerned with the Diaghilev era, while their
respective legacies, visual and verbal, have suffered a similar, ignominious fate, fragment-
ed, sold piecemeal, and scattered throughout Europe, Russia, the United States and Asia.
The unique collection of books and papers that Benois amassed during his emigration,
for example, was simply dismantled as a result of unscrupulous private sales and auctions
in the 1980s,[3] while Bakst has become a favorite target of numerous forgers, some very
skilful. Obviously, this diffusion and distortion of materials do not facilitate enquiry into
the careers of the two artists, especially outside the popular subject of the Ballets Russes.
Even so, one purpose of this exhibition and its catalog is to focus attention on the less
familiar, but formative years of Benois and Bakst, especially their interaction with the
World of Art group, rather than to repeat basic information that is already widely avail-

3. Photograph of Alexandre Benois by S. Branzburg published to mark his collaboration with the Moscow Arts Theater. Reproduced in *Solntse Rossii,* Petrograd 1915, May, p. 12

2. Photograph of Alexandre Benois in his study, St. Petersburg, ca. 1914. Photograph courtesy of Natalia Aleksandrova, Moscow

4. Photograph of Alexandre Benois by Eugène Lipnitzki, ca. 1949.
Reproduced in N.D. Yantchevsky, *Apollon en flammes,* Le Groupe initiatif des artistes et amateurs d'art, Paris 1949, p. 21

5. Georgii Vereisky (1886-1962),
Portrait of Alexandre Benois, 1922
Lithograph.
Reproduced from Georgii
Vereisky, *Portrety russkikh
khudozhnikov,* Committee
for the Popularization of Artistic
Editions at the Russian Academy
of Material Culture, St. Petersburg
1922, unpaginated

6. Photograph of Léon Bakst,
1906. Photographer unknown.
Courtesy of Aurora Publishers,
St. Petersburg.
The booklet visible on the left
hand side of the table is
the catalog of the Russian Section
of the "Salon d'Automne" (D41)
that Sergei Diaghilev organized
in Paris in 1906 and for which
Bakst designed the sculpture
garden. The two prefaces
to the catalog were written
by Diaghilev and Alexandre
Benois and the cover was designed
by Ivan Bilibin. The stuffed raven
in the middle of the desk would
indicate that Bakst shared
the Symbolist vogue for Edgar
Allan Poe

9. Photograph of Léon Bakst.
Reproduced in *Stolitsa i usadba,*
St. Petersburg, 1914, 20 April,
p. 18 (photographer unknown).
See D47

8. P. Choumoff (P.I. Shumov),
Photograph of Léon Bakst
in his Paris studio at 112,
Bd. Malesherbes, ca. 1920.
He is holding a Chinese porcelain
figure. See D17

7. Léon Bakst,
Self-Portrait, 1906
Colored crayon and sanguine,
75.8 × 51.8 cm
Moscow, State Tretiakov Gallery

10. Photograph of Léon Bakst. Reproduced in *Iskusstvo,* Petrograd 1917, No. 5-6, between pp. 12-13 (photographer unknown)

11. Photograph accompanying Léon Bakst's obituary in the journal *Zhar-ptitsa* (Fire Bird), Berlin 1925, No. 13, p. 17 (photographer unknown).

able. After all, Diaghilev's Ballets Russes and Benois' and Bakst's involvement have been described on numerous occasions, the chronology has been established, audience reaction documented, and interrelationships defined thanks to the extensive publications on Benois, Bakst, Diaghilev, Michel Fokine, and Igor Stravinsky within the context of the ballet.[4]

But if Benois and Bakst shared many things, they were also competitors and antagonists. Each possessed his own emotional and artistic psyche (Benois the man of reason, Bakst of desire), each followed his own religious and ideological orientation, and each occupied his own social and familial station (Benois the faithful husband and affectionate father of three, Bakst the divorcee, constantly tempted by "jeunes ballerines en chemises de nuit").[5] Benois was the cosmopolitan *intelligent* of Russia's Silver Age, Bakst was the provincial Jew, painfully aware of his unstable place in the social mesh of the Russian Empire. Yet, for all his fortune and fertility, Benois was – and still is – overshadowed by his rival and it is Bakst, not Benois, who is now advocated as the foremost stage designer of our time, and perhaps he already realized this when, in a huff and a puff, the "Jesuit" Shura insulted the "Levantine" Levushka after the *Petrushka* episode in June, 1911 thus suspending their close personal and professional interaction.[6] When Bakst died in 1924 Benois chose not to write an obituary, although he did mollify his attitude in later years.

A primary aim of this exhibition is to address difference rather than similarity and to remove Benois and Bakst from the confining template of the Ballets Russes or, rather, to present them as perpetrators of many different creative actions both inside and outside of Diaghilev's perimeter. After all, Benois was also a fine book designer and a perspicacious historian, while Bakst left a deep imprint on the *hautes coutures* of St. Petersburg and Paris. In particular, Benois should be recognized as much for his essays on Russian and European art and architecture as for his paintings and designs and he was also a masterful chronicler of the momentous events that transformed his country, to which his diaries – excerpts of which are published below – bear strong witness. The real stature of Benois the scholar, the critic, and the connoisseur has yet to be delineated and it is to be hoped that, in this regard, the documentary section of this catalog will prove to be of particular benefit. Recent research on Benois and Bakst both in Russia and the West has done a great deal to fill lacunae and rectify imbalances, but much has yet to be done, especially with regard to their early, pre-balletic careers: this exhibition is offered, therefore, as a tribute to their diverse accomplishments in the hope that it will bring into deeper relief the disparity and multiplicity of their creative personalities.

The World of Art

In order to understand why Benois and Bakst developed in the ways that they did, the researcher is bound to direct primary attention to their various activities within the group of artists, writers, and musicians known as the World of Art (*Mir iskusstva*).[7] To a considerable extent, the attitudes, preferences, and rituals of the World of Art informed and predetermined the early careers of the two artists and many of their subsequent conjunctions and disjunctions can be explained by reference to this.

By the late 1890s a group of artists, esthetes and critics had come together in St. Petersburg united in their hostility towards both the Academy of Arts and the canons of didactic Realism. Led at first by Benois and the writer Dmitrii Filosofov, this self-styled Society of Nevsky Pickwickians was joined in 1890 by Filosofov's cousin, Sergei Diaghilev (Fig. 20), who eight years later welded the group into the World of Art: and it was this circle of young men that launched the famous magazine of the same name (*Mir iskusstva,* 1898-1904), organized two series of important exhibitions (1899-1906; 1910-24), and propagated Russian art and music so successfully in the West (Fig. 12), especially through the spectacular productions of the Ballets Russes. While not a painter or a

12. Photograph of Sergei Diaghilev (1872-1929), New York, 1916. Photograph courtesy of private collection, New York.

13. Photograph of Sergei Diaghilev (1872-1929), 1928, carrying the dedication "A mon cher ami King avec mes meilleurs souvenirs. Serge Diaghilev, 1928" Reproduced in *Les Ballets Russes de Serge de Diaghilev, 1909-1929*. Catalog of exhibition à l'Ancienne Douane, Strasbourg, 1969, unpaginated.

14. Léón Bakst, *Portrait of Alexandre Benois*, 1898 Watercolor and pastel, 64.5 × 100.3 cm St. Petersburg, State Russian Museum

15. Photograph of the Boudoir by Léón Bakst at the Contemporary Art Showrooms, St. Petersburg, 1902-1903. Photograph courtesy of Iskusstvo, Moscow

16. Photograph of the dining room by Alexandre Benois and Evgenii Lancéray (1875-1946) at the Contemporary Art Showrooms, St. Petersburg, 1902-1903. Benois' panneau *Diana* (Cat. 6) can be recognized in the background. Photograph courtesy of Iskusstvo, Moscow

poet, Diaghilev was an accomplished musician, an inde-fatigable organizer, and a perceptive critic, and it was thanks mainly to his efforts that the World of Art attract-ed the financial support of the wealthy patrons Savva Mamontov and Princess Mariia Tenisheva.

The World of Art artists never issued a written mani-festo, but it would be fair to summarize their initial credo as "art for art's sake", and their attention to artistic craft, their cult of retrospective beauty, and their comparative alienation from socio-political reality linked them imme-diately with the Russian Symbolist writers, many of whom frequented their meetings. The major figures of the group, Bakst, Benois, Ivan Bilibin (Fig. 21), Mstislav Dobujinsky, Evgenii Lancéray, Anna Ostroumova-Lebedeva (Fig. 61), Nicholas Roerich, Valentin Serov, and Konstantin Somov (Fig. 62), shared, above all, the desire to recapture a formal discipline which, they felt, had been lost with the technical laxity of 19th century Russian nar-rative painting. Thus we find that some of the greatest achievements of the World of Art painters are to be found in those art forms that dictate concentration on linear discipline or are governed by rigid conventions – the miniature, the silhouette, book illustration, and stage design. This is not to say, of course, that the *miriskusniki* ignored other areas of pictorial endeavor: Bakst and Somov produced remarkable portraits of their contempo-raries, such as of the writers Andrei Bely, Alexander Blok, and Zinaida Gippius and most members of the group were fine landscapists.

The World of Art covered a multiplicity of artistic phenomena – the demonic art of Mikhail Vrubel and the stylizations of the early Vasilii Kandinsky, the graphics of Aubrey Beardsley and the German Simplicissimus group, the Art Nouveau designs of Charles Rennie Mackintosh and the poetry of Konstantin Balmont, the retrospec-tivism of Benois and the exoticism of Bakst. Still, there were certain principles that drew the World of Art artists and writers together, for example, their mutual striving to create a *Gesamtkunstwerk* – manifest, for example, in the general enthusiasm for Richard Wagner (on whom Benois wrote on several occasions). True, the World of Art empha-sized the visual and the performing arts, but it was in touch with the leading representa-tives of all the humanistic disciplines and acted as a platform for the cross-fertilization of esthetic concepts. The *miriskusniki* were also bound by a common fascination with remote epochs, such as Ancient Greece, pagan Russia, the Middle East and Versailles, antiquities which they cultivated as the embodiment of moral and social integration. They also tended to interpret art as "craft" rather than as "religion" and to deny it an immediate social or political use. In other words, the World of Art served as a cultural intersection, rather than as the advocate of a single idea, for, it was, as one of its mem-bers remembered, "the cult of dilettantism in the good and true sense of the word".[8]

Beginning their real careers under the auspices of the World of Art, both Benois and Bakst designed and illustrated numerous publications, including *Mir iskusstva,* with ele-

17. *Souvenir Program for the Russian Opera and Ballet at the Royal Theatre, Drury Lane* (London season), 1914, with set and costume designs by Léon Bakst. Paris, Brunoff, 1914. See D43

18. *Souvenir Program for Serge de Diaghileff's Ballet Russe* (New York season), with set and costume designs by Léon Bakst, New York, Morris Gest, 1916. See D44

19. *Souvenir Program for "The Sleeping Princess"*, Alhambra Theatre, London, with set and costume designs by Léon Bakst, Brunoff, Paris 1921. See D45

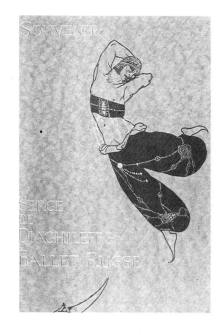

20. Alexandre Benois,
Portrait of Sergei Diaghilev, 1907
Ink and pencil. 34.1 × 37 cm
St. Petersburg, State Russian
Museum.

21. Ivan Bilibin,
Fragment of a page from a sketch
album, 1905
Pencil and watercolor,
24.3 × 16.2 cm
St. Petersburg, Artist's family.
Reproduced in S. Golynets,
Ivan Yakovlevich Bilibin,
Leningrad, Khudozhnik RSFSR,
1970, between pp. 112 and 113.
Courtesy of Sergei Golynets

gant vignettes, title-pages, and tail-pieces (some of which are included in this exhibition) and often collaborated on common ventures such as Diaghilev's *Ezhegodnik Imperatorskikh teatrov* (Annual of the Imperial Theaters) for 1899-1900 (D23) with contributions by Bakst and Somov. Benois and Bakst were also eager supporters of the later Modernist journals such as *Zolotoe runo* (Golden Fleece, D55), *Apollon* (Apollo, D2); Fig. 22), and *Lukomore* (The Shore, Fig. 71). Indeed, a salient characteristic of the World of Art group was its endeavor to integrate the arts into synthetic disciplines such as the book and the opera, while emphasizing individual interpretation – principles also identifiable with the Ballets Russes, especially of the first phase (1909-14). As Serge Lifar asserted,[9] the Ballets Russes can and should be perceived as an immediate extension of the artistic "ideology" of the St. Petersburg group. But how did Bakst, Benois, Diaghilev, Somov and their colleagues regard the medium of the theater in 1900 and what exactly were the creative links between their own artistic principles and those of the Ballets Russes? What is important to remember here is that, in its initial phase, the World of Art was not especially interested in the ballet as such and the subject received very little discussion on the pages of the journal. On the other hand, as Benois recalled, they were all driven by a "mania for the theater",[10] even if they preferred opera to dramatic theater and the ballet. Benois, for example, was so fascinated by the stage that as early as 1905 he was "dreaming of holding to just one enduring cause in the future. And insofar as I know myself, I would do best of all in the theater".[11] In opera Benois and Diaghilev, at least, had very definite opinions: paying homage to a vogue of their time, they praised Wagner and the operatic drama, especially *Tristan und Isolde*, *Die Walkyrie*, and *Die Götterdämmerung*.[12] "I'm fed up with Beethoven", wrote Benois in 1896, "What is he in comparison with Bach!! Or Wagner!!!"[13]

Diaghilev's abrupt disengagement from his administrative position at the Mariinsky Theater after the abortive *Sylvia* episode in 1901[14] and his general intolerance of the cumbersome state bureaucracy impelled him rapidly towards the establishment of his own troupe in 1909. Nevertheless, it would be wrong to assume that all was unwell in the Imperial Theaters in the late 19th and early 20th centuries. After all, most of Diaghilev's key dancers received their training within the Imperial ballet system and a number of Diaghilev's experimental ballets actually had their premieres (albeit in tamer versions) on the Imperial stage. For example, *Egyptian Nights*, which became *Cléopâtre* in 1909 in Paris, was first produced by Fokine at the Mariinsky in 1908, as was *Le Pavillon d'Armide* in 1907.

These remarks notwithstanding, stage design became probably the most exciting and enduring area of activity for the World of Art artists. As far as Diaghilev's Ballets Russes was concerned, it was the stage designs that astounded, angered or perplexed the Edwardian public at least as much as Nijinsky's leap or Stravinsky's brave discordance. Yet ironically – in view of the success – not one of Diaghilev's Russian designers was actually trained as a designer or decorator and all came to the stage by way of studio painting. Moreover, most of the artists were graduates not of the St. Petersburg Academy of Arts, but of private schools and studios more often than not in Munich and Paris. Some, perhaps even Benois, were simply brilliant amateurs, but far from hindering Diaghilev's designers, the absence of a strict, academic mentality provided them with a necessary flexibility, enabling Benois, for example, to move easily from France in *Le Pavillon d'Armide* or Russia in *Petrushka* to China in *Le Rossignol* (Cat. 32), and Bakst from Ancient Greece in *Hippolytus* (Cat. 42) or 19th century St. Petersburg in *La Fée des Poupées* (Cat. 43) to 17th century France in *The Sleeping Princess* (Cat. 52-55; D31, 45).

The World of Art artists looked backwards rather than forwards, although their reveries were not limited to any one historical epoch. Apart from Egypt, Greece, and Versailles, they also cultivated a strong interest in the Middle Ages and even in 'primitive'

24. Kuzma Petrov-Vodkin
(1878-1929), *Portrait
of Alexandre Benois,* 1912
Pencil, 52.5 × 42 cm
St. Petersburg, State Russian
Museum

22. Léon Bakst, Frontispiece
for the journal *Apollon* (Apollo),
St. Petersburg 1909. No. 1.
See D2.

23. (Mikhail Vrubel).
Photograph taken at the funeral
of Mikhail Vrubel (1856-1910).
Standing from right to left
are Boris Kustodiev, Alexander
Benois, Valentin Serov,
Ivan Bilibin, Léon Bakst,
Nicholas Roerich, Elena Roerich,
Nadezhda Zabela-Vrubel (?),
and Alexander Blok.
Photograph courtesy of Institute
of Modern Russian Culture,
Los Angeles

25. Elizaveta Kruglikova (1865-1941), *Silhouette of Léon Bakst,* 1914. Photograph courtesy of Khudozhnik RSFSR, Moscow

26. Elizaveta Kruglikova (1865-1941), *Silhouette of Alexandre Benois and his Wife, Anna Karlovna,* 1916. Reproduced in *Stolitsa i usadba,* Petrograd 1916, 15 December, No. 72, p. 26

cultures as is demonstrated by their deep reverence for Vrubel (Fig. 23), whose art they regarded as the incarnation of an archaic, barbaric force, a world of ancient myth and elemental unity. Bakst's integration of ethnographical fact and magic fantasy in his interpretations of Hellas (as in his curtain for Komissarzhevskaia's Dramatic Theater in 1906 – Cat. 40 – or in his vast painting called *Terror Antiquus* of 1908) crystallized the Symbolists' demand that humankind recapture an earlier, more pristine condition, a concept that Bakst discussed in his lead article of 1909 on "The New Paths of Classicism": "Painting of the future calls for a lapidary style, because the new art cannot endure the refined (...) Painting of the future will crawl down into the depths of coarseness..."[15] But Bakst was anticipating not only the advent of a fresh and adolescent culture, but also the demise of the World of Art itself, for its crafted elegance was no match for the abrasive pressure of the new generation, i.e., the Russian avant-garde, a term, incidentally, that Benois seems to have coined in 1910.[16]

27. Front cover of the journal *Stolitsa i usadba* (Town and Country), Petrograd, 1916, No. 60-61, 1 July, showing a scene from *Petrushka*. See D48

As a titled society the World of Art existed in Russia until 1924, the year of its last exhibition in Leningrad. By then the society differed substantially from the original composition, for it was no longer at the forefront of artistic experiment, lacked the albeit cantankerous leadership of Diaghilev and functioned basically as an exhibition forum. True, when the society was recreated in 1910, it attracted most of the original members and the continued presence of Benois, Bilibin, Dobujinsky, Igor Grabar, Roerich, and Somov ensured a continuity of style and taste. Younger converts such as Egor Narbut, Alexandre Jacovleff, Kuzma Petrov-Vodkin (Fig. 24), and Vasilii Shukhaev upheld the properties of restraint and common sense and their work (e.g. Elizaveta Kruglikova's silhouettes – Figs. 25, 26 – and Narbut's alphabet) reflected these principles. In emigration, too, the World of Art survived throughout the 1920s, organizing titled exhibitions in Paris in 1921 and 1927, but by then it had lost its esthetic denominator and sense of purpose. Even so, without the World of Art, neither Bakst, nor Benois would have attained the heights that they did and, in spite of cardinal differences, were both molded by its "cult of dilettantism" and its perverse interplay of reason and desire.

Alexandre Benois

How difficult it is to offer an adequate appreciation of the artistic and intellectual career of Alexandre Benois. His erudition was extraordinary and he wrote on the most diverse subjects, from Watteau to toys, from Palestrina to snuff boxes; between 1912 and 1917 he issued twenty-two fascicles of his monumental *Istoriia zhivopisi vsekh vremen i nardorov* (The History of Painting of All Times and of All Peoples),[17] and he published numerous reviews and essays in leading newspapers both in Russia [e.g. in *Rech* (Discourse)] and in France [e.g. in *Poslednie novosti* (Latest News)]. In his achievements, visual and verbal, Benois manifested a moderation and sobriety where Diaghilev was impetuous, a restraint where Bakst was lavish, a precision where Roerich was liberal. His friend Dobujinsky (Cat. 1) once wrote that good taste could be defined as being a "sense of measure",[18] and Benois, indeed, possessed this measured reason, a property, however, that sometimes degenerated into an overly cautious pedantry – contravening Dostoevsky's assertion that "Dreams (...) are impelled not by reason, but by desire".[19] No doubt, with such a worldview, Benois felt more at home in the 17th and 18th centuries than in the 20th and his immersion in the culture of Versailles (Cat. 3, 4; D14) is clear evidence of this. After all, the most celebrated artist of our century, Picasso, was for Benois no more than a symptom of our "deplorable culture" (which also included Cézanne, Rodin, Rousseau, and Van Gogh).[20]

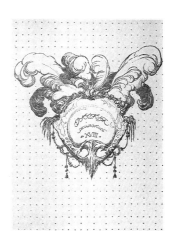

30. Léon Bakst, Frontispiece for Sergei Diaghilev, *Russkaia zhivopis v XVIII veke. D.G. Levitsky, 1735-1822* (Russian Painting in the18th Century. D.G. Levitsky, 1735-1822), St. Petersburg 1902. See D24

Many of the statements that Benois published on the history and function of visual culture seem to extend the same principles of that very status quo which the World of Art claimed to renounce. This is inherent in his attitude towards the Academy of Arts

28. Léon Bakst,
Illustration to Volume 3,
Chapter III, of Nikolai Kutepov's
Velikokniazheskaia i tsarskaia okhota na Rusi, s X po XVI vek
(Hunting in Russia by the Great Princes and the Tsars),
St. Petersburg 1902. See D30 (a)

29. Alexandre Benois,
Illustration to Volume 4,
Chapter V, of Nikolai Kutepov's
Velikokniazheskaia i tsarskaia okhota na Rusi, s X po XVI vek
(Hunting in Russia by the Great Princes and the Tsars], St.
Petersburg, 1911. See D30 (b)

in St. Petersburg and to academies in general, for, on the one hand, he condemned them as representing the "domination of traditions (...) over free creativity (...) and a tendency to use ready-made schemes"[21] and refused the title of Academician in 1912 (Bakst, however, accepting it in 1914), yet, on the other, he was incensed when angry young artists dared to undermine the classical esthetic. The ambivalence may derive from his own brief and unhappy tenure at the Academy, a moment of "shameful failure".[22] In any case, like his World of Art colleagues, Benois still supported an art that was figurative, insisting that what was important in art was the clear definition and purpose of plastic form and, consequently, he had little patience with radical digressions from hallowed tradition. Yet any history or historiography of modern Russian art must take full account of Benois, for not only did he describe in vivid detail the artistic events of his time, participate in numerous exhibitions, enter into a vast correspondence with luminaries at home and abroad, but in some degree he also epitomized the salient characteristic of his generation – eclecticism. Just as his forebear, Louis-Jules Benois, *maître de bouche* to Paul I, had achieved a solid reputation for his tasteful confections, so Benois amazes by his esthetic and critical versatility. As Ostromuova-Lebedeva recalled, Benois' "intellect was a creative one and this creative principle was inexhaustible. Everything he apprehended (...) underwent a processing by this brilliant mind. His speed of perception was astounding and he had the rare gift of being able to orient himself in unfamiliar territory".[23]

All the more curious, therefore, that Benois, resentful of the weight of the Academy and eager to explore fresh fields and pastures new, at least in the theater, was so adamantly opposed to the epicurean individualism of his time. On the one hand, he could welcome fresh and radical talent – for example, he recommended that Natalia Goncharova be designer for *The Golden Cockerel* in 1914 – but, on the other, could refer to the art of her generation as being analogous to the "puerility, chaos, and unruliness of savages".[24] Identifying these qualities as the consequence of social irresponsibility, Benois expressed grave concern for the welfare of the sense, measure, and reason that he promoted: "Artists have crawled into their own corners, they seek consolation in their own self-delight, fight shy of mutual influences and try to be 'themselves', whatever the cost. Chaos reigns, something turbid, having hardly any value and, strangest of all, any physiognomy".[25]

A principal reason for the velocity and diversity of Benois' intellect lay simply in his upbringing. His father, Nikolai Leontievich, was an architect and academician, his maternal grandfather, Albert Kavos (Alberto Cavos), had been largely responsible for the design of the old Mariinsky and Bolshoi Theaters in St. Petersburg (Cat. 5) and for the reconstruction of the Bolshoi Theater in Moscow after the fire of 1853, his mother Kamilla was an accomplished musician, his uncle Albert was a celebrated watercolorist, while his elder brother, Leontii, was an architect. From his youngest days Benois was surrounded by art: Guardi sepias, 18th century furniture, language of conversation that combined French and Russian, frequent excursions to the theater and to Pavlovsk and Peterhof, a condition that generated the "historical sentimentalism"[26] to which Benois returned again and again. Deeply attached to the sweet experiences of his childhood, Benois gave them particular attention in his memoirs and some of his most enduring achievements such as the designs for the Russian alphabet (Cat. 38 ; D7), for toys (Cat. 39), and *Petrushka* (Cat. 18-31; Fig. 27) evoke the innocent pastimes of his childhood spent with puppets, tin soldiers, charades, and fairy-tales. So deeply ingrained was this "childishness" that Benois even applied what he felt were the metaphorical values of toys to subjects of serious artistic discourse, dismissing Böcklin, Klinger, and Stuck, for example, as "broken toys" and, therefore, as worthless.[27]

A 'Benois connection' can be recognized in many cultural phenomena of the Russian *fin de siècle,* a phenomenon, however, that sometimes elicited indignation and accusations of nepotism, especially on the part of the avant-garde.[28] Conversely, Benois' own scholarship and connoisseurship informed the taste of an entire generation of Russian artists and critics, as the designer Dimitri Bouchène indicated in a letter to Benois of 1931: "From the moment that I first saw your works in 1908, I think, and read what you wrote, your words have served me as a guiding star (...) I realize that no-one could ever do more for me".[29] Writers, too, such as the novelist Boris Zaitsev, regarded Benois as their mentor, especially if Versailles was the subject of discussion: "In this Benois was at home, he knew everything, explained everything, and we listened with reverence. We really felt like pupils, like children from far off Muscovy. For Benois all these palaces, galleries of mirrors, and Trianons were totally his

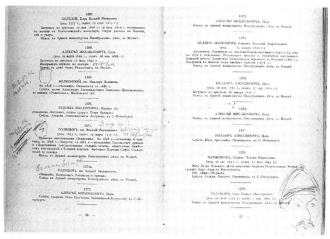

31. Alexandre Benois, Handwritten emendations on pp. 50-51 of the catalog of Sergei Diaghilev's "Exhibition of Russian Portraits" at the Tauride Palace, St. Petersburg, 1905.

own (in general, I think that he was closer to France and the West than to Russia...)".[30] It should also be mentioned that Benois was a model and paragon for Russia's new generation of critics such as Pavel Ettinger, Sergei Makovsky, Nikolai Punin, Alexander Rostislavov, Yakov Tugendkhold, and Nikolai Vrangel who, while each pursuing a different critical course, nevertheless, paid homage to Benois' knowledge, integrity, and clarity of argumentation.

Of course, Benois owed a great deal to his classical education, for, after graduating form Karl Mai's prestigious *Gymnasium* in 1890, he enrolled in the Department of Law at St. Petersburg University, an academic path, incidentally, that many of his colleagues pursued, including Bilibin, Diaghilev, Dobujinsky, Grabar, and Kandinsky. While he was at university (through 1894), he became president of the Society for Self-Education, an extension of the group of so called Nevsky Pickwickians, which brought together many of the future members of the World of Art. The lectures and discussions of this group of amateurs were marked by "dilettantism (...) versatility (...) encylopedism" [without which] "there would never have been a World of Art or any of the things springing therefrom, including the Ballets Russes".[31]

Benois' first professional appointment came in 1895 when he assumed curatorship of the collection of European and Russian paintings and drawings belonging to Princess Tenisheva. The Princess was a magnanimous, if self-willed, lady, and her initial enthusiasm for Benois' energy and sensibility soon waned as she came to understand the incalcitrance and obdurateness of her ward. Still, Benois "influenced her taste and talked to her about subsidizing a journal"[32] and convinced her to donate part of the collection to the Russian Museum of Alexander III in 1898, an action that led to several relevant publications by Benois (D8). Above all, it was thanks to the Princess that Benois also made his first trip to Paris in 1896 in the company of Bakst and Somov, visiting Versailles, the Louvre, and even attending classes in Whistler's studio.

32. Alexandre Benois, Frontispiece of *Tsarskoe selo v tsarstvovanie Imperatritsy Elizavety Petrovny* (Tsarskoe Selo in the Reign of Elizabeth Petrovna), Golike and Vilborg, St. Petersburg 1910. See D9

Benois was attracted to Gallic culture of the late 17th and 18th centuries by more than a caprice of fashion. His passion for Versailles ("he would go there and paint six or eight studies a day")[33] transformed his attitudes to painting, criticism and the history of art; it was almost as if Benois, by some perverse anachronism, had been born two centuries earlier, for, as he himself admitted, "a great deal of the past seems to me to be very familiar, perhaps even more familiar than the present".[34] The critic and poet Sergei Makovsky also noticed this spiritual alliance, remarking that "The dream of Versailles seemed to find an ancient friend in Benois, in the penchant of his taste and soul for the country of his ancestors (...) for the luxury of the Sun King, the refined and majestic Baroque and the smiling enchantment of the 18th century".[35] For Benois Versailles symbolized the culmination of the Renaissance, a natural conclusion to the flowering of Western reason and whatever contradicted that supreme principle was for him anathe-

33. Alexandre Benois,
Tail-piece for Alexander Pushkin,
Pikovaia dama (Queen of Spades),
Golike and Vilborg, St. Petersburg
1911. See D39

ma. But in the rational splendor of Versailles Benois also identified a theatrical impulse, dwelling on the exquisite costumes of Louis XIV and his courtiers, on their controlled gestures, on the ritualized landscapes and water artistries as if Versailles were some magnificent Rococo backdrop against which the Sun King was acting out his brilliant reign. Obviously, Benois drew upon his knowledge of Versailles when he came to design *Le Pavillon d'Armide* (Cat. 8, 9) in 1907 which, like the very era in which it was cast, represented an "irresolvable contradiction between the private destinies of the people and the magnificence of the architectural ensemble".[36] In many of the Versailles paintings (Cat. 3, 4) Benois presents his subject as a theatrical space in which the figures resemble marionettes, playing automatic and preconditioned roles. Benois transmits not only the elegance and symmetry of Versailles with its "cult of frozen beauty",[37] but also his own instinctive gravitation towards the scenic arts.

Benois' fascination with Versailles also left its mark on the activities of the World of Art society, especially on the contents of its journal, of which he became coeditor with Diaghilev in 1904. Although he did not publish in the journal until the sixth issue for 1899, Benois became a regular contributor of articles and reviews and his scenes of Versailles were often reproduced. Upset by the emphasis on Russian Neo-Nationalism in the first issue, Benois was quick to criticize Diaghilev and to insist that the direction shift to more elegant subjects such as Versailles, Peterhof, and 18th century Russian portraiture. Indeed, Benois seemed to look at much of early Russian culture "through the lorgnette of reminiscences"[38] and many of his critical endeavors reflected this – including the journal *Khudozhestvennye sokrovishcha Rossii* [Artistic Treasures of Russia] which he founded in 1901 and *Starye gody* [Bygone Years, D46] which he coedited between 1907 and 1916. Benois' call to reassess the traditions of Petrine and post-Petrine Russia prompted or paralleled a number of related projects. In 1902, for example, Benois and Bakst contributed illustrations to the third volume of Nikolai Kutepov's de luxe panorama of the Imperial hunt (D30; Figs. 28, 29); also in 1902 the Society of St. Eugenia began to publish historical postcards (cf. Cat. 39) and Diaghilev published his catalogue raisonné of Levitsky's portraits (D24, with frontispiece by Bakst, Fig. 30), three years later, with the close consultation of Benois (and interior design by Bakst), Diaghilev organized the "Exhibition of Russian Portraits" at the Tauride Palace (D25; Fig. 31), while in 1910 Benois published his magnificent study of Tsarskoe Selo (D9; Fig. 32) and the following year became vice-president of the St. Petersburg Society for the Protection and Preservation of Russian Monuments of Art and Antiquity.

From his Parnassian heights, Benois chose not to involve himself in political campaigns for sudden change and was certainly disturbed by the actual and potential damage to antiquities wrought by the 1905 and 1917 revolutions (something that his diary for 1916-18 demonstrates very clearly). Benois' philosophical escapism – and geographical escape to France – vexed many of his colleagues who accused him of burying his head in the sand while Russia was burning: "I don't understand your fear of Socialism...", wrote Lancéray to him in 1906, "I don't like you immersing yourself in the past as if you're insulted by the reality of the present".[39] At the same time, Benois' alienation from socio-political involvement enabled him to indulge in retrospective meditation and scrupulous archaeology, qualities that informed many of his own artistic activities, including his studio paintings and his book and stage designs. For Alexander Pushkin's poetical masterpiece, *The Bronze Horseman* (D38; Fig. 73), for example, perhaps Benois' most celebrated cycle of literary illustrations, he evoked a fantastic combination of Petrine and Pushkinian St. Petersburgs. In the manner of an early 19th century bibliophile, Benois intended to produce a miniature travel book with an illustration on every page and, to some extent, the actual illustrations do remind us of antique engravings or woodcuts. Although they are less ornamental than analogous designs by Bilibin or

Somov, they function well as a sequential interpretation of the text and as independent artifacts. Grabar, in particular, was impressed by the "contemporaneity" of the illustrations[40] and Bakst even regarded them as Benois' "most important *oeuvre*".[41] The critic Alexei Fedorov-Davydov had this cycle in mind when he remarked that Benois was the inspiration to an entire school of St. Petersburg graphic artists[42] and in the words of Yurii Annenkov Benois was the "initiator of an unexpected renewal" in the Russian graphic arts as a whole (Fig. 72).[43] The school included Vladimir Konashevich, Dmitrii Mitrokhin, Viktor Zamirailo, and many others.

35. Photograph of the Mariinsky Theater, St. Petersburg, ca. 1910. The Theater was designed by Alexandre Benois' maternal grandfather, Albert Kavos, in 1860

What must have attracted Benois so strongly to *The Bronze Horseman* is Pushkin's evocation of a fantasmagoric and magical St. Petersburg, for this appealed to the artist's personal love of the fabulous and the whimsical, an "infantile" view of the world in which objects could become people (the tapestry coming to life in *Le Pavillon d'Armide*, Cat. 7) or monsters come out at night (*Petrushka* curtain, Cat. 22). In this sense, we can understand Benois' fascination with Pushkin's story of the *Queen of Spades*, (D39; Fig. 33) in which the occult power of cards inspires passion, death, and madness and his illustrations to the 1911 edition carry some of that mystery. Benois tried to maintain the world of make believe of his childhood throughout his life and even as a grown man found solace in a "tiny five-inch doll (...) dressed in the costume of Louis XIV which served him apparently as a mannequin".[44] Benois' "childishness" is evident on many levels, but especially in his delectable alphabet of 1905 (D7; Fig. 34), his postcards on the theme of toys (Cat. 39), his own collection of toys[45] and his evocation of the *balagan* and the Punch and Judy show in *Petrushka* (D48). After all, for Benois the theater was all these things, because "it is a world of illusions, this is its chief fundamental, its prerogative of miracle".[46]

Benois inherited a veritable cult of the theater from his mother and even as a young boy, impressed by productions of *Sleeping Beauty* and *The Queen of Spades,* he resolved to become a stage designer. But although he created all manner of theatrical bagatelles in the 1890s such as sets and costumes for *Orfeo ed Euridice* in 1895 and *Masquerade in the Reign of Louis XIV* in 1898 (not produced), he did not commit himself to an actual production until 1902 with Alexander Taneev's opera *Cupid's Revenge* at the Imperial Hermitage Theater (cf. Cat. 41, 43), which, however, as Benois himself recalled, "had no success (...) and my setting could not be called successful either, although the theme – a French park of the 18th century – seemed to be a suitable one".[47]

34. Alexandre Benois, The letter "I" for "*Igrushki* (Toys)" in his *Azbuka v kartinakh Alexandra Benua* (The Alphabet in Pictures by Alexandre Benois), Department for the Preparation of State Papers, St. Petersburg 1905. See Cat. 39 and D7

Greater resonance came with Benois' designs for the production of Wagner's *Götterdämmerung* at the Mariinsky Theater in January, 1903 (Fig. 35). For Benois, as for Diaghilev and the poet Viacheslav Ivanov, Wagner was the first modern composer to create a convincing integration of the various arts into the single *Gesamtkunstwerk* of which the Symbolists dreamed and of which Benois himself often spoke. For them Wagner was also the "author of a new Dionysian creation, the first precursor of a universal myth-creation"[48] and, as such, required a grandiose and imposing visual setting which, however, Benois failed to provide. Diaghilev even criticized him for a tedious naturalism and a lack of imagination, although Benois, of course, thought otherwise, welcoming the converse, laudatory comments on his "authenticity".[49] Certainly, Benois' work on *Le Pavillon d'Armide* for the 1907 and 1909 productions and for *Petrushka* in 1911 proved that he could tinge authenticity with imagination and reason with desire; if he had not, Diaghilev, "close friend and cruel enemy"[50] would not have invited him to enter the Ballets Russes virtually as artist-in-residence, even if that status proved to be a brief and

36. Auguste Bert, Photograph of Tamara Karsavina in *Le Pavillon d'Armide*, 1909. Reproduced in Valeriian Svetlov, *Sovremennyi balet,* Golike and Vilborg, St. Petersburg 1911, between pp. 114-115. See D50

37. E.D. Hoppé, Photograph of Tamara Karsavina and Adolph Bolm in *Le Pavillon d'Armide,* 1912. See D76

38. Karl Fisher, Photograph of Vaslav Nijinsky in *Le Pavillon d'Armide,* 1909. Photography courtesy private collection, St. Petersburg

embittering experience – and even if, strange to say, he was not, on his own admission, a "devotee of the ballet or even a *balletomane*".[51]

Benois returned to Russia from France in the spring of 1907, responding to an invitation from Michel Fokine who required a designer for his production of *Le Pavillon d'Armide.* Its composer, Nikolai Cherepnin, had intimated that he would be pleased if Benois would assume this responsibility and Benois, still nostalgic for the "charming lie"[52] of Versailles, accepted the commission with enthusiasm. With the exception of a few designs for his mute autobiographical ballet called *The Prodigal Son* (1907, not produced), *Le Pavillon* was Benois' first professional engagement since 1903. What distinguished Benois' sets and costumes and what drew applause in St. Petersburg and Paris was the deft combination of historical accuracy and fragile fancy within the three-dimensional box of the stage, something that can also be identified with what Bakst called "the very great success"[53] of *Les Sylphides* of 1909 also choreographed by Fokine and designed by Benois for the Ballets Russes (Cat. 17). As Fokine recalled of *Le Pavillon*: "Alexandre Nikolaevich seemed to be – immediately and exclusively – a theatrical artist. All his colours, his lines related directly and obviously to the particular juncture on stage. The costumes, the sets, the lighting – everything was aimed at expressing the content of the piece".[54] Benois demonstrated clearly how well he understood the historical era – especially in his celebrated decors for Scene 2 (Cat. 9) and his numerous costumes such as the Marquis de Fierbois and the Cavalier (Cat. 10,12,13). After all, the first ballet that Diaghilev presented to Paris in his new cycle of Russian performances was *Le Pavillon* and it was *Le Pavillon* that "brought forth the first ovations" (Figs. 36, 37, 38).[55]

Although Benois was sometimes guilty of pedantic compilation of historical detail, this failing was not especially evident in *Le Pavillon* or in any of the early productions such as *Le Festin* (1909, costumes only), *Giselle*, *Petrushka*, and *Le Rossignol*. For example, Benois' designs for *Giselle* were so well received at its Paris premiere that the original Benois version was reconstructed many times thereafter. Benois' lyrical evocation of Giselle, his fantastic castle, and romantic cemetery of the Wilis became images enjoyed by many audiences – in spite of Diaghilev's initial reluctance to produce this particular ballet. But both Diaghilev and Benois knew quite well that the French also expected a measure of "barbarism" from the Russians, and, of course, Diaghilev satisfied this desire with his productions of *Petrushka* and *Le Sacre du Printemps*, presenting the "pagan" music of Stravinsky to the Paris audiences. The dancer Nathalie Trouhanova, who was not an enthusiast of Diaghilev's company, admitted grudgingly that *Petrushka* did, indeed, evoke the sense of play, although for her it was the "cretin" Nijinsky who stole the show.[56]

How curious that in 1911 a staid, urbane, and middle-aged man would have scored such a resounding success with the violent, exuberant ballet *Petrushka* (Fig. 39). Yet the plot and characters of *Petrushka* were very close to Benois and, in creating the sets and costumes, he seemed to be eliciting fond memories of a childhood when the *balagany,* the street vendors, and the Gypsy fortune tellers and the bazaars of Butterweek were still a part of St. Petersburg reality. Seen against this emotional background – and in the intellectual context of the Russian cult of the Commedia dell'arte in the 1900s – Benois' eager evocation of Pierrot, Harlequin, and Columbine can be understood. Benois recalled: "If Petrouchka is the incarnation of (...) the poetic principle, if his lady, Columbine, the ballerina, proved to be the personification of *Das ewige Weibliche,* then the 'luxurious' Blackamoor became the incarnation of the absurdly captivating principle of the powerful and the virile".[57] Benois not only expressed the enchantment of a childhood fantasy, but also enhanced Stravinsky's discordant music with his bold color contrasts and raucous crowd of incompatible individuals. The fortunate union prompted Benois and Stravinsky to join forces again for Diaghilev's production of *Le Rossignol* in 1914, for which Benois applied a quaint *chinoiserie* to sumptuous backdrops and dynamic costumes, culminating in what he felt was among his most successful syntheses. What Benois once wrote of the Bibienas, Ricci, and Pozzo, could be applied with equal justification to his fanciful inventions in all three ballets: "they braid the imagination with such convincing mendacity that (...) you lose the faculty of prudent criticism".[58]

39. Auguste Bert, Photograph of Bronislava Nijinska (Street Dancer), Konstantin Kobelev (Barrel Organ Grinder), and Liudmila Shollar (Gypsy) in *Petrushka*, 1911. Reproduced in Valeriian Svetlov, *Sovremennyi balet,* Goliike and Vilborg, St. Petersburg 1911, between pp. 128 and 129. See D50.

But *Petrushka* was also Benois' undoing and its tale of triangular affections was also a prophetic allegory. Mercurial moods and temper tantrums were peculiar to many of the World of Art members, not least Bakst and Diaghilev, and Benois, too, was quick to perceive slight where not intended and to cast aspersions where unjustified. The story of the rupture of relations between Benois and Bakst over the latter's "improvement" of the former's portrait of the Showman in Scene 2 has been related many times, but even so the hysterical intensity with which Benois reacted seems quite out of keeping with this man of reason and common sense: "As soon as Benois appeared at the *répétition générale* (...) he saw that the portrait was an entirely new one. He thereupon flung down all the sketches for *Petrushka* that he was carrying under his arm and left the theatre in a rage".[59] No doubt, Benois' anger was exacerbated further by his memory of the dissension which had arisen between Bakst, Diaghilev and him over *Schéhérazade* of the year before: Benois felt that the ballet was "his", but in the program Diaghilev ascribed the authorship to Bakst, which, his fleeting sylphs paling before the lushness of Bakst's sultanas, Benois contested strongly. In May, 1911 Bakst "broke with Benois forever",[60] vexed at the latter's needling jealousy and constant carping. Although Benois returned to collaborate with both Diaghilev and Stravinsky on *Le Rossignol* in 1914, he could not forget the *Petrushka* incident and harbored the grudge throughout his life: when Stravinsky presented him with a copy of his 1935 *Chronique de ma vie* carrying the dedication "De la part de l'auteur, absent de Paris", Benois was quick to add "et absent de ma vie".[61] We might contrast this with Stravinsky's 1921 portrait of Bakst carrying the affectionate "A mon ami Bakst/son ami Igor Strawinsky/Paris Oct. 1921".[62]

Benois' success as a designer for *Le Pavillon d'Armide* and *Petrushka* confirmed his artistic vocation and during the next several years he was involved in numerous stage projects in Russia and abroad, an activity that has received only sporadic attention. In the 1910s and in contrast to Bakst, Benois collaborated on many dramatic, operatic, and balletic productions for Russian theaters, incuding the Antique Theater (for which Benois also designed the drop curtain) and the Bolshoi Dramatic Theater in St. Petersburg and the Moscow Art Theater. Beginning in 1913 Benois designed no less than six dramatic productions of plays by Molière, Pushkin and Goldoni for Konstantin Stanislavsky – whom he praised as a "man of deed rather than of word who has succeeded in creating a grandiose and lasting whole, a real monument with real style".[63] No doubt, the Moscow Art Theater with its emphasis on a restrained Realism, on reason rather than desire, appealed to Benois' mentality and he seemed content to reproduce the costumes and accoutrements of his favorite historical environments. But it is for *Petrushka* of 1911 and not for *Le Malade Imaginaire* or *The Stone Guest* that we now remember Benois the stage designer.

42. Pietro Gonzago (1751-1831), *Staircase in Fantastic Architecture,* undated Ink wash, 31.5 × 20.5 cm Formerly in the collection of Alexandre Benois. Auctioned as Lot 41 at "Collection Alexandre Benois. Collection J. de Vichet" at Hôtel Drouot, Paris, 16 November, 1984

Indeed, in some sense *Petrushka* marked the zenith of Benois' career as a stage designer – and perhaps Benois himself was aware of this, for he undertook many later reconstructions of his ballet. Of course, this is not to say that Benois' activities as designer, painter, illustrator and historian suddenly ceased; on the contrary, his artistic and intellectual curiosity and energy continued unabated. Until his final emigration from Leningrad to Paris in 1926 and thereafter in Paris, London, Milan and other cities, Benois worked for many companies, pleasing audiences with his Rococo lightness and playful moderation, identifiable, for example, with *La Princesse Cygne, Swan Lake* (Cat. 35), and *Les Deux Tisserands* (Cat. 36, 37). He designed regularly for la Comédie Française, l'Opéra, and l'Opéra-Comique, and between 1947 and 1958 worked on more

41. M. Brodsky, Group Photograph taken in the Paris apartment of Alexandre Benois, ca. 1955. Standing from left to right Issar Gourvitch, Alexandre Tcherkessoff (son of Anna Benois-Tcherkessoff), Hélène (Elena) Benois; sitting from left to right, Anna Benois-Tcherkessoff (Cherkesova), Alexandre Benois, unidentified woman and man.
Photograph courtesy of Dimitri Vicheney, Paris

40. Photograph of Alexandre Benois in his Paris apartment, 1950, (photographer unknown). Photograph courtesy of Dimitri Vicheney, Paris

than twenty productions for La Scala in Milan. Throughout these years Benois also continued to write profusely, publishing articles and reviews in the Russian, Soviet and then émigré press, always expanding the repertoire of his interests. For example, just before and after the October Revolution Benois was especially concerned with the question of how to conserve and restore historic buildings, emphasizing the need to record and inventorize works of art in private and public collections and in this regard he contributed much to the development of a Soviet science of museology. Benois also led the design team for the interior decoration of Kazan Station in Moscow in 1914-17, participated in numerous committees and conferences, was appointed director of the Painting Gallery at the Hermitage in 1918, and travelled constantly in Russia, France, Germany, Italy, Switzerland, and the Crimea.

As in St. Petersburg, his Paris apartment became a center for the Russian artists and writers abroad who sympathized with the World of Art movement (Figs. 40, 41). The painter Giorgio Sciltian remembered that ambience: "His house was full of beautiful objects, including two superb drawings by Guardi and many relics and souvenirs of life in St. Petersburg. The cream of the Russian intelligentsia attended his receptions (...) Merezhkovsky, Gippius, Bunin, Zaitsev, Osorgin (...) Alexandre Jacovlev (...) Somov, Dobujinsky, Serebriakova and so many others".[64] In Paris, Benois pursued his interests in attribution and connoisseurship and as late as 1952 was compiling the catalogue raisonné of the collection of Russian paintings belonging to Alexandre Popoff.[65] In emigration Benois also continued his comprehensive survey of world art, interrupted by the First World War and Revolution, completing lengthy sections on Italian painting and scenography of the 17th and 18th centuries (Fig. 42). Those, after all, were his favorite centuries and if he approached our own era with the light reason of the Directoire, he compels us to remember that the triumph of the Ballets Russes owed as much to the weight of sense as to the flight of sensuality. As Orio Vergani wrote in the catalog of the first major retrospective exhibition of the Benois family in 1955: "his virtues, which may seem antique, have the youth of genius".[66]

Léon Bakst

Of all the artists of the original World of Art group Léon Bakst is the most celebrated. During the first seasons of the Ballets Russes Bakst received the highest – although not universal – praise[67] and it seemed that his youthful dream to be "the most famous artist in the world" was about to be fulfilled.[68] Bakst's reputation has not waned, his accomplishments continue to be the subject of monographs and exhibitions, and, of course, his work is an integral part of the many surveys of Diaghilev and the Russian ballet that galleries across Russia, Europe, and the Americas continue to organize.

When Bakst and Valentin Serov were travelling in Greece in 1907, they happened to visit a museum of Hellenic antiquities. One of the main attractions for Bakst was a large pediment and statuary from the Temple of Zeus and his head was soon aching from craning his neck. Much to the consternation of the custodian and with sketchbook in hand, Bakst climbed up on to the pediment, an impetuous action dictated by his desperate desire to "run my hand over the marble, to find out what Niobe's shoulders are like, what her breasts are like...".[69] This incident illustrates not only Bakst's fascination with the ancient civilizations of Greece and the Orient (and for Bakst the "East" included Greece),[70] but also his essential perception of art as a sensual and tactile experience. This

44. Michel and Vera Fokine in *Schéhérazade*. Photograph by S. Branzburg. Reproduced in *Solntse Rossii*, Petrograd 1915, 3 January, No. 258, p. 14

43. Photograph of the final scene of *Schéhérazade*, 1910 (photographer unknown). Courtesy Iskusstvo, Moscow

45. Léon Bakst (Lev Rozenberg),
King Lear and the Fool.
Illustration for Alexander Kanaev
(after William Shakespeare],
Korol Lir, ili Neblagodarnost detei
(King Lear or the Ungratefulness
of Children), Alms House
for Waifs, St. Petersburg 1888.
Courtesy of Sergei Golynets

was a code that aligned him with certain colleagues in the World of Art, above all, Diaghilev, the "incorrigible sensualist",[71] and yet divided him from others, notably Benois and Dobujinsky. Moreover, it was his skilful manipulation and translation of the sensual into startling, but always elegant, compositions that provided his art with its internal resilience and public attraction, especially in the portraits and designs for the stage.

Bakst did not hail from an especially privileged family or milieu. Born in Grodno, Bakst (who in 1889 replaced the family name of Rozenberg with a modification of his maternal grandmother's name of Baxter) grew up in a lower middle-class Jewish family, but entered a St. Petersburg *Gymnasium* when his father's business affairs caused the family to move to the capital.[72] In 1883 the school organized a portrait competition to mark the centenary of the birth of the Romantic poet Vasilii Zhukovsky, Bakst won the competition with his rendering and from then on he was convinced of his vocation. In 1883 Bakst received permission to audit classes at the Academy of Arts (at that time no mean feat for a Russian Jew), but three years later was advised to leave after producing an "unconventional" interpretation of the *Pietà* for a Silver Medal Competition – and he resigned under the pretext of a "worsening eye disease".[73] This was one of many unsavory incidents that Bakst experienced throughout his public and private life – from the bitter conflicts with Benois and Diaghilev to the humiliation at being refused a St. Petersburg residency permit in 1912 because of his ethnic origin. Actually, Bakst himself was not altogether innocent, for his temperament, vain and irascible, did not always inspire affection. His fond remembrance of a day in the park of Pavlovsk when, as a little boy of eight, he happened to be travelling in a carriage "while others were on foot",[74] epitomized his constant ambition to surpass and his eventual megalomania.

Even so, Bakst was "dazzling" (to use one of his favorite words) and when we look at his designs for *Cléopâtre* or *Schéhérazade* (Cat. 45; Figs. 43, 44, 66) we might be tempted to repeat the exclamations of his audiences – "barbaric", "hedonistic", "decadent" – and such pieces rely for their effect not only on bold colors and occult symmetries, but also on total control of the medium. Bakst may have been an artist of desire, but he tempered this with reason, for he painted and designed according to a strict etiquette, using color and line as organizational devices and calculating the emotional impact. Unlike Benois, Bakst rarely improvised or doodled, seeming always to know in advance what the ultimate rendering of his vision would bring. Bakst attained a high degree of technical fluency thanks in part to his initial training at the Academy, where he took lessons from Pavel Chistiakov, Russia's primary engraver. On leaving the Academy, Bakst started work as an illustrator and copier for Alexander Kanaev (Fig. 45), writer and also owner of a lithographic studio specializing in pedagogical aids, which, in turn, prepared him for his engagement as professional illustrator for the popular journals *Khudozhnik* (Artist), *Peterburgskaia zhizn* (Petersburg Life) and other presses. Although these commissions dictated a simple, narrative approach to the subject, they endowed Bakst with valuable experience of typography, lithography and xylography – which he applied to good effect as technical supervisor of the World of Art journal in 1898 onwards.

In the spring of 1890, the "not so young, ugly, but sympathetic Bakst"[75] met Benois and was introduced to the Society of Nevsky Pickwickians. Ill-versed in the newest European movements, Bakst preferred to discuss the conventional styles of his time, so when the Society invited him to give a lecture, he talked about Russia's *pompiers* such as Konstantin Makovsky and Genrikh Semiradsky – the very artists that Benois, Diaghilev and Bakst himself would soon condemn. Still, Bakst's early enthusiasm for the Orientalist Semiradsky should not be disregarded, because, after all, the feasting Romans, Greek dancers, and fanatical martyrs that decorate Semiradsky's melodramatic paintings return in Bakst's own evocations of Mediterranean and Oriental cultures. But in the 1890s Bakst (like the provincial

Diaghilev) was in desperate need of cultural nourishment and his proximity to Benois, Filosofov, and Walter Nouvel could not fail to improve his taste in art and literature; here was an educational experience that provided him with a new appreciation of the Italian Renaissance, contemporary French and German art, Symbolist poetry, and the music of Wagner. In a direct sense Benois, his junior by four years, was then his principal mentor.

47. Semeon Erber, Parody of the "Exhibition of Paintings of the St. Petersburg Society of Artists" published in *Shut*, St. Petersburg 1896, 8 March, No. 10, p. 5.
The work numbered 151 is called *Vision* and is ascribed to Bakst

Bakst made his first trip abroad in 1891, visiting Germany, Belgium, France, Spain, and Italy, and the same year began to exhibit with the Society of Watercolorists in St. Petersburg. In the following years he continued to travel widely, especially to Paris where, sporadically, he took lessons from various celebrities, including Albert Edelfeldt and Jean Léon Gérôme and, perhaps remembering Benois' preferences, studied the Barbizons, the Old Masters, and the new German Realists. In fact, Bakst's portraits of this time of, for example, Nouvel (1895), Filosofov (1897) and Benois (1898, Fig. 14) betray the strong influence of Franz von Lenbach and Adolf von Menzel and not, as one might expect, of the the *fin de siècle* Decadents such as Aubrey Beardsley and T.T. Heine. Still, Bakst soon digressed from the Realist path to explore more experimental styles and subjects as in his provocative *Supper* of 1902 (D49; Fig. 46). The sensuality of the theme (a lady of the night smiles at the viewer while waiting for her companion), the sinuous brushstrokes of heavy paint, the table cascading, as it were, into our own reality – these elements now bring to mind the expressive allegories of Edvard Munch and Félicien Rops. Here are the lunatic despair of late night cafés and cabarets and the solitude of the flowers of the night that the French and Russian Symbolists described so poignantly in their poetry, even though Bakst maintained that there was nothing especially transgressive about *Supper*. Whatever its derivation, *Supper* scored a *succès de scandale* in Paris and St. Petersburg, was used as a cover for the October, 1903 issue of *Jugend* and inspired a numer of plagiarisms, one of which Bakst contested in court[76] – although he himself may have paraphrased the theme from Anglada-Camarosa's painting called *Morphine Addict*.[77] His status as a St. Petersburg Decadent seemed assured (Fig. 47).

Bakst's move away from external Realism to a more individual and evocative approach coincided with the rapid orientation of the World of Art towards a retrospective or elegiac style, supported by Benois, Diaghilev, and Somov. Encouraged by the eclectic taste of his friends, Bakst began to collect Japanese colored engravings, including Hokusai, Siamese artifacts (in the wake of the St. Petersburg performances by the Royal Ballet Troupe of the Siamese Court in 1900)[78] and other knick-knacks, including a stuffed raven *à la Edgar Allan Poe* (Fig. 6). He followed Benois' passion for Versailles and Somov's for *Jugendstil,* painted a few salon portraits (Fig. 48), and made numerous vignettes for books and magazines – especially for the "World of Art" (D34).

46. Front cover of the journal *Stolitsa i usadba* (Town and Country), Petrograd 1917, No. 80, 30 April, showing Bakst's painting *Supper*. See D49

The general conception of the "World of Art" magazine belonged, of course, to Diaghilev, that "amazing energy machine", as Bakst once described him (Fig. 49).[79] But it was Bakst who attended to the intricate details of type selection, page layout and decoration, and distribution of reproductions. In other words, Bakst was in charge of the mechanical organization of the journal, although the only acknowledgement that he received for this was a reluctant entry in the list of technical collaborators at the end of the first volume. Benois recalled Bakst's dedication to the cause: "Levushka Bakst, the next victim of Seriozha's [Diaghilev's] despotism, spent entire days inventing elegant titles for the drawings and retouching the photographs (...) The good-natured and easygoing Levushka would have sudden fits of rebellion and indignation (...) but more often

48. Léon Bakst,
Portrait of a Woman, 1906
Oil on canvas, 100 × 82 cm
Ukraine, Simferopol Art Museum

49. Léon Bakst, *Portrait of Sergei Diaghilev and his Nanny Avdotia Alexandrovna,* 1906
Oil on canvas, 161 × 116 cm
St. Petersburg, State Russian Museum.

50. Léon Bakst, Logo
for the journal *Mir iskusstva*
(World of Art), St. Petersburg
1898-1904. See D34-D36

he spent his time manipulating Indian ink and Paris white".[80] But if Bakst was being exploited by his despot, he did not seem to be unduly upset, for it was an exciting time of artistic discovery and innovation and the journal served as a common departure-point for so many individual explorations and improvements. Grabar was quick to notice the difference in the Bakst of "before" and "after": "I didn't realize that the Lev Bakst whose drawings in the *World of Art* so enchanted me was the same Rozenberg, the caricaturist of lower than average accomplishment (...) There was now something different in him (...) Now he was a dandy, dressed like a new pin, in patent leather boots, with a fantastic tie and a lilac handkerchief tucked away coquettishly in his shirt sleeve".[81]

Bakst made many graphic decorations for the "World of Art" and also designed its promotional materials (D36), including the insignia (Fig. 50) – silhouetted against a sickle moon and stars, an eagle perches on a snowy peak (Bakst drew the eagle from nature in the St. Petersburg Zoo). In a letter to Benois dated 24 October, 1898, just before the first number of the "World of Art" came out, Bakst explained the allegory: "'The World of Art' is higher than anything earthly, it is next to the stars where it reigns haughtily, mysteriously, and in solitude like an eagle on a snowy peak and in this case we have an 'eagle of the midnight countries', i.e. of the north of Russia".[82] One wonders whether the vignette of an eagle wounded and falling from the sun against a black sky that Bilibin drew in 1905 (Fig. 21) might not be another allegory, this time of the collapse of the World of Art journal as well as of the tragic events of the First Revolution. What is immediately striking in Bakst's graphic decorations is the precision of line and clarity of composition. Just as Bakst himself, by 1900, seems to have "grown up", so his technique became more assertive, more deliberate, more experimental while his vocabulary became more titillating and more sensuous. This is evident, for example, from the revivalist *style empire* covers for the "World of Art", No. 2 for 1902 and Vasilii Vereshchagin's survey of ex-libris designs of the same year (D51; Figs. 51, 52), which, in the attention to the fine tracery, the oval format, and severe contrast between white and black, bring to mind the concurrent work of Julius Dietz, T.T. Heine and Somov.

Bakst also contributed to the various de luxe publications sponsored by the World of Art such as the 1900 folio of fifteen lithograph portraits of Russian artists and writers (including Isaak Levitan, Nikolai Gogol, Filipp Maliavin and Benois) and made sketches of the members of the Editorial Board. That Bakst and Benois respected each other's talents at this time is indicated by many other joint projects – Bakst's graphic ornaments for Benois' appreciation of Arkhangelskoe in the last number of the *World of Art* (D34), his covers for Benois' surveys of the Russian Museum of Alexander III (D8), their parallel involvement in the intimate productions for the Imperial Hermitage Theater, their respective interior designs for Contemporary Art (Cat. 6; Figs. 15, 16), and their lively correspondence.

However, Bakst was more interested in the ancient civilizations than in the pleasantries of the 19th century and the recurrent motifs in his designs for the journal come more from artifacts of the Ancient Greeks – amphorae, Doric columns, clusters of grapes, vestal maidens, mythological deities. In combining these motifs often in a witty and whimsical manner, Bakst seems to be applying the expertise of some eccentric archaeologist who takes poetic liberty in order to emphasize the exotic splendour of the era that he is investigating. Like the writers Viacheslav Ivanov and Vasilii Rozanov, Bakst was fascinated by Hellas and paid homage to that culture even if inappropriate: one wonders, for example, wherein lies the relevance of Bakst's headpiece to Balmont's poem "Predestination" (1901, No. 5) or of his illustration to Rozanov's "Stars" (1901, No. 7). In other words, some of Bakst's graphic ornaments seem to have been generated more by his own thematic predilections than by the exigencies of the text, an artistic licence, however, that he exploited in his stage designs where sheer visual effect was often more important than ethnographical accuracy (Cat. 59).

Bakst pursued a rather different esthetic approach to his portraits and landscapes. His images of the poets Andrei Bely (1905) and Zinaida Gippius (1906) or his self-portrait of 1906, for example, are wonderful exercises in psychological Realism and derive little from *Jugendstil* and *Art Nouveau.* The remarkable rendering of Gippius which, as a matter of fact, she did not like, reveals at once the inner contradictions of a complex psyche, refined yet affected, malicious yet frail. Certainly, in his treatment of her pose and face Bakst seemed to echo what his colleague Alexander Golovin once said of the poetess, "sometimes rather venomous, sometimes a little arrogant".[83] In his portrait of Diaghilev and his old nanny, Avdotia Alexandrovna, of 1906 (Fig. 49), Bakst also engages our attention by eliciting something of his friend's haughty, if not despotic, character, his passion for art, his Wildean self-consciousness (the besilvered streak of hair), and his deep emotional attachment to his nanny. Bakst's self-portraits, however, do not rely on external props or characters, but focus on the sitter's quizzical and challenging gaze as if to insist on his (illusory) autonomy (a notable exception being the autobiographical *Vase* of 1906 with its subtext of conjugal distance and division).

Bakst's portraits are curiously "untheatrical" and in their freedom and immediacy rarely evoke associations with stage, wings, framing, controlled gesture. Moreover, Bakst painted rather few portraits of actors and dancers and even his somewhat desultory sketch of Isadora Duncan dancing (that "inebriated, crazy Amazon")[84] of 1907 scarcely reflects the initial enthusiasm and popularity that she enjoyed at that time. Perhaps because of his feverish activity as a stage designer Bakst simply did not have time to portray the stars to whom he was so close such as Karsavina and Nijinsky or the hostesses to whom he was so drawn in the 1910s. His letters to Diaghilev are full of such complaints: "I'm being torn to pieces on all sides, each moment seems to be unfailingly important without which everything would collapse. Not to mention my purely animal fear of failing with this ridiculously enormous workload (...) Of course, your continual changes (...) create a loathsome impression and I think that in my place anyone else would have given up".[85] Whatever the reason, this lacuna is one of the most peculiar in Bakst's *oeuvre,* for the magnificent early portraits of, say, Gippius or Diaghilev, promised much for a future as a master portraitist. On the other hand, perhaps as a product of that Decadent era, the rather misanthropic Bakst was drawn more towards the outward trappings of the costume than to the capricious diva who wore it.

Be that as it may, Bakst felt at home in the theater and, like Georgii Yakulov, the Constructivist designer whom Diaghilev commissioned for the 1927 production of *Le Pas d'Acier,* he "carries the theater within himself".[86] Bakst shared the extraordinary enthusiasm for the theater that Benois describes in his memoirs and that brought the *miriskusniki* to the theater "nine times in one week".[87] He also followed closely the scenographical experiments of the older generation such as Konstantin Korovin, Viktor Vasnetsov, and Vrubel who had been designing for Savva Mamontov's troupe in the 1880s – and whom Benois, at least, regarded as the prelude to the imminent revolution in Russian stage design. Recognizing the new plasticity of gesture and bold decorative resolutions that the new theaters presented, including Princess Tenisheva's theater at Talashkino, the Moscow Art Theater (opened in 1898), and, of course, Diaghilev's Ballets Russes, Bakst had every reason to believe that his vocation was that of stage designer. Beginning in 1901 Bakst expressed an increasing preference for the theater, at first for innocuous baubles such as *Le Coeur de la Marquise* (Cat. 41; Fig. 53) and then, of course, for the great displays of sex and violence that Diaghilev showed the world in 1909 onwards.

Bakst's career as a stage designer has been the subject of many exhibitions and publications and there is no need to repeat the basic information here. Suffice it to recall that Bakst's first professional involvement in the theater was as codesigner of the Delibes bal-

53. Léon Bakst, Frontispiece for Valeriian Svetlov, *Sovremennyi balet,* Golike and Vilborg, St. Petersburg 1911, between pp. 114 and 115. See D50. Bakst had also used this design as the program cover for the production of *Le Coeur de la Marquise* at the Imperial Hermitage Theater, St. Petersburg, in 1902. See Cat. 41 and D50

51. Léon Bakst, Customized pigskin cover designed by Bakst for Vasilii Vereshchagin, *Russkii knizhnyi znak/L'ex-libris russe*, Golike, St. Petersburg 1902. The binding was made by Alexander Shnel of St. Petersburg expressly for Tsar Nicholas II to whom this copy belonged. See D51 and Fig. 52

52. Léon Bakst, Frontispiece for Vasilii Vereshchagin, *Russkii knizhnyi znak/L'ex-libris russe*, Golike and Vilborg, St. Petersburg 1902. See D51 and Fig. 51

let *Sylvia* that Diaghilev prepared for the Mariinsky Theater in 1901. Although *Sylvia* was not produced, Bakst's participation in the project gave him practical experience of theatrical space, of how to transfer an idea from studio to the stage and of how to collaborate with performers, technicians, and patrons, and he built on this experience in the years to come.

Bakst's debut as an independent designer for a real production came with *Le Coeur de la Marquise* (Cat. 41) for which he designed a Rococo pavilion and period costumes and this, in turn, prepared him for his collaboration with the Legat brothers on the two act ballet *Die Puppenfee* the following year for the Hermitage and Mariinsky Theaters. Transferring the latter ballet from its legitimate location in Germany to a mid-19th century St. Petersburg and interpolating the original music with dances by Anatolii Liadov, Anton Rubinstein and Tchaikovsky, Bakst and the Legats attempted to make the result more Russian and more appealing. However, Bakst was not altogether pleased with the result, complaining to Benois that the scene painters had misunderstood his instructions (a constant lament in the years to come) and that the result was "candy-box tones".[88] Even so, this was an important event in Bakst's career, not only because Matilda Kchessinskaya danced the doll and the Imperial Family attended the premiere, but also because Bakst was suddenly acknowledged as being a "wonderful designer, refined, with great taste, limitless imagination, absolutely exquisite and aristocratic".[89]

Although *Die Puppenfee* evoked a historical moment dear to some of the World of Art artists and, on one level, even anticipated Benois' *Petrushka* of 1911, it was not Bakst's favorite time. Ancient Greece was, of course, his historical and philosophical commitment and it was fortunate, indeed, that between 1902 and 1904 Bakst was able to indulge his Hellenic imagination in three consecutive productions, *Hippolytus* (Cat. 42), *Oedipus at Colonus* (Cat. 44) and *Antigone* (1904), which, as we can see from the surviving sets and costumes, already embodied Bakst's key principles of theater design. In these early productions, Bakst was moving away from the *bella prospettiva* and ethnographical pedantry of the traditional stage towards the sweeping diagonals and exuberant curves of ballets such as *Schéhérazade* and *Le Dieu Bleu* (Cat. 47-49; Fig. 54). He was already viewing the body on stage as a kinetic mechanism that defined, and was defined by, the surrounding space, so much so that, according to one observer, the Greeks in *Hippolytus* seemed "real".[90] Similarly, the costumes for *Oedipus at Colonus* (Cat. 44), with the loose folds, belts, bangles, and braids, emphasized the dynamic principle of the performance – just as the feathers and veils maintained the momentum of the dancer's dance in *Cléopâtre* and *Schéhérazade*. Inspecting the Acropolis in May, 1907 Bakst himself was struck by the coincidence in "tone and form" with his *Oedipus at Colonus*, even though in "tragedy everything is more colossal than in life".[91] Remembering Ida Rubinstein's svelte and slender form (Fig. 55), we can understand her own enthusiasm for these Greek costumes and the alacrity with which she made her own private début as Antigone in April, 1904, wearing a robe specially designed by Bakst. Of course, the fascination with Greece stayed with Bakst for many years, inspiring the stage curtain *Elysium* (Cat. 40), his panneau *Terror Antiquus* (1908), his friendship with the Classical scholar and poet Viacheslav Ivanov,[92] and, of course, the major commissions for *Narcisse, Daphnis et Chloé, Hélène de Sparte* (Cat. 50), *Phaedra* (Cat. 61), and *Artemis Troublée* (1922). "Bakst is immersed in Hellas (...) Bakst is obsessed with Hellas", wrote Benois in 1910.[93]

Bakst understood that the set, costume and the performer were of equal importance within the spectacle, and he perceived the stage in three dimensions, not as a mere extension of the easel – something that is immediately apparent from his major achievements such as *Cléopâtre, Schéhérazade* and *Le Dieu Bleu* (Cat. 47-49). True, Bakst did not believe in audience participation and he distinguished emphatically between the proscenium and the auditorium, but his concentration on elements such as diagonal axis, occult symmetry, and rhythmicality of the body broke the pictorial, i.e. painterly, convention of 19th century stage design, and, therefore, built a solid bridge between performer and public. Bakst's approach to stage design was an exciting one because, while joining "l'outrancière d'un barbare au raffinement sensuel d'un décadent",[94] he also made every effort to coordinate the decoration and the human figure. Like the Constructivist designers of the 1920s, especially Alexandra Exter, Liubov Popova and Varvara Stepanova, Bakst regarded the body as a dynamic force that was to be exposed and amplified in its movements, not enveloped and disguised. Instead of the constrained, static unit that the body tended to represent on the academic stage (a tradition that Benois never finally rejected), Bakst tried to make the body itself an expressive totality and to liberate its movement – while exerting reason and proportion and to argue, therefore, for the retention of the corset.[95] He also supplemented the physical motions of the body either by attaching appendages such as veils, feathers and jewelry (e.g., La Péri, Cat. 46) or by creating intricate abstract patterns of dress (e.g., the Pilgrim, Cat. 47) – so as to extend and emphasize the body's movement through space.

54. Auguste Bert, Photograph of Vaslav Nijinsky in *Le Dieu Bleu,* 1912. Photograpy courtesy private collection, St. Petersburg

Bakst, of course, emancipated the body from its conventional disguise on stage, but he did not expose it merely for erotic appeal, although his langourous sultanas captivate with their explicit and luscious proportions. Bakst regarded the nude body as an esthetic totality whose artistry had been forgotten under the weight of social and theatrical dress. As he indicated in his contribution to Nikolai Evreinov's survey of nudity on stage in 1911, he felt that the Ancient Greeks had known and praised this physical beauty and, in ths regard, he welcomed the antique evocations of Isadora Duncan and Olga Desmond. At the same time and however much Bakst loved the human anatomy, he saw its beauty to lie in the tension between the seen and the unseen, something that he achieved so masterfully in his costume for La Péri in the ballet of the same name (Cat. 46). Indeed, Bakst's gravitation towards exotic ballets – *Cléopâtre, Schéhérazade, Le Dieu Bleu, La Péri* – coincided, too, with the fashion for a lustful Orient that affected Moscow and St. Petersburg almost as much as it did Paris and London. Occasionally, Bakst might descend into a playful pornography as in his explicit filigrees for Alexei Remizov's tale of Tsar Dodon (D40; Fig. 56), but such sallies were few and far between.

In any case, while Bakst was fascinated by the exotic vision of the East as a place of sensual desire and consumption, it would be wrong to associate him too closely with the fashion for nudity and 'sex' on stage. By nature Bakst was retiring rather than flamboyant and his "Magdalenian" personality[96] sometimes dictated restrained and sober artistic forms as is manifest, for example, in his simple clothes designs for *Jeux* of 1913. Indeed, it is not very distant from this monochrome, functional sportswear to the *sportodezhda* (sports clothes) of Stepanova, the multi-use costumes of Nina Aizenberg or even Liubov Popova's blue denims for the workers in *The Magnanimous Cuckold* (1922), the moreso since the action of *Jeux* was cast in the year 1925. Bakst's knee-length skirt for the female tennis player represented an audacious development in fashion, at once enhancing her sexuality and, at the same time, symbolizing woman's freedom from the strictures of her 19th century social round. In this respect, Bakst was actually continuing his search for a new *haute couture* that he began in 1912, and the dynamism of sports, obviously, attracted him no less than the dynamism of the dance. As he implies in his several statements on women's fashion, he even wondered whether one day sports might not replace ballet and whether sportswear might not become the *haute couture.*

By 1914 Bakst had become a "legislator of fashion"[97] in Paris and St. Petersburg and although his reputation relied substantially on his successes as a stage designer, he continued to receive tributes for his many other activities – fashion designer, portrait painter, book illustrator, and lecturer. In broad terms, Bakst evolved from line to color: "From a graphist I've turned into a pure painter", he wrote to the critic Ettinger in

55. Fedor Boasson,
Photograph of Ida Rubinstein
wearing a costume by Léon Bakst
in *Salomé*. Reproduced
in Valeriian Svetlov, *Sovremennyi
balet*, Golike and Vilborg,
St. Petersburg 1911, p. 75

56. Léon Bakst,
Cover for Alexei Remizov,
Tsar Dodon, Petrograd 1921.
See D40

1910.[98] "It's easier to sense and to synthesize form through paint – it turns out more authentically, more tangibly," he wrote to Ostroumova-Lebedeva the same year.[99] In his Paris stage productions, between 1909 and 1914 (twelve of which he designed for Diaghilev), Bakst astounded audiences by his munificence of color and tactile forms. His exposure of the mobility of the human body was a simple and radical development and contrasted sharply with the traditional notion of the theatrical costume as an ornamental disguise. If his costumes and sets could be criticized at all, it was that they were too visual – "the spectacle dominates the music too much".[100] Although Bakst himself was aware of this incongruity, he was unable, and perhaps never really wished, to resolve it. Sometimes he did adjust his design to external demands, even though he was aware of the swiftness with which fashion and style changed, but, inevitably, he compromised or exaggerated, especially in some of his later commissions such as *The Sleeping Princess* of 1921 (Cat. 52-55 and D31).

Among Russian stage designers, Bakst enjoyed and still enjoys the widest recognition. His success was meteoric, but at great cost to his psychological and physical wellbeing, as is clear from his intimate correspondence with friends and colleagues: "I go to bed worn out and fall into depression several times a day. Want to give it all up and run off somewhere!"[101] There was something overripe, something fateful about Bakst's art, as if it mirrored his own morbid hypochondria. In 1913, at the height of his fame, Bakst remarked: "It's strange to feel horribly indifferent and almost despondent".[102] One paradox of Bakst's career lies in the fact that the surfeit of his colors and the lushness of his forms seem to draw their strength from desire consumed, but not gratified – and from an era fast receding, doomed to imminent destruction.

Coda

A history of modern Russian culture would be unthinkable without the names of Alexandre Benois and Léon Bakst. Both contributed directly to the brief, but brilliant artistic renaissance that Russia entered a century ago and their esthetic explorations, both sensible and sensual, left a profound and lasting influence on many artistic developments in both Russia and the West. Of course, Benois and Bakst possessed very different personalities, for if caution and measure can be associated with Benois, transgression and exuberance are synonymous with Bakst. Ultimately, however, both triumphed as critic and artist, observer and participant, and they did so because, albeit in varying degrees, they acknowledged the salubrity of reason, while delighting in desire. That the synthesis of reason and desire is an indispensable ingredient of the creative process – and of the artistic experiments of Benois and Bakst – is inherent in Benois' impassioned defense of the ballet: "Attempt to destroy any of its conventions and this will not only fail to lead to any improvement (...), but will appear as a crude invasion of reason, an attack against its very nature".[103] Surely, this formula can be applied to the constructs and artifacts of both Benois and Bakst, for, desirous of reason, they reasoned their desire.

[1] Schematic bio-bibliographies of Benois and Bakst are included in the List of Works. Unless indicated otherwise, abbreviated references in the footnotes below are to this source.
[2] Letter from Sergei Diaghilev to Elena Diaghileva dated 1909-10. Quoted in I. Nestiev, *Diagilev i muzykalnyi teatr XX veka*, Muzyka, Moscow 1994, p. 89.
[3] See the auction catalogs of his Paris estate, i.e. 1) *Bibliothèque Alexandre Benois et à divers,* Nouveau Drouot, Paris 1984, 29 October; 2) *Collection Alexandre Benois. Collection J. de Vichet et à divers amateurs,* Hôtel Drouot, Paris 1984, 16 November; 3) *Collection Alexandre Benois et à divers amateurs,* Hôtel Drouot, Paris 1985, 20 March. Some idea of the diversity of Benois' library in his St. Petersburg apartment on Glinka Street can be gained from the partial inventory that he made from memory in emigration. See "S-te Petersbourg (dit Petrograd, dit et maudit Léningrad)" in the Alexandre Benois Archive at the Harry Ransom Center, University of Texas, Austin (hereafter: Benois Archive, HRC). Call No.: Box 5, File 16 (eight pages).
[4] Apart from LRC and TBC, both of which contain extensive bibliographies, the following sources should be consulted for further information on Diaghilev and the Ballets Russes: R. Buckle, *Diaghilev,* Atheneum, New York 1979; I. Zilbershtein and V. Samkov (eds.),

Sergei Diagilev i russkoe iskusstvo, Izobrazitelnoe iskusstvo, Moscow 1982 (two volumes); *Strawinsky. Sein Nachlass. Sein Bild.* Catalog of exhibition at the Kunstmuseum, Basel 1984; *The Art of Enchantment. Diaghilev's Ballets Russes 1909-1929.* Catalog of exhibition at the Fine Arts Museums of San Francisco, 1988; L. Garafola, *Diaghilev's Ballets Russes,* Oxford University Press, New York 1989; R. Sheade, *Ballets Russes,* Seacaucus, Wellfleet, New Jersey 1989; *Diaghilev, Creator of the Ballets Russes.* Catalog of exhibition at the Barbican Art Gallery, London 1996; *Overdädets konst. The Art of Extravagance.* Catalog of exhibition at the Dansmuseet, Stockholm 1996; A. Schouvaloff, *The Art of Ballets Russes. The Serge Lifar Collection of Theater Stage Designs and Paintings at the Wadsworth Atheneum, Hartford, Conn.,* Yale University Press, New Haven 1997.

[5] Letter from Bakst to Emile Vuillermoz dated 29 May (1924). Carlton Lake Archive at the Harry Ransom Center, University of Texas, Austin.

[6] Letter from Bakst to Liubov Bakst dated 27 July, 1911. In I. Zilbershtein and V. Samkov (eds.), *Valentin Serov v vospominaniiakh, dnevnikakh i perepiske sovremennikov,* Khudozhnik RSFSR, Leningrad 1971, Vol. 1, p. 610. Shura is a diminutive of Alexander, Levushka of Lev (Leo). Liubov Pavlovna Bakst (née Tretiakova; first married name, Gritsenko, 1870-1928) was Bakst's wife from 1904 until 1910. For information on Bakst's "Levantinism" see Spencer, *Leon Bakst,* pp.13-24; *Russian Jewish Artists in a Century of Change 1890-1990.* Catalog of exhibition at the Jewish Museum, New York, 1995, passim.

[7] For information on the World of Art group see A. Benois,*Vozniknovenie Mira iskusstva,* Komitet populiarizatsii khudozhestvennykh izdanii, Leningrad 1928; N. Sokolova, *Mir iskusstva,* Gosizdat, Moscow-Leningrad 1934; V. Petrov, *"Mir iskusstva",* Izobrazitelnoe iskusstvo, Moscow 1975; J. Kennedy, *The "Mir iskusstva" Group and Russian Art, 1898-1912,* Garland, New York 1977; N. Lapshina, *"Mir iskusstva",* Iskusstvo, Moscow 1977; J. Bowlt, *The Silver Age, Russian Art of the Early Twentieth Century and the "World of Art" Group,* ORP, Newtonville, (Mass.) 1979; V. Petrov and A. Kamensky, *The*

World of Art Movement, Aurora, Leningrad 1991; S. Parshin, *Mir iskusstva,* Izobrazitelnoe iskusstvo, Moscow 1993.

[8] Statement attributed to Filosofov. Quoted in A. Grishchenko and N. Lavrsky, *A. Shevchenko,* IZONKP, Moscow 1919, p. 5.

[9] See S. Lifar, *Serge Diaghilev. His Life, His Work, His Legend,* Putnam, London 1940, Part III.

[10] Benois, *Memoirs,* Vol. 2, p. 26.

[11] Letter from Benois to Walter Nouvel dated 20 October, 1905, in RGALI. Call No.: f. 938, op. 1, ed. khr. 46.

[12] See D[iaghilev], "K postanovke 'Tristan i Izolde'" in *Mir iskusstva,* St. Petersburg, 1899, Vol. 1, Khudozhestvennaia khronika, pp. 135-37; A. Benois, "Postanovka Valkirii", *ibid.*, 1900, Vol. 1, Literaturnyi otdel, pp. 241-43; S. Diaghilev, "Gibel bogov", *ibid.*, 1903, No. 4, pp. 35-38.

[13] Letter from Benois to Walter Nouvel dated late November, 1898 in RGALI. Call No.: f. 938, op. 1, ed. khr. 46, l. 45.

[14] For details on Diaghilev's brief administrative position in the Imperial Theaters and his conflict with Sergei Volkonsky after *Sylvia* see Lifar, *Serge Diaghilev,* pp. 112-16.

[15] L. Bakst, "Puti klassitsizma v iskusstve" in *Apollon,* St. Petersburg 1909-10, No. 2, pp. 63-78; No. 3, pp. 46-61. For other extracts see *Selected Writings by Alexandre Benois and Léon Bakst* below.

[16] A. Benois, "Vystavka 'Soiuza'. I-IV" in *Rech,* St. Petersburg 1910, 26 February and 5,13, and 19 March. Quoted in Etkind, *A.N. Benua,* p. 187.

[17] Benois continued to supplement or modify his world history of painting in emigration. The Benois Archive, HRC, for example, contains manuscript chapters on Italian painting of the 17th and 18th centuries. Call No.: Box 1, Folder 4.

[18] M. Dobujinsky, "Vozniknovenie". Unpublished, undated manuscript, p. 50, New York, Columbia University, The Russian Archive. Call No: Box P7-3, No. 23.3.2.1.

[19] F. Dostoevsky, "A Strange Man's Dream" in D. Richards, ed., *The Penguin Book of Russian Short Stories,* Penguin, London 1981, p. 105.

[20] A. Benois, "Vystavka Pikasso" in *Poslednie novosti,* Paris, 1930, 21 March. Quoted in Etkind, *A.N. Benua,* p. 383.

[21] Benois, "Zhivopis Italii v XVII i

XVIII vekakh", Benois Archive, HRC, *op. cit.,* Box 1, Folder 4, p. 27. Benois' manuscript on Italian painting of the 17th and 18th centuries seems to have been intended as a continuation of his *Istoriia zhivopisi,* two volumes of which, treating of early Italian painting, were published by Shipovnik, Moscow, in 1912.

[22] Benois, *Zhizn khudozhnika,* Vol. 2, p. 357.

[23] A. Ostroumova-Lebedeva, *Avtobiograficheskie zapiski,* Soiuz sovetskikh khudozhnikov, Leningrad 1935, Vol. 1, pp. 188-90.

[24] A. Benois, "Obzor khudozhestvennoi zhizni" in *Rech,* St. Peterburg, 1909, 1 January, p. 3.

[25] A. Benois, "Khudozhestvennye eresi" in *Zolotoe runo,* Moscow, 1906, No. 2, p. 80. See *Selected Writings by Alexandre Benois and Léon Bakst* below.

[26] Benois, *Zhizn khudozhnika,* Vol. 2, p. 57.

[27] According to Etkind, *A.N. Benua,* p. 132.

[28] The avant-garde painter and poet, David Burliuk, even compiled a mosaic of statements by Benois culled from his newspaper reviews, publishing these in the form of a burlesque conversation between Benois, the Realist painter, Ilia Repin, and himself. See D. Burliuk, *Galdiashchie "benua" i novoe russkoe natsionalnoe iskusstvo,* Soiuz molodezhi, St. Petersburg 1913.

[29] Letter from Bouchène to Benois dated 28 February, 1931. Benois Archive, HRC, Box 6.

[30] B. Zaitsev, *Dalekoe,* Inter-Language Literary Associates, Washington D.C. 1965, p. 83.

[31] Benois, *Reminiscences,* pp. 156-57.

[32] Benois, *Vozniknovenie,* p. 20.

[33] N. Berberova, *Kursiv moi,* Fink, Munich 1972, p. 333.

[34] Benois, *Zhizn khudozhnika,* Vol. 1, p. 261.

[35] S. Makovsky, *Portrety sovremennikov,* Chekhov, New York 1955, p. 403.

[36] Parshin, *Mir iskusstva,* p. 16.

[37] Sokolova, *Mir iskusstva,* p. 117.

[38] Etkind, *A.N. Benua,* p. 145.

[39] Letter from Lancéray to Benois dated January, 1906. Quoted in E. Gomberg-Verzhbinskaia, *Russkoe iskusstvo i revoliutsiia 1905 goda,* Leningrad University, Leningrad 1960, p. 112.

[40] Letter from Grabar to Benois dated 25 March, 1904. In T. Kazhdan and V. Lazarev (eds.), *Igor Grabar. Pisma, 1891-1917,* Nauka, Moscow 1974, p. 151

[41] Letter from Bakst to Benois

dated 18 January, 1906. Quoted in Etkind, *Aleksandr Nikolaevich Benua,* p. 72.

[42] A. Fedorov-Davydov, "Leningradskaia shkola graficheskikh iskusstv" in V. Polonsky (ed.), *Mastera sovremennoi graviury i grafiki,* Gosizdat, Moscow-Leningrad 1928, p. 206.

[43] Yu. Annenkov, *Dnevnik moikh vstrech,* Inter-Language Literary Associates, New York 1966, Vol. 2, p. 202.

[44] M. Tenisheva, *Vpechatleniia moei zhizni,* Russkoe Istoriko-Genealogicheskoe obschestvo vo Frantsii, Paris 1933, p. 194.

[45] A few toys from Benois' collection were included in the exhibition "Benois and the Hermitage" at the Hermitage, St. Petersburg, 1994.

[46] Letter from A. Benois to Nikolai Benois dated 19 March, 1935. Quoted in Etkind, *A.N. Benua,* p. 400.

[47] Benois, *Reminiscences of the Russian Ballet,* p. 205.

[48] V. Ivanov, "Vagner i dionisovo deistvo" in *Po zvezdam,* Ory, St. Petersburg 1909, pp. 65-66.

[49] A. Ostroumova-Lebedeva, *Avtobiograficheskie zapiski,* Moscow-Leningrad, Iskusstvo, 1945, p. 37.

[50] Etkind, *A.N. Benua,* p. 227.

[51] Benois, *Reminiscences,* p. 5.

[52] A. Benois, *Istoriia zhivopisi v XIX veke,* Evdokimov, St. Petersburg 1901, p. 12.

[53] Letter from Bakst to Benois dated July, 1910. In Zilbershtein and Samkov, *Valentin Serov,* Vol. 1, p. 607.

[54] M. Fokine, *Memoirs of a Ballet Master,* Constable, London 1961, p. 188.

[55] Aleksandrova, *Aleksandr Benua,* Vol. 2, p. 473.

[56] N. Trukhanova, "Ogni rampy. Vospominaniia" in RGALI. Call No., f. 1403, op. 1, ed. khr. 932, l. 74.

[57] Benois, *Reminiscences,* p. 197.

[58] Benois, "Zhivopis Italii v XVII i XVIII vekakh", p. 44.

[59] S. Grigoriev, *The Diaghilev Ballet 1909-1929,* Constable, London 1953, pp. 53-54.

[60] Letter from Bakst to Liubov Bakst dated 28 May, 1911. In Zilbershtein and Samkov, *Valentin Serov,* p. 189.

[61] See *Collection Alexandre Benois. Collection J. de Vichet et à divers amateurs,* Lot 116.

[62] For a reproduction see, for example, Pruzhan, *Bakst* (1975), p. 208.

[63] A. Benois, "Artists and Their Participation in the Theater" in *Selected Writings by Alexandre Benois and Léon Bakst* below.

[64] G. Sciltian, *Mia avventura,* Rizzoli, Milan 1963, p. 324.

[65] See Benois Archive, HRC, Box 2, Folder 1.

[66] O. Vergani, "Alessandro Benois" in *Mostra dei Benois,* p. 22.

[67] The artist Maria Vorobev (Marevna), for example, felt that Bakst's décor for *Schéhérazade* was "uninspired". See M. Vorobev, *Life in Two Worlds,* Abelard-Schuman, London 1962, p. 193.

[68] Benois, *Memoirs,* Vol. 2, p. 66.

[69] L. Bakst, *Serov i ya v Gretsii,* Slovo, Berlin 1923, p. 26. See *Selected Writings by Alexandre Benois and Léon Bakst* below.

[70] Letter from Bakst to Liubov Bakst dated 20 May, 1907. In Zilbershtein and Samkov, *Valentin Serov,* Vol. 1, p. 604.

[71] S. Diaghilev, "V chas itogov" in *Vesy,* Moscow, 1905, No. 4, p. 46.

[72] Information on Bakst's early life, his Jewish milieu, and change of name is confusing and contradictory. For commentary on this problem see Spencer, *Leon Bakst,* pp. 13-17.

[73] According to Pruzhan, *Bakst* (1975), p. 10.

[74] Bakst, *Serov i ia v Gretsii,* p. 53.

[75] Letter from Eugene Somoff to Mstislav Dobujinsky dated 30 May, 1944. The Russian Archive, Columbia University, New York. Call No., Box P1-2, No. 23.2.71.

[76] According to *Vystavochnyi vestnik,* St. Petersburg 1906, No. 6, p. 5.

[77] Bakst would have seen Anglada's painting *Morphine Addict* in the special Anglada section of *Mir iskusstva,* 1904, No. 8-9, between p. 227 and p. 232.

[78] For information on the Siamese ballet in St. Petersburg see N. (=V.) Svetlov, "Siamskii balet" in L. Gelmersen (ed.), *Ezhegodnik Imperatorskikh teatrov. Sezon 1900-1901,* Imperial St. Petersburg Theaters, St. Petersburg 1901, pp. 293-98; reprinted in V. Svetlov, *Terpsikhora,* Marks, St. Petersburg 1906, pp. 159-66. On Bakst's response to the Siamese ballet see N. Misler, "Ex Oriente Lux: Siamese Dancing and the Ballets Russes" in *Annali dell'Istituto Universitario Orientale,* Naples 1986, Vol. 46, pp. 187-219.

[79] Letter from Bakst to Liubov Gritsenko dated 17 February, 1903. In Zilbershtein, Samkov, *Valentin Serov,* Vol. 1, p. 591.

[80] Benois, *Reminiscences,* p. 188.

[81] I. Gabar, *Moia zhizn: Avtomonografiia,* Iskusstvo, Moscow-Leningrad 1937, p. 158.

[82] Benois, *Vozniknovenie,* p. 42.

[83] A. Golovin, "Vstrechi i vpechatleniia" in A. Movshenson, ed., *Aleksandr Yakovlevich Golovin,* Iskusstvo, Leningrad-Moscow 1960, p. 98.

[84] Letter from Bakst to Benois dated 1903. Quoted in Pruzhan, *Bakst* (English version), p. 220.

[85] Letter from Bakst to Diaghilev dated 3 April, 1911. In Zilbershtein and Samkov, *Sergei Diagilev,* Vol. 2, pp. 114-15.

[86] N. Giliarovskaia, *Teatralno-dekoratsionnoe iskusstvo za 5 let,* Kombinat izdatelstva i pechati, Kazan 1924, p. 15.

[87] A. Benois, "Konstantin Korovin" in Zilbershtein, *Aleksandr Benua razmyshliaet,* p. 210.

[88] Letter from Bakst to Benois dated 1901. Quoted in Pruzhan, *Bakst* (1975), p. 55.

[89] Statement by Anna Ostroumova-Lebedeva. *Ibid.,* p. 58.

[90] Yu. Beliaev, "Ippolit" in *Novoe vremia,* St. Petersburg, 1902, 16 October. Quoted in Pruzhan, *Bakst* (1975), p. 63.

[91] Letter from Bakst to Liubov Bakst dated 10 May 1907. In Zilbershtein and Samkov, *Valentin Serov,* Vol. 1, p. 602.

[92] Viacheslav Ivanov delivered a lecture on Bakst's painting *Terror Antiquus* in 1909. See V. Ivanov, "Drevnii uzhas" in his *Po zvezdam, op. cit.,* pp. 393-424.

[93] A. Benois, "Eshche o vystavke 'Salon'" in *Rech,* 10 February, 1909. Quoted in Pruzhan, *Bakst,* p. 221.

[94] Boll, *Du Décor de théâtre,* p. 56.

[95] Text of a lecture that Bakst gave in the United States. Quoted in Bespalova, p. 10.

[96] Letter from Bakst to Nouvel dated 3 November, 1897 in RGALI. Call No.: f. 938, op. 1, ed. khr. 46, l. 66.

[97] Movshenson, *op. cit.,* p. 68.

[98] Letter from Bakst to Pavel Ettinger, dated 15 September, 1910. Quoted in Pruzhan, *Bakst* (1975), p. 135.

[99] Letter from Bakst to Ostroumova-Lebedeva dated 12 November, 1910. *Ibid.*

[100] Movshenson, *op. cit.,* p. 88.

[101] Letter from Bakst to Liubov Bakst dated 10 May, 1911. In Zilbershtein and Samkov, *Sergei Diagilev,* p. 189.

[102] Letter from Bakst to Liubov Bakst dated 17 June, 1913. Quoted in Pruzhan, *Bakst* (1975), p. 185.

[103] A. Benois, "The Décor and the Costume" in C. Brahms (ed.), *Footnotes to the Ballet,* Holt, New York 1936, p. 210.

57. E.D. Hoppé,
Photograph of Léon Bakst, 1916
See D56

Witnesses to Russia's Silver Age, Léon Bakst (Fig. 57) and Alexandre Benois were major contributors to the artistic renaissance that Russia – and St. Petersburg in particular – experienced at the turn of the 20th century and their intimate circle, the World of Art (*Mir iskusstva*), founded one hundred years ago, symbolized their noble aspiration to endow Russian poetry, painting, and music with a new vision and vitality. Subsequently, however, theirs was a culture that elicited only disdain and defamation by the Bolshevik *régime* and for long decades both Bakst and Benois were regarded as foreigners in their native land. True, most members of the World of Art and of the Silver Age in general emigrated just before or after the October Revolution, leaving only Alexander Golovin and Evgenii Lancéray to bear the banner of the World of Art into the Soviet era. In this way, the artistic beauty of that era fell victim to a total sublimation, becoming redundant and irrelevant to the exigencies of the Soviet apparatus.

But I had the good fortune to learn about Bakst (Fig. 58), Benois, and their colleagues as a child. My father, Alexander Pavlovich, the celebrated Soviet stage designer, president of the Union of Theater Artists, and academician, was an enthusiastic collector of Modernist reviews such as *Mir iskusstva* (World of Art), *Zolotoe runo* (Golden Fleece), *Apollon* (Apollo), and *Stolitsa i usadba: Zhurnal krasivoi zhizni* (Town and Country: A Journal of Beautiful Living) and our home even boasted several volumes of Benois' history of Russian painting. So it was precisely from these publications, from their half-tone and sepia illustrations, that I learned about Bakst and Benois as a student in the 1960s. For the longest time the Tretiakov Gallery did not exhibit works by the World of Art, so when canvases such as Bakst's *Terror Antiquus* or Konstantin Somov's *Lady in Blue* suddenly went on public display, there were no limits to our joy.

In the 1970s I enrolled in the Studio-School of the Moscow Art Theater, established by Konstantin Stanislavsky and Vladimir Nemirovich-Danchenko also, incidentally, a century ago. One of my teachers in the Department of Stage Design was Tatiana Borisovna Serebriakova, daughter of the painter Zinaida Serebriakova – a niece of Benois – who had emigrated to France in the 1920s. Tatiana Borisovna preserved the highest traditions of Russian culture, for she had trained at the Vaganova School in St. Petersburg in the same class as Alexandra Danilova (destined to become one of Diaghilev's prima ballerinas attired in the costumes of Bakst and Benois). The Studio-School happened to have a costume storage area, i.e. a depository of vintage costumes left over from previous productions at the Art Theater, and that is where I first saw original costumes that had been designed by World of Art artists (Figs. 59, 60). In fact, in his endeavor to improve the design level of his productions, Stanislavsky had invited three *miriskusniki* to come and work for him: Benois, Mstislav Dobujinsky, and Golovin.

Dobujinsky achieved particular recognition for his sets and costumes for *A Month in the Country* (Turgenev) and *Nikola Stavrogin* (adapted from Dostoevsky's novel *The Devils*) and is also remembered for his new designs for Griboedov's *Woe from Wit*. Benois joined the Art Theater as designer for new productions of the Pushkin *Little Tragedies* – as well as of Molière's *Tartuffe* and *Le Malade Imaginaire,* because the France of Louis XIV was especially close to him, 17th century Paris and Versailles being his passion. Golovin was also very active in the Art Theater, designing Beaumarchais' *Le Mariage de Figaro* and Shakespeare's *Othello.* During my time at the School these old costumes just lay around in obscurity gathering dust such as Benois' unique and wonderful Renaissance jackets for Pushkin's *Feast in the Time of the Plague,* although they were still in very good condition inasmuch as the production had not run for very long so they had not suffered wear and tear. Imagine my delight when, at the beginning of my career, I was allowed to use these costumes in my design scheme for the production of Robert Bolt's *Vivat! Vivat! Regina!*

After emigrating to France in 1982, I immersed myself in the traditions of the World of Art artists once again and by the good graces of Zinaida Serebriakova's son and daughter, Alexandre and Catherine, and the Lancéray and Benois families, I made the acquaintance of Dobujinsky's son, Rostislav, who invited me to assist him with the production of *Sortilège.* How valuable it was for me then to rediscover the behests of the World of Art – still hale and hearty in Paris. That is when I met Dimitri (Dmitrii) Dmitrievich Bouchène, the last of the *miriskusniki* and the *protégé* of Benois. He told me so much about Benois and, with scrupulous attention to detail, described Benois' faculty for rendering theatrical perspective that he had borrowed from the traditions of the 18th century Venetian theater. At that time Mila Markovna Bakst, Bakst's niece, was still alive, whose family ties linked her to the *regisseur* André Barsacq.

It is thanks to Maia Plissetskaia, prima ballerina at the Bolshoi, that I came to work as a costume and set designer for the ballet. As fate would have it, I happened to meet many survivors from the Diaghilev era in Paris, although at that time the principal custodian of the Diaghilev ballet tradition was Nicolas Beresoff, formerly an assistant of Michel Fokine, then living in London. His restorations of *Petrushka, Schéhérazade, Carnaval,* and *L'Après-midi d'un faune,* designed so many years before by Bakst and Benois, were brilliant and it is hard to imagine my delight when, in New York, I first saw the Joffrey Ballet's restorations of Fokine's ballets. Music and color, form and movement fused into a single totality, providing rich food for thought and reverie.

However, perhaps the most jealous guardian of the Diaghilev legacy was Olga Morozova de Basile, previously prima ballerina with the Ballets Russes de Monte Carlo which in the 1930s and 1940s won over audiences in North and South America, Europe, and Australia. After Diaghilev's death in 1929, the greater part of his estate (designs and décors) passed to the troupe founded by Colonel de Basile (Vasilii Voskresensky) and, until the 1960s, was the property of Olga Morozova when it was sold under the auspices of Diamantidi. Morozova, incidentally, received nothing from the sale, but that's another story.

At least three of my dear friends danced in the Bakst costumes for *Schéhérazade* – Tatiana Leskova and Tamara Grigorieva (both of whom are living in South America) and the late Valentina Kashuba (she passed away in Madrid recently aged 99). One-time members of the De Basile Company, they told me how the fabrics for the Bakst costumes had actually been painted and how in reality they were not transparent, even though the designs themselves seemed to be very light – and in this lay a notable difference between Bakst's costumes and those of Benois. If, for the former, a drawing or

60. E.D. Hoppé,
Photograph of Tamara Karsavina
in *The Firebird,* 1912
See D72

59. Auguste Bert,
Photograph of Vaslav Nijinsky
in *Le Festin,* 1909
Reproduced in Arthur Applin,
The Stories of the Russian Ballet,
Everett, London 1911,
between pp. 63 and 64

58. Léon Bakst, *Cupid Playing the Violin. Design for the Lid of a Snuffbox,* 1904
Watercolor, gouache, Indian ink, 13.7 × 8.3 cm
Moscow, State Tretiakov Gallery
Courtesy of Sergei Golynets

design carried expression and movement, a graphic lightness and transparency, then for the latter the design carried more static detail and a historicism, its apparent and natural elegance notwithstanding. Nevertheless, in my opinion, Bakst's costumes stand to less advantage on stage than do those of Benois, a *grand connoisseur* of fabrics and accessories and – the main thing – of scenic proportion.

To me it was Valentina Ivanovna Koshuba who really made the era of Bakst and the early Benois come alive. She danced with the Diaghilev troupe in 1914-18 and travelled with him throughout his European and American tours, accompanying him on his trips to the museums of Italy and Spain. Never parting with her Kodak, Valentina Ivanovna created a unique cycle of amateur snapshots which captured the costumes of Bakst and Benois with particular clarity and immediacy.

The World of Art is an indefeasible part of me. I have breathed its ether deeply and have imbibed its flavor – and I regard myself as its modern disciple. In Russia the pull of tradition is very strong, but I never realized that its effect upon me would be just as strong in France. I am gratified, indeed, that the Villa Favorita has organized such a remarkable exhibition in this centennial year: once again we can delight in a dazzling art, in an unfading radiance still playing in the refractions of the omnipotent prism of time.

Richard Buckle

Thoughts on Alexandre Benois*

61. Anna Ostroumova-Lebedeva
(1871-1944), *Portrait
of Alexandre Benois,* 1924
Watercolor, 44 × 42 cm
Moscow, Collection
of Svetlana Lancéray

* This is a revised version of the original article that appeared in the catalog of the exhibition "Alexandre Benois" organized by Hazlitt, Gooden and Fox, London, in 1970. We are grateful to Richard Buckle and to the publishers for their kind permission to reprint the text.

I never knew my own godfathers as both were killed in the First World War without ever setting eyes on me, but if I could have chosen one for myself – or wished one on the children of my dearest friends – it would have been Alexandre Benois (Figs. 61, 62). He always seemed to me the ideal fairy godfather.

In the forties and fifties I used to send Benois my monthly magazine *Ballet,* and it may have been by way of a thank you for this that he painted me a Christmas card showing three mysterious characters from ballets he had designed. His inscription read: "Les trois Mages ayant d'autres obligations à remplir ces jours-ci, j'ai demandé à trois magiciens de mes amis de vous porter, cher Mr. Buckle, mes meilleurs souhaits ainsi que l'assurance de ma très grande et sincère sympathie". The three magicians, he went on to explain, in case I was in any doubt, were the Charlatan from *Petrushka,* Councillor Drosselmeyer from *Casse-Noisette,* and King Hydraot from *Le Pavillon d'Armide* (Cat. 10). The first, with crafty eyes gleaming above his long white beard, brandished the flute with which to animate his puppets and charm the crowd; the second, patch over eye and parcel under arm, held up the big painted wooden nutcracker which would come to life and guide the child Clara through the snow kingdom to the land of gingerbread, sugarplums and candy; the third, with mantle, crown and staff, glanced sideways at the spectator, assessing his potential worth as a victim for the fair witch Armida. Did Benois see himself, as indeed I saw him, as one who, having learnt – not the black arts, but – the crimson-and-gold trickery of these dead enchanters, brought them to life again in little watercolors of his own, and sent them forth through the Fifth Column of the world's theatres, to subject us by their potent spells until the end of time?

Cocteau wrote of Diaghilev: "Il avait beau chercher des mécènes, le mécène c'etait lui" and one might echo his paradox in writing of Alexandre Benois. To find a magician he only had to look in the glass.

From childhood Benois had felt the magic of St. Petersburg, that "Palmyra of the North", and he immortalised in *Petrushka* (Cat. 18-31) his early memories of its pre-Lenten carnival, the Butterweek fairs, for which booths were erected on the square between the Admiralty, with its slender gilded spire, and the gilded dome and four belfries of St. Isaac's Cathedral; from his university days he had fallen under the spell of Tchaikovsky, attending some of the first performances of *The Sleeping Beauty* and *The Queen of Spades,* then in 1892 the first production of the composer's last ballet *Casse-Noisette,* all of which he designed later; and from the time of his first journey to France in 1896, overpowered by the beauty of Versailles (Fig. 63), he had begun to dwell in his imagination in the *grand siècle*, in the baroque and *rococo* periods, later revived by him in his first ballet – and the first that Diaghilev showed in the West, i.e. *Le Pavillon d'Armide*.

Both *Casse-Noisette* and *Armide*, incidentally, were based on stories by writers of the Romantic period, the former by E.T.A. Hoffmann, the latter by Théophile Gautier. Benois never lost his youthful love for the eerie atmosphere of Hoffmann's tales; and it is typical of his peculiar, allusive mind that – taking his cue from long-haired Gautier, who, though the staunchest of *hugolâtres*, still dreamed (no less than Baudelaire and the brothers Goncourt) of Watteau's *fêtes champêtres* – he should have cast a shadow of early nineteenth-century mystery across the ordered groves of golden Armida.

It was a long trek out to Benois' studio in a gloomy district off the Quai de Javel, far beyond the Eiffel Tower. I first went there in January 1947. The studio was vast, with an expanse of glass windows, a big work table and many portfolios of designs; and it was somehow divided by the barriers of bookcases and sofas and by the spiral staircase to the sleeping quarters (whither I never penetrated) into painting-room, sitting-room and library. I recorded our first meeting: "Alexandre Benois, the father of modern ballet, received me at the door of his studio in a fur-collared overcoat and a blue knitted cap. Paris is short of fuel. "It was in your magazine that I first saw a photograph of the realisation of the *Raymonda* designs I sent to America." He spoke of the ballet in Imperial Russia: "Gerdt, [the original René in his first *Armide*] had a style and nobility which I have never since seen, although later dancers could boast a far more remarkable technique". Of the first production of *Le Spectre de la Rose* – "Nobody wanted to do it. Fokine and Bakst were worn out with their other ballets that season, Nijinsky was tired". He showed me sketches of a complete version of *Le Lac des Cygnes*, including a marvelous dappled dawn over the lake for the apotheosis. When I spoke of the future of ballet and speculated on the possibility of another golden age, he cried immediately: "Il faut remonter *La Fille mal gardée*". He explained to me how to get back to the centre of Paris by *métro*, and where to change trains, saying "I shall give you the thread of Ariadne to lead you through the Labyrinth", and he handed me a *métro* ticket (which I shall always keep). Finally, a blessing – "J'ai une grande sympathie pour votre revue".

That summer Benois came to see me in London, commented on the Italian Baroque paintings and those of the Dutch *caravaggisti* which I then collected, and recalled seeing a picture by Abraham Bloemaert hanging in a small hotel he had stayed at near the church of St. Mary, Wyndham Place. I visited him more than once during the next ten years. The old man was very bent, which accentuated his patriarchal aspect and made him appear all the more a benevolent magician. As I sat beside him on a formal French sofa he would pat my knee and call me "dear". He always wore his wands of magical office – his pencils – in the breast pocket of his coat, as Fokine had noticed forty years before, "signifying his immediate willingness to draw a bit of scenery or an architectural detail on any available piece of paper..."

When I was gathering material for the Diaghilev Exhibition of 1954 he helped me generously, and besides lending his work, taught me how to spot a fake Bakst, wrote an introduction to the catalogue and painted a frontispiece for it in grey and *bistre*.

Although it was Benois who had first opened Diaghilev's eyes to the enchantment of ballet – and even earlier had guided his musical taste and vetted his tentative essays in art criticism – and although it was his *Pavillon d'Armide* (Cat. 7-16) which, along with the novel choreographic ideas of Fokine and the transcendent talents of Pavlova and Nijinsky, had decided Diaghilev to take the Russian ballet to Western Europe, Benois' theatrical genius had from the first Russian season of 1909 been eclipsed by the more spectacular achievements of Bakst. Indeed, Benois himself described how *Cléopâtre*, with Ida Rubinstein in the Egyptian décor of Bakst, even more than the genius of Chaliapin, Pavlova, Karsavina and Nijinsky, was the outstanding attraction of the first *Saison russe*.

62. Konstantin Somov
(1869-1939), *Portrait
of Alexandre Benois*, 1895
Charcoal and crayons
St. Petersburg, State Russian
Museum

63. Alexandre Benois,
Front cover of his book *Versailles*,
Akvilon, St. Petersburg 1922.
See D14

Only perhaps in his fantastic Chinese designs for Stravinsky's *Rossignol* in 1914 (now in the Ashmolean Museum, Oxford) did Benois compete in colour and exoticism with his friend. Although his *Giselle* of 1910 and his *Petrushka* of 1911 were perfect in their ways, they could hardly vie with such cataracts of colour and such cornucopias of pattern as flowed from Bakst to adorn Fokine's *Schéhérazade, Dieu Bleu, Narcisse* and *Daphins et Chloé*, or Nijinsky's *L'Après-midi d'un Faune*. Benois' calligraphic, Tiepolesque way of scribbling his costume designs appeared unimpressive beside the erotic contorsions or Beardsleyesque audacities of Bakst; and his delicate gradations of tone looked anaemic beside Bakst's areas of pure colour. Bakst always had one eye on the public and thought of his costume designs as finished pictures which would eventually be sold: indeed he had them copied by assistants so that they never risked damage at the dressmaker's. Benois thought only of making everything clear to the costumier. His sketches were often covered with written instructions (If you ever find a "Bakst" with writing all over you may be fairly sure it is a copy made by a pupil, although annotated by the artist himself. Exceptions to this rule are certain designs for Diaghilev's *Sleeping Princess* of 1921, for which several hundred sketches had to be produced in two or three months). Then, although Bakst died in Paris in 1924 shortly before Benois abandoned Russia for good, Benois found that Diaghilev, with his hunger for experiment, had left him far behind and dismissed him as intolerably old-fashioned. The comparative neglect of Benois has continued almost to the present day.

Yet Benois had a deeper love for the theatre than Bakst: it was in his blood. His great-great grandfather Giovanni Cavos was director of a theatre in Venice; his great-grandfather Catarino composed ballets in Italy before migrating to St. Petersburg, where he became Director of Music and encouraged Glinka; his grandfather, Alberto Camille Cavos, was the architect of the Mariinsky and Bolshoi Theatres in St. Petersburg and the restorer of the Moscow Bolshoi after the fire in 1853. While Benois' mother's ancestors were Venetian, his paternal forebears were French and German. His grandfather Louis-Jules Benois, born in the reign of King Louis XV, left France for Russia after the Revolution, and became supervisor of the Emperor Paul's kitchens. When this French Catholic married a German Lutheran they agreed that their male children should be brought up in the Roman, their female in the Protestant faiths. Echoes of this liberal-minded cosmopolitanism in Alexandre Benois' ancestry may be applauded today in the polyglot clowning of his grand-nephew Peter Ustinov, the Falstaff (albeit an honest one) of our second Elizabethan age, no less than in the latter's good work for UNESCO. Benois' father Nicolas was an architect, like his father-in-law, and built the Imperial stables at Peterhof, inspired by Hampton Court.

It must not be forgotten that Benois was an art historian and book-illustrator as well as a stage designer. From 1918 until 1926 he was Curator of the Hermitage. Then, few memories of childhood are so fascinating as his. During his lifetime, two volumes of *Memoirs* appeared, besides his *Reminiscences of the Russian Ballet*. I do not know how often I have read these books. The *Gemütlichkeit* of the artistic family's home in Nikolskaia Street, from whose windows one could look left towards the Bolshoi Theatre (destroyed in 1886 to make way for the Conservatoire of Music) and the towers of St. Nicolas' Cathedral, is conveyed by a sepia wash drawing, done in 1895 by the father of Alexandre, in which the old architect shows himself in the library, seated on a Chippendale chair at a huge double-sided desk in the cosy light of a hanging lamp, surrounded by his family portraits, his children and grandchildren. You can almost feel the heat from the corner stove. Alexandre ("Shoura"), not yet his father's most famous son, is drawing by the light of another lamp at a table beneath one of the tall curtained windows, watched by his nephew Eugène Lancerey, who did some of the best black and white illustrations for Diaghilev's magazine, *The World of Art*. Two other rooms, more brightly illuminated, are seen *en enfilade* through the open door. It was a large, happy and talented family. "Everyone in our house played the piano", wrote Alexandre Benois.

It was in this Benois' flat, and doubtless in this very room that the young provincial Sergei Diaghilev received from Alexandre in 1890 his first hints at a more sophisticated approach to the arts than he had acquired in far off Perm. He soon surprised his mentor, two years his senior, by leaping, as Benois wrote, "from indifference to enthusiasm, from total ignorance to unusual expertise... How amazed we should have been [Benois was referring to his friends Kostantin Somov and Diaghilev's cousin, Dmitri Filosofov, who had been at school with him, and to Bakst] to know that we had just welcomed the one who was to become in so few years 'Captain' of our team, the man who would help us to realise all our dreams in the varied fields of art!"

Benois evoked something of the winter glamour of his old home though on a more grandiose scale, in his designs for the opening scene of *Casse-Noisette*, in which a Christmas party of about 1800 was held in the *rococo* setting of an eighteenth century German *haut burgeois* house. Benois also recreated this work for the London Festival Ballet in 1957.

Benois realised no less than eleven productions of *Petrushka* (Cat. 18-31). This famous work had its origin in a *Konzertstück* which Stravinsky began in Switzerland during the summer of 1910, then continued in the South of France; its first designs were made in the artist's flat in St. Petersburg to the sound of revelry in Count Bobrinskoy's stables next door; its last bars were orchestrated to the music of the Barberini fountains in Rome in 1911; and its first production, with the inspired performances of Nijinsky (Fig. 59) and Karsavina (Figs. 60, 64), took place in Paris that spring. The resulting masterpiece was Benois' enduring tribute to the St. Petersburg he loved (shown not in the time of his own youth, but in that of Tsar Nicholas I), the city to which he persisted in referring in the time-honoured way – although "certain people", as he wrote to me in 1954, "are in the habit of giving it, quite unjustifiably, another name". Most of the other designs for this Diaghilev production are, as Benois told me, in the Tretiakov Gallery, Moscow. In later versions the fairground booths are decked with more flags or adorned with different popular paintings, but the frame, a sort of proscenium which helps to make the artist's joke about the boundaries between "life" and "art" – to suggest that we are watching a theatre within a theatre within a theatre – is always cobalt blue and overhung by looped crimson curtains fringed with gold; Zakharov's Admiralty spire nearly always appears in the background; and on the act drop, usually crossed by speeding demons of the night, there always looms over the switch-backs or *montagnes russes*, the vast edifice of Montferrand's St. Isaac's Cathedral. Not only Benois' sketches for the scenes and costumes, but his little notes for architectural details, for the cake and sweet stall, for samovars and for paintings to adorn the *balagani* give evidence of such knowledge, such careful thought and such love!

Benois designed four productions for *Giselle*, the first for Diaghilev in 1910, the others for the Paris Opéra and La Scala, Milan. His autumn wood with a distant castle on a crag, and his haunted moonlit glade give him the opportunity, as did his Gothic graveyard for *Les Sylphides*, to evoke the era of Carlotta Grisi and Marie Taglioni, which we only know from old prints and music covers. The student can seek proof of how subtly Benois saw his sketches for the Prince's squire in Diaghilev's production of *Giselle* by examining them in the London Theatre Museum.

64. Photograph
of Tamara Karsavina
in *Le Chant du Rossignol,* 1920.
Reproduced in Joseph Gregor
and René Fülöp Miller,
Das russische Theater, Amalthea,
Wien 1928, Ill. 117

Studying the old designs – and one surviving on-stage photograph – of Diaghilev's 1909 production of *Le Pavillon d'Armide*, I always thought that Armida's pavilion in the background must derive from the Piedemontese palaces of Juvara (which I only know from books), with perhaps a touch of St. Petersburg about the spire. After reading in 1979 Anthony Blunt's wonderful book on Borromini, so thrilling a revelation after so many years of that architect's strange genius, I realised that Benois must surely have been inspired by that baroque master, born by Lake Lugano – where Benois loved to spend his holidays – though he worked chiefly in Rome. The concave recesses, with columns at their projections, which surround a circular building, resemble those of the lantern of St. Ivo alla Sapienza, and derive, like the Temple of the Sun at Stourhead from the Temple of Venus at Balbeek. The artist had first planned *Armide* in 1907 for the Mariinsky Theatre, for which, after the ballet's Paris production in 1909, he revived it in 1919. In the original St. Petersburg production Armida's garden and palace were seen at an angle, and the latter had no spire; in the Paris production the building had a rectangular portico without pediment. The architectural sketches which he showed me, carefully hoarded by the artist in a folder inscribed "1907" and "1909", were evidently first thoughts for the earlier productions. He adapted these baroque ideas for *Les Noces de Psyché et de l'Amour* (arranged by Bronislava Nijinska for Ida Rubinstein) in 1928 and for the garden scene in *The Sleeping Beauty* at La Scala in the 1950s – for which last the artist gave me a little coloured design.

Alexandre Benois was an artist to whom the theatre's magic, the dust, the greasepaint, the tarlatan skirts and the smell of size, were the breath of life. He was a great and revolutionary designer, though he devoted himself mainly to reviving the glories of days gone by. He had the courage in an age when novelty was in demand, to follow the old masters, and at a time when scale was highly rated to concentrate on refinement of detail. The designs of Alexandre Benois remain modest and self-effacing in their tender perfection, even though the movement he initiated shook the world.

Alexander Schouvaloff

Léon Bakst, the Indispensable Designer

65. Léon Bakst, *Self-Portrait*, 1893
Oil on board, 34 × 21 cm
State Russian Museum,
St. Petersburg

From time to time for one reason or another a theatrical performance assumes the status of a legend. The first night of the ballet *Schéhérazade* on 4 June 1910 at the Opéra in Paris is such a performance (Cat. 45; D61, D66, D67; Figs. 66, 67). Although rave reviews and descriptive reports exist and can be read in newspapers of the time there is now no one left who remembers it or who can say whether those reports are true or not, whether those assessments are accurate or not. Had nothing like it been seen before in the west ? Did the performance truly create such a sensation ? Were Bakst's set and costumes quite so original? Did he in fact alter fashion and revolutionize theater design?

Unusually for legends there was an opportunity a few years ago to try to answer these questions and verify the claims. Michel Fokine, the original choreographer of the ballet, had performed *Schéhérazade* at the Stockholm Opera in January 1914 in a set and costumes made under Bakst's direct instructions to be identical to the ones used in Paris. The set was then preserved and mercifully, instead of being scrapped, was given to the Stockholm Dance Museum in 1971. In 1993 the Museum agreed to lend this original scenery for a revival of the ballet by the Stockholm Opera. I was in the audience in the full and expectant theater on the first night on 29 April. The house lights dimmed, the curtain went up on that famous set, and after a moment's stunned silence we all burst into spontaneous and prolonged applause. We had all suddenly understood something of what it must have been like on that night in Paris in 1910. Even with all our inherited experience we realized that the claims had been true.

Léon Bakst was an extraordinary artist. He was also fiercely ambitious and tried for a number of years to become a successful painter, but he achieved only minor distinction as a portraitist (Fig. 65) until he was introduced in 1890 along with Serge Diaghilev and others into the magic circle led by Alexandre Benois which later became known as *Mir iskusstva* (The World of Art). This in turn developed under Diaghilev's magisterial direction into the Ballets Russes. It was to be the making of Bakst, although he was already thirty-five when he designed his first derivative work for the theater in 1901. This was a production of Léo Delibes' ballet *Sylvia*, a co-operative hotch-potch of an effort by several members of the World of Art group which was canceled before it took place. But Bakst had finally found his true vocation. His talent was spotted and he was asked to design other productions. His technique followed that of other easel painters who had been encouraged to design for the stage: he was unaware of, or ignored the novel ideas of theater design being expounded by the minimalist Appia or the realist Antoine. His heroes were Matisse and Maurice Denis. His productions of *Le Coeur de la Marquise* and

57

Hippolytus in 1902 were followed by *Die Puppenfee* in 1903 and *Oedipus at Colonus* in 1904 (Cat. 41-44). Bakst's designs were for the most part in a rather dull and conventional style of landscape painting and book illustration, although he began to vary his style in some of his designs for the two Greek plays. Already obsessed by ancient Greece, Bakst spent many days researching in the basement of the Hermitage to ensure that his designs were archaeologically correct without necessarily being realistic; but some of his costume designs were also beginning to be more flamboyant indicating character and movement.

66. E.D. Hoppé, Photograph of Tamara Karsavina in *Schéhérazade,* 1911. See D66

Bakst did not find his unique style until after his visit to Greece and Crete in May 1907. This journey, with his friend the painter Valentin Serov, fulfilled a dream and profoundly affected him as an artist. Having derived his knowledge of ancient Greece from museums and books he only half accepted the scholarly view that the classical world was refined and pale. He had suspected a world of brilliant color and now he saw it: the journey was both a revelation and a confirmation. Bakst and Serov spent some days looking at, and being staggered by, the disclosures then being made by Sir Arthur Evans who was uncovering the ruins of the Palace of Minos at Knossos. The sketches Bakst made in Greece of figures in landscapes, people in boats, painted houses, polychromed architectural details, bare-breasted Cretan women with details of jewelry, ornaments and decorative geometric patterns remained in his memory and were henceforth reflected, sometimes with accuracy, sometimes with variation, sometimes with distortion, in all his subsequent work for the theater. Above all, his palette blossomed into the startling range of brilliant colors which he used in the theater with such freshness and originality.

His colors, for they soon became personalized, first found their true expression in the set and costumes for *Cléopâtre* which was the last of the new ballets performed at the Châtelet Theater in Paris on 2 June 1909 during the first ballet only season of the Ballets Russes. It was an eye-opener for Parisians and a triumph for Bakst. The historian Huntly Carter wrote of Bakst's work: "*Cléopâtre* illustrated his mastery of chromatic combinations, and the use of the five primary colors in endless harmonies, as well as his right understanding of the note of style to be found in coherence and uniformity. The whole was held together by a tremendous design or framework into which he poured characteristic Egyptian motives which were caught up and repeated in the movements, costumes, and even in the ornaments worn by the dancers. This dominant mood flowed uninterruptedly from beginning to end and thus his contribution to the Ballet was seen to be the essential line and color of one great rhythmic movement. He provided, indeed, the connecting links of a whole series of rhythms".[1] Substitute the title for any other later production, change the adjective 'Egyptian' for another appropriate label and this appreciation could be equally applied to all his subsequent work for the theater summarized by the word 'Bakstian' which itself became an adjective.

67. Auguste Bert, Photograph of Vaslav Nijinsky in *Schéhérazade,* 1911 St. Petersburg, photograph private collection

Bakst's great innovation and originality as a theater designer was in determining the right "band of color" (as he called it) for any given production and then following it through, or, as he explained once in a letter to Diaghilev, "the whole essence of my designing for the theater is based on the most calculated arrangement of patches of color against the background of a set with costumes which correspond directly to the physique of the dancers".[2] Bakst was the first to use the whole stage peopled with performers as a canvas in this way. It was not just a question of a band of color but how it was used. The floor of the stage was as important an element of the set as the ceiling. Furniture was carefully designed. Lighting, often set by Diaghilev, was also crucial. The costumes, often supplied by the Parisian costumier Marie Muelle, had to be made to the highest specifications using the best materials, as were the shoes and props. Make-up and wigs too were precisely detailed. He was a painter in more than three dimensions: the movements of the costumed characters within the painted set over a certain period of time were all part of his carefully prepared design plan. This is why he always insisted on seeing a detailed libretto

and participated in discussions about choreography. But of course Bakst had to rely on others to execute his designs. However, in a medium in which the desired result is so often subject to compromise he compromised as little as possible. He never took short cuts, and always insisted on maintaining overall control. This was all part of his innovation, but his pernickety attention to every detail, this insistence on perfection, while being much admired, also often irritated his colleagues. He used to have furious rows with Diaghilev who shouted back but generally let him have his way because the results were so magnificent.

68. (Léon Bakst)
Photograph of the Oriental Quadrille at the Costume Ball hosted by Countess Mariia Kleinmikhel, St. Petersburg, January 1914. Bakst was responsible for many of the fancy dresses here – one of the last great balls of the Russian nobility. Reproduced in *Stolitsa i usadba*, St. Petersburg, 1914, 15 February, No. 4, p. 21. See Fig. 69 and D47. For further commentary, including identification of some of the individuals, see Boris Ometev and John Stuart, *St. Petersburg. Portrait of an Imperial City,* The Vendome Press, New York 1990, p. 129.

If *Cléopâtre* had introduced Bakst's originality and splendor to Parisian audiences then *Schéhérazade* confirmed his uniqueness in their minds. It completely realised Benois' opinion that Bakst had been "nursing a secret ambition to be a "great and remarkable artist'".[3] It also made him one of the busiest designers for the theater. Between 1911 and the beginning of the First World War he designed nine ballets for Diaghilev, four plays for Ida Rubinstein with casts of hundreds, a ballet for Anna Pavlova, various other sets and costumes for operas and a revue in London, many individual costumes for fancy-dress balls usually "à la *Schéhérazade*" (Figs. 68-70) and had as well one-man shows in Paris, London, Berlin and the United States. Also, between the end of 1912 and the beginning of 1913, as a kind of relaxation, away from the frenetic demands of the theater, Bakst made his series of drawings called "Fantasies on Modern Costume" (Cat. 64). These delicately sensual pin-up girls with modest sex-appeal dressed in adaptations of contemporary fashion were gentle fantasies and were called after Greek goddesses and nymphs, 'Nike,' 'Atalante', 'Alcyone', or after fashionable seaside resorts such as 'Deauville'. The dresses, made up by the *couturier* Jeanne Paquin, were launched in Paris at the end of March 1913. Bakst said: "A woman's dress is my most cherished dream. In spite of my many productions for the theater, every morning, when I wake up, I create one or two dresses with which I adorn, sometimes in my imagination, sometimes in actual fact, elegant women with beautiful bodies".[4]

69. Léon Bakst, Design for the Oriental Costume for Princess Natalia Gorchakova at Countess Mariia Kleinmikhel's Costume Ball, January, 1914. Reproduced in *Stolitsa i usadba*, St. Petersburg 1914, 20 April, p. 19 (photographer unknown). Princess Gorchakova wearing the costume can be seen in the group photograph of the Ball. See Fig. 68 and D47

Schéhérazade prompted critics to use words like "sensual", "erotic", and "sumptuous" to describe Bakst's work, words which stuck and were often repeated in descriptions of later productions. The set and costumes for *Schéhérazade* were full of dazzling greens, blues, reds, oranges and yellows contrasting with each other, but his colors only underlined and confirmed the violence and eroticism of the music, choreography and dancing. Although he was never afraid of using violently clashing colors, his designs never clashed with the action of any particular ballet.

While later productions varied enormously in style and period as well as in manner of drawing, Bakst's approach to the design of the sets and costumes was constant. He also elaborated a symbolic use of color. In an interview for the *New York Tribune* he said: "I have often noticed that in each color of the prism there exists a gradation which sometimes expresses frankness and chastity, sometimes sensuality and even bestiality, sometimes pride, sometimes despair. That is what I tried to do in *Schéhérazade*. Against a lugubrious green I put a blue full of despair, paradoxical as it may seem. There are reds which are triumphal and there are reds which assassinate. There is a blue which can be the color of St. Madeleine, and there is a blue of Messalina (...) My method is generally to take a simple motif and vary it indefinitely, so as to create a harmony of color and line".[5] Among the large number of productions that Bakst designed there were more 'oriental' style ballets such as *Le Dieu Bleu* (Cat. 47-49) in which pure white, the most difficult color, was predominant in the costumes against orange rock and a deep blue starry sky, ancient Greek style ballets such as *Daphnis et Chloë* and the plays for Rubinstein, and

Hélène de Sparte (Cat. 50) *Phaedre*, with costumes patterned with Greek motifs against sun-scorched landscapes. There were exotic ballets such as *Thamar* (D58, D59), romantic such as *Carnaval* (D73, D84, D86), or Biedermeier-romantic-botanic such as *Le Spectre de la Rose* (D68, D77), and even anthropomorphic such as *L'Après-midi d'un Faune*. Only Bakst could have got away with designing a costume for a rose without the dancer looking ridiculous, or a costume for a faun without him looking foolish. But then Nijinsky was probably the only dancer who could be believable as the spirit of a rose and convincing as a faun cavorting with nymphs on a sultry afternoon. Both these productions also quickly became legendary.

70. (Léon Bakst)
Photograph of the Ball of Colored Wigs hosted by Anastasia Leonard, St. Petersburg, on 22 March, 1914. Bakst was responsible for many of the dresses and the hairstyles. Reproduced in *Stolitsa i usadba*, St. Petersburg 1914, 1 May, No. 9. p. 27

The Sleeping Princess in 1921 (D80) was the last production Bakst designed for Diaghilev and it was on a bigger scale, more splendid and more extravagant than any earlier production. 'Sumptuous' was again the most appropriate word to use to describe it. Using for the most part his previous work for Anna Pavlova for *The Sleeping Beauty* in New York in 1916 he applied his basic principle of theater design to startling and memorable effect. The critic of *The Dancing Times* gave a graphic impression of the production: 'The principle upon which the decor was generally arranged was the same throughout the various scenes (...) It solely consisted in arranging the sets in dull colors, and grouping the dancers on opposite sides of the stage costumed in opposing or contrasting colors".[6] Bakst's designs were neither original or new but *The Sleeping Princess* is generally considered to be his crowning achievement (Cat. 52-55; D31, D45). This is perhaps because there are still some people who can remember it while no one can remember *Schéhérazade*.

Revivals of productions without the presence or participation of the original designer often deteriorate into mediocrity. That perceptive chronicler of the Ballets Russes in London, Cyril W. Beaumont, was disappointed by an early revival of *Schéhérazade* in 1918 and wrote that "the Bakst scenery, however, was only a shadow of its former self. The lamps had vanished and the whole set appeared to have been crudely simplified, and to have lost its subtleties of color and lighting, in particular the mysterious shadows at the base of the walls, which hinted at so much".[7] Last year I saw a revival of *Schéhérazade* by the Kirov ballet for which they acknowledged having used Bakst's set and costume designs. They had done nothing of the kind. The set and costumes were quite wrong in color and construction and the atmosphere created was merely gaudy. Bakst could be often garish, sometimes even crude in his use of color, but he never descended into kitsch. He always maintained a wonderfully refined good taste. He made himself indispensable because in supervising every detail he ensured consistent excellence. This is why I will never forget that night at the Stockholm Opera in 1993 nor, I am sure, will anyone else who was there;. We all felt as if Bakst was present and had himself participated in a genuine revival. Our applause at the sight of his set was not out of reverance for an old master but in recognition of a thrilling and still amazingly original piece of theater.

[1] H. Carter, *Catalogue of an Exhibition of Drawings by Léon Bakst with a Prefatory Note by Huntley [sic] Carter*, The Fine Art Society, London 1912, p. 4. repeated in a slightly different introduction in *Catalogue of an Exhibition of Drawings by Léon Bakst for Ballets, Plays and Costumes*, The Fine Art Society, London 1913, p. 4.
[2] Bakst in Paris to Sergei Diaghilev in Monaco in a letter dated 15/18 April 1911 quoted in I. Zilbarshtein and V. Samkov, *Sergei Diaghilev i russkoe iskusstvo* Izobrazitelnoe iskusstvo, Moscow 1982, Vol. 2, p. 116.
[3] A. Benois, *Reminiscences of the Russian Ballet*, Putnam, London 1941, p. 160.
[4] Quoted in "La Comédie de la Mode", "Robes Modernes de Léon Bakst", *Comoedia Illustré*, Paris, 20 Feb. 1913, p. 479.
[5] In R. Strunsky, "Léon Bakst on the Modern Ballet", *New York Tribune*, New York, 5 Sept. 1915.
[6] "Notes on Decor, The Sleeping Princess", *The Dancing Times*, London, Dec. 1921, p. 283.
[7] C.W. Beaumont, *The Diaghilev Ballet in London*, Putnam, London 1940, p. 119.

Alexandre Benois

Alexandre Benois
*Portrait of Mstislav Dobujinsky
on the Terrace of the Villa du Midi,
Lago di Lugano*, 1908
Watercolor, 22 × 27.5 cm
London, Collection of Nina
and Nikita D. Lobanov-Rostovsky
(Cat. 1)

Alexandre Benois
Lago di Lugano, 1913
Watercolor, indian ink, pencil
on paper, 32 × 43 cm
Moscow, State Tretiakov Gallery
(Cat. 2)

Alexandre Benois
Versailles. Parterre d'eau, 1906
Watercolor, gouache,
31 × 49.5 cm
Moscow, State Tretiakov Gallery
(Cat. 4)

Alexandre Benois
*Versailles. L'Allée
des philosophes*, 1905
Watercolor and gouache,
40.8 × 33.5 cm
Moscow, State Tretiakov Gallery
(Cat. 3)

Alexandre Benois
*The Bolshoi Theater,
St. Petersburg, in 1885*, 1939
Gouache and watercolor,
34 × 60 cm
New York, Collection
of Alex Rabinovich
(Cat. 5)

Alexandre Benois
The Gardens of Diana
Panneau for the Contemporary Art
Showrooms, St. Petersburg, 1902
Colored indian ink, whitening,
watercolor, pencil on paper
on board, 37.7 × 61.9 cm
Moscow, State Tretiakov Gallery
(Cat. 6)

Alexandre Benois
Design for the Gobelin, 1907
Watercolor, 44 × 40.5 cm
(with mount); 33 × 35.3 cm
(without mount)
Moscow, State Bakhrushin
Theater Museum
(Cat. 7)

Alexandre Benois
*Stage Design for Armide's
Garden, Scene 2*
(preliminary sketch), 1907
Watercolor and ink,
18.5 × 26.5 cm
San Antonio (Texas),
Collection of Robert Tobin
(Cat. 8)

Alexandre Benois
*Stage Design for Armide's
Garden, Scene 2*, 1909 (?)
Watercolor, india ink, pencil,
and gouache, 47.5 × 63.2 cm
London, Collection of Nina
and Nikita D. Lobanov-Rostovsky
(Cat. 9)

Alexandre Benois
*Costume Design
for the Cavalier*, 1907
Watercolor, pencil, whitening,
bronze and silver paint
38.3 × 26.5 cm
St. Petersburg, State Museum
of Theater and Music
(Cat. 11)

Alexandre Benois
*Costume Design
for a Dancer*, 1907 (?)
Watercolor, pencil, whitening,
bronze paint on brown paper
33.3 × 25.5 cm
Moscow, State Bakhrushin
Theater Museum
(Cat. 13)

Alexandre Benois
*Costume Design
for the Marquis de Fierbois
Dressed as King Hydraot*, 1907 (?)
Watercolor, pencil, whitening,
silver and bronze paint
38.6 × 22.2 cm
Moscow, State Bakhrushin
Theater Museum
(Cat. 10)

Pav[?] de
Armide

Le roi
Hidart

1909

(Sons Paris)

Alexandre
Benois

Alexandre Benois
Costume for the Cavalier, 1907
Cotton, silk and metal lame
St. Petersburg, State Museum
of Theater and Music
(Cat. 12)

Alexandre Benois
Jacket for the Buffoon, 1907
Taffeta, brocade, braid,
lace, buttons
St. Petersburg, State Museum
of Theater and Music
(Cat. 15)

Alexandre Benois
Cloak , 1907
Silk, rep, braid, embroidery
St. Petersburg, State Museum
of Theater and Music
(Cat. 16)

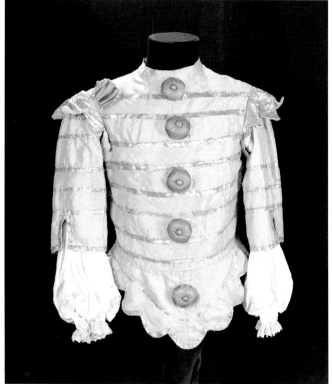

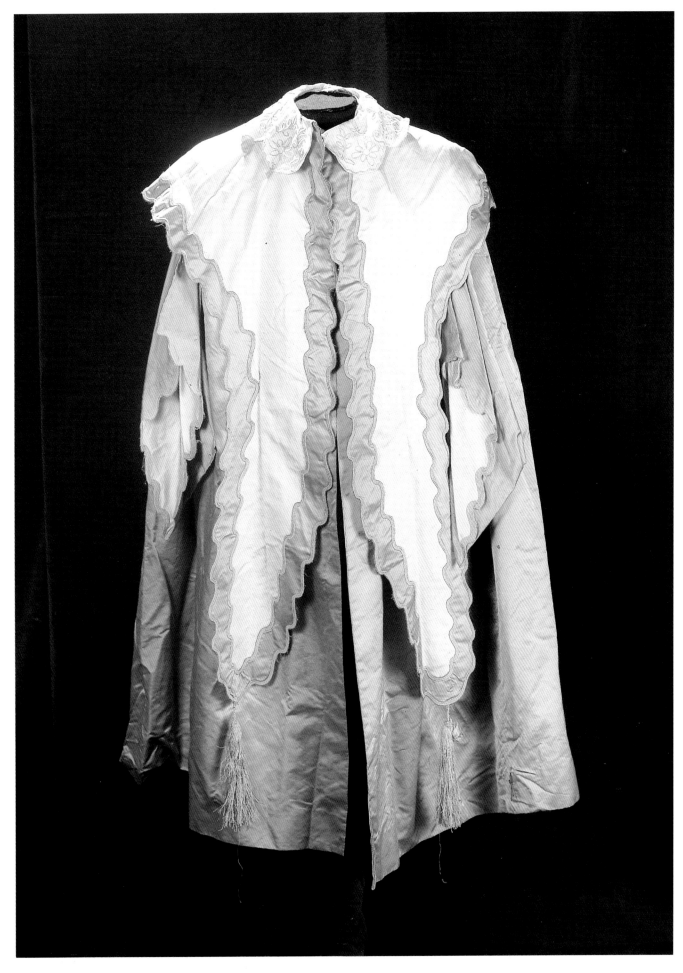

Alexandre Benois
Design for Two Costumes, 1907
Watercolor, pencil, whitening,
bronze and siver paint
34 × 37.3 cm
St. Petersburg, State Museum
of Theater and Music
(Cat. 14)

Valentin Aleksandrovich Serov
(1865-1911)
*Poster advertising
the inauguration of the first
"Russian Season" at the Théâtre
du Chatelet, Paris, in May-June,
1909*
Lithographic poster in black
and white on a blue background
254 × 192 cm
Moscow, State Bakhrushin
Theater Museum
(Cat. 17)

THÉÂTRE DU CHÂTELET
SAISON RUSSE
MAI
JUIN
1909
OPÉRA ET BALLET
ADMINISTRATION G. ASTRUC & Cie
PAVILLON de HANOVRE. 32, Rue Louis-le-Grand
EUGÈNE VERNEAU, 108, rue Folie Méricourt, Paris

Alexandre Benois
Backdrop for the Fair,
Scenes 1 and 4, 1947
Watercolor, gouache,
and pencil, 32.5 × 47.5 cm
London, Collection of Nina
and Nikita D. Lobanov-Rostovsky
(Petrushka, Cat. 18)

Alexandre Benois
*Backdrop for Petrushka's Room,
Scene 2*, 1948
Watercolor, gouache
and ink 23.5 × 35.5 cm
London, Collection of Nina
and Nikita D. Lobanov-Rostovsky
(Petrushka, Cat. 19)

Alexandre Benois
*Backdrop for the Moor's Room,
Scene 3*, 1956
Pencil ink, watercolor
and gouache, 27 × 40 cm
Lugano, Thyssen-Bornemisza
Collection
(Petrushka, Cat. 20)

Alexandre Benois
*Design for the Curtain with Night
Scene, Fantastic Creatures in the
Sky, and the Admiralty Tower
in the Background*, 1957
Watercolor and ink, 32 × 49 cm
London, Collection of Nina
and Nikita D. Lobanov-Rostovsky
(Petrushka, Cat. 22)

Alexandre Benois
*Sketch for the Scene
where Petrushka Kisses
the Ballerina*, 1945
Watercolor, pencil and black
ink, 13 × 18 cm
London, Collection of Nina
and Nikita D. Lobanov-Rostovsky
(Petrushka, Cat. 21)

Alexandre Benois
Petrushka, 1947
Watercolor, ink and pencil,
27.5 × 19 cm
London, Collection of Nina
and Nikita D. Lobanov-Rostovsky
(Cat. 23)

Alexandre Benois
The Ballerina, 1947
Watercolor, gold, ink and pencil
27.5 × 19 cm
London, Collection of Nina
and Nikita D. Lobanov-Rostovsky
(Petrushka, Cat. 24)

Alexandre Benois
The Moor, 1947
Watercolor, silver paint, ink,
and pencil, 27.5 × 19 cm
London, Collection of Nina
and Nikita D. Lobanov-Rostovsky
(Petrushka, Cat. 25)

Alexandre Benois
The Moor with a Sword, 1947
Watercolor, black ink, gold paint
and pencil, 23 × 16 cm
London, Collection of Nina
and Nikita D. Lobanov-Rostovsky
(Petrushka, Cat. 26)

At page 80
Alexandre Benois
*The Second Barrel
Organ Grinder*
Watercolor and black ink,
31 × 23 cm
London, Collection of Nina
and Nikita D. Lobanov-Rostovsky
(Petrushka, Cat. 27)

At page 81
Alexandre Benois
Lady with Her Son
Watercolor, ink
and pencil, 26 × 18 cm
London, Collection of Nina
and Nikita D. Lobanov-Rostovsky
(Petrushka, Cat. 28)

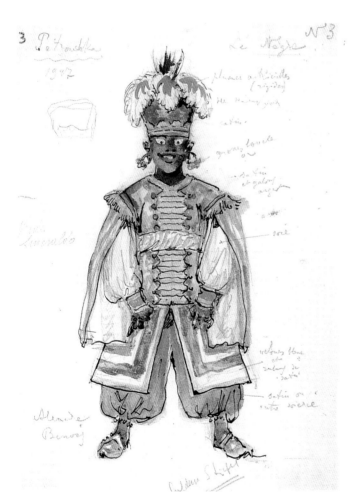

Petrouchka
clochettes
N°7
Second Organ Grinder
Второй шарманщик
cuivre
drap en loques
très usé

Alexandre Benois
*Young Girl Disguised
as a Polish Maid*, 1956
Watercolor, ink and pencil,
31 × 24 cm
London, Collection of Nina
and Nikita D. Lobanov-Rostovsky
(Petrushka, Cat. 29)

Alexandre Benois
*Balloon Vendor and Boy
from the People*, 1956
Watercolor and ink, 31 × 23.5 cm
London, Collection of Nina
and Nikita D. Lobanov-Rostovsky
(Petrushka, Cat. 30)

Alexandre Benois
Costume for a Lady, 1911 (?)
Velvet, silk, cloth, braid
and cord with metal thread
and metal buttons
St. Petersburg, State Museum
of Theater and Music
(Petrushka, Cat. 31)

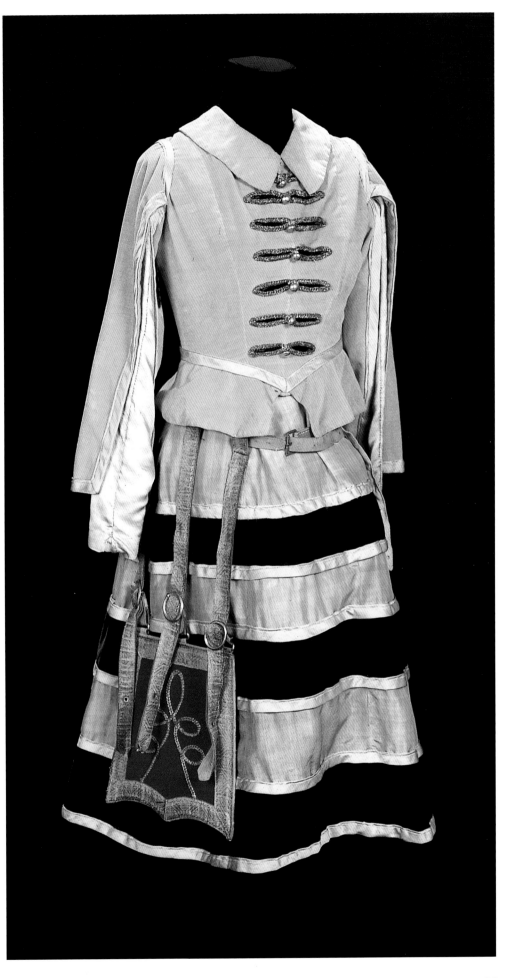

Alexandre Benois
Décor for Act III, Scene 2:
On the Quay of the Neva, 1919
Pencil, watercolor
and gouache, 37.5 × 61.6 cm
Lugano, Thyssen-Bornemisza
Collection
(Queen of Spades, Cat. 33)

Alexandre Benois
The Throne Room.
Décor for Act III, 1914
Gouache on paper laid down
on canvas, 99 × 109.5
San Antonio (Texas), Collection
of Robert Tobin
(Le Rossignol, Cat. 32)

Alexandre Benois
*Décor for Scene 2:
The Miraculous Apparition
of the Town of Ledenets*
Pencil, watercolor
and gouache, 44 × 61 cm
Lugano, Thyssen-Bornemisza
Collection
(Le Princesse Cygne, Cat. 34)

Alexandre Benois
Handwritten letter on four
pages from Alexandre Benois
to Cyril Beaumont dated
29 April, 1947 carrying
a watercolor sketch for
Tchaikovsky's ballet *Swan Lake*
Watercolor, pencil and ink,
22.5 × 17.5 cm (paper size)
New York, Collection
of Alex Rabinovich
(Cat. 35)

Alexandre Benois
Décor for Scene I, 1940
Pencil, ink, waterfolor
and gouache, 27.8 × 38.4 cm
Lugano, Thyssen-Bornemisza
Collection
(Les Deux Tisserands, Cat. 36)

Alexandre Benois
Décor for Scene 4
Pencil, ink, watercolor
and gouache, 27.8 × 38.4 cm
Lugano, Thyssen-Bornemisza
Collection
(Les Deux Tisserands, Cat. 37)

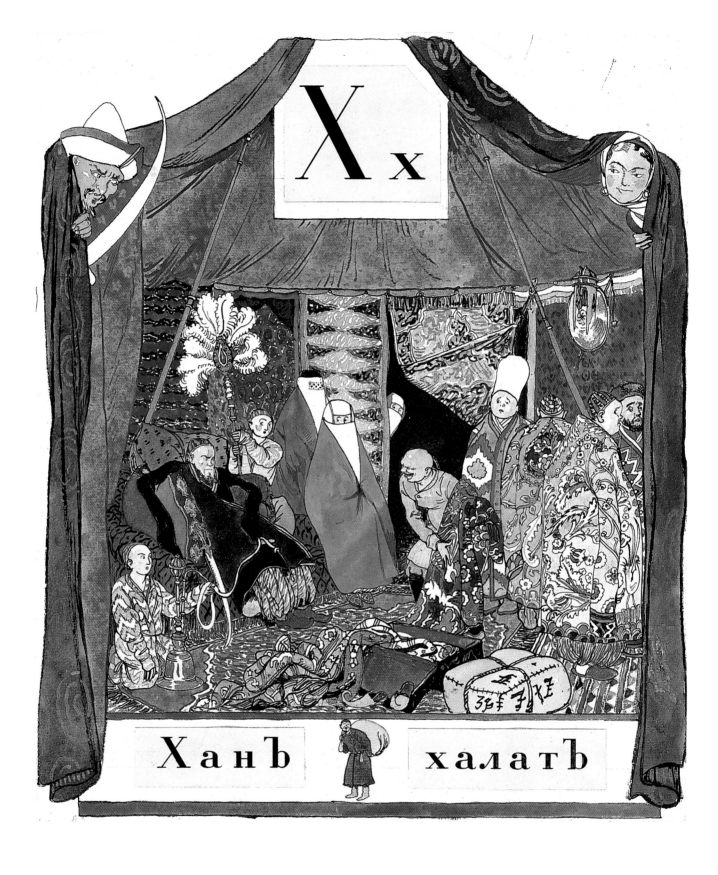

Х x

Ханъ **халатъ**

Alexandre Benois
The Letter "Kh" for Khan, Khalat
(Khan, Dressing-Gown)
Gouache, Indian ink, bronze paint,
watercolor, 36.5 × 30.8 cm
Moscow, State Tretiakov Gallery
(Cat. 38)

Alexandre Benois
Eight Postcards
on the Theme of Toys, 1904-20s
Each card, 9 × 14.2 cm
i) *The Monastery* (untitled)
ii) *The Country Estate*
Oxford (Ohio), Collection
of C. and A.L. de Saint-Rat,
(Cat. 39)

УСАДЬБА.

Alexandre Benois
Eight Postcards
on the Theme of Toys, 1904-20s
iii) *First Acquaintance*
iv) *Choir of Wetnurses*
Oxford (Ohio), Collection
of C. and A.L. de Saint-Rat,
(Cat. 39)

ХОРЪ КОРМИЛИЦЪ

Alexandre Benois
Eight Postcards
on the Theme of Toys, 1904-20s
v) *Poultry Yard*
vi) *Infantry*
Oxford (Ohio), Collection
of C. and A.L. de Saint-Rat,
(Cat. 39)

Птичій дворъ.

Пѣхота.

изъ міра фантастичнаго I.

Alexandre Benois
*Eight Postcards
on the Theme of Toys*, 1904-20s
vii) *From the World
of the Fantastic, No. 1*
viii) *Russian Toys*
Oxford (Ohio), Collection
of C. and A.L. de Saint-Rat,
(Cat. 39)

List of Works

Measurements are in centimeters, height preceding width. Works are on paper unless stated otherwise. Inventory numbers are in parentheses. The works in the Thyssen-Bornemisza Collection are also reproduced in color and described in detail in TBC. The reader is urged to consult this source for further commentary on individual items.

Schematic bio-bibliographies of Benois and Bakst are included in the List of Works. Unless indicated otherwise, abbreviated references in the footnotes below are to this source

Alexandre Nikolaevich Benois*

Born 21 April, 1870, St. Petersburg; died 9 February 1960, Paris.

Son of Nikolai Leontievich Benois, academician and architect, and of Kamilla Albertovna (née Kavos), a musician; uncle of the artists Evgenii Lancéray and Zinaida Serebriakova; 1885-90 attended Mai's Gymnasium, St. Petersburg, where he met some of the future members of the World of Art group; 1887-88 audited classes at the Academy of Arts, St. Petersburg; 1890 travelled in Germany; met Léon Bakst; 1890-94 studied law at St. Petersburg University; 1894 married Anna Kind; 1895 appointed curator of Princess Mariia Tenisheva's collection of contemporary paintings and drawings; 1896 organized a Russian section for the Munich Secession; made his first trip to Paris; began to paint scenes of Versailles, a favorite theme for the rest of his life; 1898 cofounded the World of Art, becoming a regular contributor to its magazine and exhibitions; contributed to Sergei Diaghilev's "Exhibition of Works by Russian and Finnish Artists"; 1899 onwards illustrated many books including Pushkin's *The Bronze Horseman* (various editions) and his own book *Azbuka v kartinakh A.N. Benua* (The Alphabet in the Pictures of A.N. Benois) (1905); 1900 made his debut as a stage designer for the one-act opera *Cupid's Revenge;* 1901 with Bakst, Lancéray, and others codesigned *Sylvia* which Diaghilev prepared for the Mariinsky Theater (not produced); 1901-02 published his *Istoriia russkoi zhivopisi v XIX veke* (History of Russian Painting in the XIX Century), the first of several major books on the history art; 1902 designed a production of *Götterdämmerung* for the Mariinsky Theater; thereafter designed or codesigned numerous stage productions in Russia and abroad; 1902-03 collaborated with Sergei Shcherbatov and Vladimir von Meck on the Contemporary Art showrooms in St. Petersburg; 1907 designed *Le Pavillon d'Armide* for the Mariinsky Theater; 1907-16 coedited the journal *Starye gody* (Bygone Years); 1908 designed Diaghilev's production of *Boris Godunov* in Paris; published monograph on Francisco Goya; 1909 designed Diaghilev's production of *Le Pavillon d'Armide* for the first Paris season; also designed *Le Festin* and *Les Sylphides;* 1910 designed Diaghilev's Paris production of *Giselle*; published his survey of Tsarskoe Selo in the reign of Empress Elizabeth; 1911 designed Diaghilev's Paris production of *Petrushka* for which he also wrote the libretto; published his guide to the Hermitage Painting Gallery; illustrated an edition of Pushkin's *Queen of Spades*; 1912 onwards designed several productions for the Moscow Art Theater, including cycles of plays by Molière and Pushkin; published the first of twenty-two fascicles (through 1917) of his *Istoriia zhivopisi vsekh vremen i narodov* (The History of Painting of All Times and of All Peoples); 1914 designed Diaghilev's Paris production of *Le Rossignol* ; began to work on the interior decoration for the Kazan Station, Moscow; 1918-26 curator of the Painting Gallery at the Hermitage, St. Petersburg; during this period continued to design many productions for Petrograd and Moscow theaters; 1924 designed *Le Médecin malgré lui* and *Philémon et Baucis* for Diaghilev in Paris, their last professional association; 1926 emigrated to Paris; one-man exhibition at the Galerie Charpentier, Paris; 1920s-50s continued to paint and publish and to design for many companies, including Ida Rubinstein, La Scala, Théâtre des Champs-Elysées, and Théâtre Pigalle; 1929 one-man exhibitions at the Galerie Charpentier and Galerie Hirshman, Paris; 1937 one-man exhibition at Arthur Tooth & Sons, London; 1941 published his *Reminiscences of the Russian Ballet;* 1954 wrote introduction to the catalog of Richard Buckle's Diaghilev Exhibition, Edinburgh and London; 1957 created new designs for *Petrushka* at Covent Garden, London (his last production).

Selected Bibliography
A. Benois, *Reminiscences of the Russian Ballet*, Putnam, London 1941.
A. Benois, *Zhizn khudozhnika*, Chekhov, New York 1955 (two volumes).
Mostra dei Benois. Catalog of the exhibition, Villa Comunale dell'Olmo, Como, 1955.
A. Benois, *Memoirs*, Chatto and Windus, London 1960-64 (two volumes).
M. Etkind, *Aleksandr Nikolaevich Benua*, Iskusstvo, Leningrad-Moscow 1965.
I. Zilbershtein (ed.), *Aleksandr Benua razmyshliaet...*, Sovetskii khudozhnik, Moscow 1968.
G. Bernardt, *Aleksandr Benua i muzyka*, Sovetskii khudozhnik, Moscow 1969.
Aleksandr Benua. Catalog of exhibition at the Tretiakov Gallery, Moscow 1972.
N. Aleksandrova et al. (eds.), *Aleksandr Benua. "Moi vospominaniia"*, Nauka, Moscow 1980 (two volumes).
Alexandre Benois. Catalog of exhibition at Hazlitt, Gooden and Fox, London, May, 1980, with introduction by Richard Buckle.
Bakst and Benois. Catalog of exhibition at the Marion Koogler McNay Art Museum, San Antonio (Texas), 1985
I Benois del Teatro alla Scala. Catalog of exhibition at La Scala, Milan, 1988.
M. Etkind, *A.N. Benua i russkaia khudozhestvennaia kultura*, Khudozhnik RSFSR, Leningrad 1989.
Aleksandr Nikolaevich Benua i Ermitazh. Catalog of exhibition at the Hermitage, St. Petersburg, 1994.
V. Volodarsky (ed.), *A. Benua: "Istoriia russkoi zhivoisi v XIX veka"*, Respublika, Moscow 1995 (=reprint of Benois' 1901 monograph on 19th century Russian painting).
V. Gusarov, *Petergof v akvareliakh Aleksandra Benua*, Iskusstvo Rossii, St. Petersburg 1996.
I. Khabarov (comp.), *Aleksandr Benua. Khudozhestvennye pisma.1930 Parizh 1936*, Galart, Moscow 1997.
For further bibliography, including a list of Benois' own publications, see Etkind, *Aleksandr Nikolaevich Benua*, pp. 198-208. For a comprehensive listing of the stage productions in which Benois was involved as designer see *ibid.*, pp. 181-98; *Alexandre Benois* (1980), unpaginated; and *Bakst and Benois*, pp. 35-42.

Paintings and Drawings

1.

Portrait of Mstislav Dobujinsky on the Terrace of the Villa du Midi, Lago di Lugano, 1908
Watercolor, 22 × 27.5 cm
Signed lower right corner
London, Collection of Nina and Nikita D. Lobanov-Rostovsky (R98)
The artist Mstislav Dobujinsky (Mstislav Valerianovich Dobuzhinsky, 1875-1957) was a close friend of the Benois family, a fellow member of the World of Art, and also a designer for the Ballet Russes. Benois made this portrait while he, Dobujinsky, and their families were residing at the Villa du Midi, a *pensione* on the shore of the Lago di Lugano. The portrait shows Dobujinsky seated on the terrace of the *pensione*. The Lago di Lugano was a favorite vacation spot for the Benois and Dobujinsky families in 1908-13 (Cat. 2), and Benois wrote of it fondly in his memoirs. Benois' daughter, Anna Benois-Tcherkessoff recalled in 1964 that "our families grew close thanks especially to the summers that we spent in Lugano in that extraordinary ambience. The chance to go for wonderful walks together, to enjoy the beautiful landscape and also to delight in the ease with which papa and Mstislav Valerianovich would sketch this or that picturesque corner or grand panorama of the surrounding moutains..."[1]
Benois created several other portraits of his friend – cf. the pencil portrait of 1911 in the collection of the Hermitage, St. Petersburg, and Dobujinsky made several portraits of Benois – cf. the pencil portrait of 1914 in the collection of Nina and Nikita D. Lobanov-Rostovsky (LRC, p. 135).

[1] G. Chugunov (comp.), *Vospominaniia o Dobuzhinskom*, Akademicheskii proekt, St. Petersburg 1997, pp. 36-37.

2.

Lago di Lugano, 1913
Watercolor, indian ink, pencil on paper, 32 × 43 cm
Moscow, State Tretiakov Gallery (1599)
Lugano had special significance for Benois ever since his first visit there on his honeymoon trip in 1894, and he found the atmosphere both physically beautiful and psychologically restful. Moreover, when he and his new family started to visit the area regularly for their summer holidays, he soon discovered a Russian connection, for it transpired that many Swiss-Italian artists who had worked for the Russian court in the 18th century hailed from Lugano, Montagnola, and other localities and, in some cases, their descendants were still living there. He remembered: "We all liked Montagnola – the soft and even climate (...) and the enchanting forests and the air (...) and the inhabitants themselves with their way of life combining the best aspects of Swiss and Italian culture".[1]

[1] Aleksandrova, *Aleksandr Benua*, Vol. 2, pp. 495-96. Between 1909 and 1913 the Benois family summered in the "little palace" of signora Camuzzi, aunt of the mayor of Montagnola, Alessandro Giliardi, on the Collina d'Oro in Montagnola. For some information on the Collina d'Oro and Benois see A. Mario Redaelli, "Materiali inediti per la storia degli architetti della Collina d'Oro", in *Quaderni la Ricerca*, Torre Camuzzi, Montagnola 1997, No. 1, p. 6.

3.

Versailles. L'Allée des philosophes, 1905
Watercolor and gouache, 40.8 × 33.5 cm
Signed and dated lower left
Moscow, State Tretiakov Gallery (21914)

4.

Versailles. Parterre d'eau, 1906
Watercolor, gouache, 31 × 49.5 cm
Signed and dated lower right
Moscow, State Tretiakov Gallery (21917)
Benois was fascinated by Versailles, by the *grandeur* of its design, by the Rococo intricacies of its landscaping and by the magic of its vistas. For Benois Versailles, with its statuary, topiary, and aquatic wizardry, symbolized the controlled luxury of the Sun King and his Court, subjects that Benois often placed in his nostalgic evocations of 17th and 18th century France. No doubt, for Benois Versailles also elicited images of his French ancestry and reinforced his love of the architecture of St. Petersburg and the Imperial palaces such as Peterhof and Tsarskoe Selo, about which he wrote so eloquently. Last, but not least, the highly ceremonial and ritualized life of Louis XIV with the unceasing round of balls, fireworks, uniforms and amorous intrigues must have appealed directly to Benois' theatrical sensibility. For Benois Versailles, like the reigns of Peter, Paul and Nicholas, and even like his own childhood, was a part of an intimate and immediate history, a "cloudless past"[1] that he depicted with both reason and desire.

[1] Berberova, *Kursiv moi*, p. 333.

5.

The Bolshoi Theater, St. Petersburg, in 1885, 1939
Gouache and watercolor, 34 × 60 cm
Signed lower right

New York, Collection of Alik Rabinovich

Benois nurtured a deep sympathy for the old Bolshoi Theater in St. Petersburg (not to be confused with the Bolshoi Theater in Moscow) not only because its function appealed to his love of the stage, but also because the Theater, opened in 1783, had been redesigned and restructured by his maternal grandfather, Albert Kavos (Cavos) in 1836. The Theater saw many productions of operas, ballets, and plays, including Glinka's *Life for the Tsar* which started the 1836 season, and witnessed the appearance of many stars, including Fanny Elssler and Marie Taglioni. Benois used a reproduction of this particular rendering as the frontispiece to his book *Reminiscences of the Russian Ballet* (Putnam, London 1941; see D16).

Stage and Interior Designs

6.
The Gardens of Diana
Panneau for the Contemporary Art Showrooms, St. Petersburg, 1902
Colored indian ink, whitening, watercolor, pencil on paper on board, 37.7 × 61.9 cm
Signed and dated lower right and lower left
Moscow, State Tretiakov Gallery (5562)

The Contemporary Art Enterprise, established in the fall of 1902 on the Bolshaia Morskaia in St. Petersburg (Figs. 15, 16), was an exhibition space and suite of showrooms specializing in interior design modelled in part on the Maison Bing in Paris. Its permanent display opened amidst much enthusiasm in January, 1903, but critics were quick to remark on the "practical inapplicability"[1] of the wares on sale and even Diaghilev felt that it was more "fantasy" than "enterprise".[2] Financed by Prince Sergei Shcherbatov and Baron Vladimir von Meck, Contemporary Art was intended to supply people of station with new, but elegant furniture and furnishings, both foreign (Japanese engravings, *panneaux* by the Nabis, glass by Lalique) and domestic. Many World of Art

artists took part in the venture: Benois and Lancéray designed the dining-room for which this panneau was intended and various chairs, Bakst the boudoir, Konstantin Korovin decorated the tea-room, Igor Grabar designed the main entrance and the Dutch stoves, Alexander Golovin transformed one room into a *terem* (Mediaeval tower-chamber), while Sergei Chekhonin, Alexander Matveev, Artemii Ober and other young artists contributed various ornaments and decorations. Unfortunately, dogged by financial mismanagement and public indifference, Contemporary Art functioned for little over a year and managed to sell "only one chair".[3] The theme of Diana was fresh on Benois' mind, since the year before he had created a set for the first scene of Léo Delibes' ballet, *Sylvia*, the expanded title of which is *Sylvia or The Nymph of Diana*.

[1] M. Batiushkov, "Na khudozhestvennykh vystavkakh. Zametki i vpechatleniia" in *Mir bozhii*, St. Petersburg 1903, No. 1, Section II, p. 11.
[2] S. Diaghilev, "Sovremennoe iskusstvo" in *Mir iskusstva*, 1903, Vol. 10, No. 3, Chronicle, pp. 23-24.
[3] A. Benois, "Russkoe sovremennoe iskusstvo" in *Rech*, 1912, 9 March, No. 67, p. 5.

Le Pavillon d'Armide

Ballet pantomime in three scenes based on Théophile Gautier's story *Omphale*. Produced at the Mariinsky Theater, St. Petersburg on 25 November, 1907, with scenario by Alexandre Benois, music by Nikolai Cherepnin, choreography by Michel Fokine and designs by Alexandre Benois. The ballet was then performed by Sergei Diaghilev's Ballets Russes at the Théâtre du Châtelet, Paris, on 19 May, 1909, becoming a primary part of the Ballets Russes repertoire.
The young Vicomte de Beaugency, caught unawares in a storm, finds himself in the castle of the Marquis de Fierbois, a magician. He is lodged in an enchanted pavilion decorated with an exquisite tapestry depicting the beautiful, but now deceased

Marquise Madeleine as Armide surrounded by her Court. At the stroke of midnight the tapestry comes to life and Love drives away Time. The Vicomte becomes infatuated with the embroidered Armide, and his happiness is crowned as Armide recognizes him as her long departed lover, René, and gives him her scarf as a mark of her love. King Hydraot enters, whom the Vicomte recognizes as none other than his host. When the Vicomte awakens, the Marquis shows him Armide's scarf resting on the clock. Observing that Armide in the tapestry no longer wears her scarf and that he is the victim of an enchantment, the Vicomte falls unconscious.

7.
Design for the Gobelin, 1907
Watercolor, 44 × 40.5 cm (with mount); 33 × 35.3 cm (without mount)
Signed on the cartouche
Moscow, State Bakhrushin Theater Museum (307229)

8.
Stage Design for Armide's Garden, Scene 2 (preliminary sketch), 1907
Watercolor and ink, 18.5 × 26.5 cm; mounted on a grey paper, 23.5 × 26.75 cm; framed, 48.3 × 54 × 1 cm
Signed and dated lower right
San Antonio (Texas), Collection of Robert Tobin (R95.10)

9.
Stage Design for Armide's Garden, Scene 2, 1909 (?)
Watercolor, india ink, pencil, and gouache, 47.5 × 63.2 cm
Signed lower left.
London, Collection of Nina and Nikita D. Lobanov-Rostovsky (R112)

10.
Costume Design for the Marquis de Fierbois Dressed as King Hydraot, 1907 (?)
Watercolor, pencil, whitening, silver and bronze paint, 38.6 × 22.2 cm
Dedication from Benois to Nikolai Kulbin
Moscow, State Bakhrushin Theater Museum (116635)

The circumstances whereby Benois presented this design to the physician and Futurist painter Nikolai Ivanovich Kulbin (1868-1917) are not known. Contrary to what the dedication might suggest, Benois did not have a very high opinion of the artistic activities of his St. Petersburg colleague, even declining to write his obituary in 1917. See Benois "Diary" below.

11.
Costume Design for the Cavalier, 1907
Watercolor, pencil, whitening, bronze and silver paint, 38.3 × 26.5 cm
St. Petersburg, State Museum of Theater and Music (GIK 17070/198)

12.
Costume for the Cavalier, 1907
Cotton, silk and metal lame, Length of shoulder, 12 cm; Bosom, 96 cm; Common length, 76 cm
St. Petersburg, State Museum of Theater and Music, (GIK 17963/20)
The costume was worn by Ivan Nikolaevich Kusov (1875-after 1922)

13.
Costume Design for a Dancer, 1907 (?)
Watercolor, pencil, whitening, bronze paint on brown paper 33.3 × 25.5 cm.
Moscow, State Bakhrushin Theater Museum (181249)

14.
Design for Two Costumes, 1907
Watercolor, pencil, whitening, bronze and silver paint 34 × 37.3 cm
St. Petersburg, State Museum of Theater and Music (GIK 10859)

15.
Jacket for the Buffoon, 1907
Taffeta, brocade, braid, lace, buttons
Length of shoulder, 13 cm; Bosom: 83 cm; length of back, 63 cm; Length of sleeve, 55 cm
St. Petersburg, State Museum of Theater and Music (GIK 17963/19)

16.
Cloak, 1907
Silk, rep, braid, embroidery
Common length, 117.5 cm
St. Petersburg, State Museum
of Theater and Music
(GIK 18069/1)
Le Pavillon d'Armide of 1907 was
Benois' first professional theatrical engagement since the St.
Petersburg production of
Götterdämmerung in 1903, and it
was an enduring success. *Le
Pavillon* provided Benois with a
theme requiring both imagina-
tive caprice and historical precision. As Fokine affirmed, each
detail received Benois' scrutiny:
"The color of a braid, of a galloon on the dress of an extra
which you couldn't even make
out on stage through your binoc-
ulars – Benois gave much
thought to these things and selected them after careful consid-
eration. He wished the galloon to
shine – but not too much. He
didn't want 'cheap' flashiness".[1]
The St. Petersburg production
received exceptional praise not
only for the enchanting sets and
costumes, but also because Anna
Pavlova danced Armide and the
aging but still elegant Pavel
Gerdt danced the Vicomte –
while Nijinsky danced Armide's
Slave and Tamara Karsavina,
Lidiia Kiasht, Lubov
Tchernitcheva, and Alexandra
Fedorova performed variations in
the Divertissement. Diaghilev's
reaction – "This must be shown
in Europe"[2] – prepared the way
for the no less auspicious production in Paris two years later.
Paris audiences saw a modified
and shortened version of *Le
Pavillon* with certain musical re-
arrangements and with a new
cast of primary roles – Mikhail
Mordkin danced the Vicomte,
Vera Karalli Armide, and Alexei
Bulgakov the Marquis, while
Karsavina, Fedorova, and
Nijinsky were retained (this was
Nijinsky's first ballet appearance
in the West). Benois also reexam-
ined his contribution and "succeeded in greatly improving the
decor and costumes, which had
been made especially for the
Paris stage. In the St. Petersburg
version I had been worried by the
neighbourhood of lilac, pink and
yellow, and by the somewhat

motley details of the decor for
the second scene. These defects I
now corrected."[3] Perhaps Benois
did not entirely remove these
"motley details" and some critics
still accused him of overemphasis
on historical bric-à-brac. Writing
in 1916 Andrei Levinson observed of Benois' *Le Pavillon* that
it "is not the luxurious and capricious dream of the colorist, ignit-
ing the canvases of the decors
with an incandescent play of colors; it is, first and foremost, the
recreation of the past".[4]
Benois had fond memories of *Le
Pavillon* and he returned to it
many times in his reminiscences,
especially in emigration. For him
the 1907 production had been a
true experience of artistic synthe-
sism in which visual art, music,
and movement had played equal
roles. Recalling the premiere almost thirty years later, he wrote
that the "performers danced and
played 'like gods' (that was the
first time that Nijinsky knew the
enthusiasm of ovations, while
there was no end to the encores
addressed to Pavlova). Indeed,
the fabulous transformation of
the pavilion into a garden aston-
ished even the most blasé by its
unexpectedness, while the costumes shone with the brilliance
of their colors and their lavish
trim."[5]

[1] M. Fokin, *Protiv techeniia.
Vospominaniia baletmeistera*,
Iskusstvo, Leningrad-Moscow p.
188.
[2] Benois, *Reminiscences*, p. 266.
[3] *Ibid.*, pp. 291-92.
[4] A. Levinson, "Russkie khu-
dozhniki-dekoratory" in *Stolitsa
i usadba*, Petrograd 1916, 1 May,
No. 57, p. 12.
[5] A. Benois, "Pavilion Armidy"
(1936). In Khabarov, *Aleksandr
Benua*, p. 280. For a detailed discussion of Benois' designs for *Le
Pavillon d'Armide*, including
many relevant illustrations, see
Alden Murray, "A Problematical
Pavilion: Alexandre Benois' First
Ballet," in *Russian History*,
Tempe, Arizona 1981, Vol. 8,
Part 1-2, pp. 23-52.

Les Sylphides
A romantic reverie in one act by
Michel Fokine based on music
by Frédéric Chopin orchestrated

by Igor Stravinsky, with addi-
tional music by Alexandre
Glazunov, Anatolii Liadov,
Nikolai Sokolov and Sergei
Taneev. Produced by Sergei
Diaghilev at the Théâtre du
Châtelet, Paris, on 2 June, 1909
with choreography by Michel
Fokine and designs by Alexandre
Benois.
Based on Fokine's *pas de deux*
from *Chopiniana*, this ballet car-
ries no concrete plot, but is in-
tended as a balletic reproduction
of Romantic engravings from the
1840s.

17.
Valentin
Alexandrovich Serov
(1865-1911)
*Poster advertising
the inauguration of the first
"Russian Season" at the Théâtre
du Châtelet, Paris, in May-June,
1909*
Lithographic poster in black
and white on a blue background
Initialed in the plate lower
right and dated 1909
254 × 192 cm
Other inscriptions in French
at the top: "Théâtre du Châtelet
Saison Russe Mai-Juin 1909
Opéra et Ballet"; lower left:
"Administration G. Astruc
& Cie Villon de Hanovre.
32 Rue Louis-le-Grand";
lower right along margin:
"Eugène Verneau, 108 Rue
Folie Mericourt, Paris".
The poster also exists
in a reduced format
(187 × 158 cm) and the original
tempera is in the collection
of the State Russian Museum,
St. Petersburg.
Moscow, State Bakhrushin
Theater Museum (KP317482)
Much has been written about the
ballet *Les Sylphides*, the title that
Alexandre Benois gave to this ensemble of Romantic movements,
and both Benois and Fokine
spoke of it fondly in their memoirs.[1] Sergei Diaghilev opened his
first Season of the Ballets Russes
in Paris on 1 May, 1909 with *Le
Pavillon d'Armide*, the *Polovtsian
Dances*, and *Le Festin* which were
followed by *Les Sylphides* and
Cléopâtre on 2 June. In his interpretation Serov presented the
ethereal Anna Pavlova dancing
the part of the First Sylphide in

Les Sylphides (Karsavina and
Nijinsky also performed), of
which Serov's friend and admir-
er, the writer Vasilii Rozanov,
commented: "A head, air, blue-
ness and nothing (...) and yet
the idea of dance has been expressed so perfectly."[2] Indeed,
most balletomanes agreed that
Serov had "caught Pavlova's
lines",[3] one observer even going
so far as to maintain that the
poster "attracted more responses
in the press than Pavlova herself".[4]
Serov often worked for the stage,
including the Ballets Russes,
codesigning (with Bakst)
Diaghilev's production of the
opera *Judith* in Paris also in 1909
and making the stage curtain for
Schéhérazade the following year.
Serov did at least one other
sketch of Pavlova and made several portraits of other dancers, including Fokine and Karsavina.

[1] See Benois, *Reminiscences*, p.
275 et seq., and M. Fokin, *Protiv
techeniia*, Iskusstvo, Leningrad-
Moscow 1962, p. 179 et seq.
[2] V. Rozanov. Quoted in
Zilbershtein and Samkov,
Valentin Serov, Vol. 2, p. 469.
[3] A. Pleshcheev, "Vidennoe i
slyshannoe" in *Vozrozhdenie*,
Paris 1935, 13 October. Quoted
in *ibid.*, p. 473.
[4] L. Novikov, "Ya delil s nei
slavu". Quoted in *ibid.*

Petrushka
Burlesque in four acts by
Alexandre Benois and Igor
Stravinsky. Produced by Sergei
Diaghilev's Ballets Russes at the
Théâtre du Châtelet, Paris on 13
June 1911 with music by Igor
Stravinsky, choreography by
Michel Fokine, and designs by
Alexandre Benois.
The scene is St. Petersburg ca.
1830 on Admiralty Square at
Carnival time. In the midst of
the merry-making there appears
the Showman or Charlatan in
oriental costume who displays
his puppets – Petrushka, the
Ballerina, and the Moor – who
proceed to perform a brisk
dance. The Showman has endowed his puppets with human
sentiments. The next scene
shows a prison where Petrushka
languishes after being cast there

by the Showman. The Ballerina visits him, but departs, frightened by his amorous overtures. She then proceeds to flirt with the Moor in his luxurious chambers. Petrushka appears on the scene, but is chased away by the Moor. Back outside the fairground booth, Petrushka suddenly runs through the crowd, pursued by the Moor who cuts him down with his scimitar. A policeman explains that Petrushka is only a puppet and, as the Showman drags the toy back to his booth, he suddenly sees the ghost of Petrushka on the roof. Alarmed, the Showman takes to his heels.

18.
Backdrop for the Fair,
Scenes 1 and 4, 1947
Watercolor, gouache,
and pencil, 32.5 × 47.5 cm
Signed in ink lower left
London, Collection of Nina
and Nikita D. Lobanov-
Rostovsky (R136)

19.
Backdrop for Petrushka's Room,
Scene 2, 1948
Watercolor, gouache and ink,
23.5 × 35.5 cm
Signed in ink lower left
London, Collection of Nina
and Nikita D. Lobanov-
Rostovsky (R137)

20.
Backdrop for the Moor's Room,
Scene 3, 1956
Pencil ink, watercolor,
and gouache, 27 × 40 cm
Signed and dated lower left
Lugano, Thyssen-Bornemisza
Collection

21.
Sketch for the Scene
where Petrushka Kisses
the Ballerina, 1945
Watercolor, pencil, and black
ink 13 × 18 cm
Signed and dated lower right
London, Collection of Nina
and Nikita D. Lobanov-
Rostovsky (R145)

22.
Design for the Curtain with
Night Scene, Fantastic Creatures
in the Sky, and the Admiralty
Tower in the Background, 1957

Watercolor and ink, 32 × 49 cm
Signed lower left in ink
in French
London, Collection of Nina
and Nikita D. Lobanov-
Rostovsky (R141)

Costumes
Unless stated otherwise, most of the following costume designs are signed and dated "Alexandre Benois 1911-1956" and seem to relate, therefore, to the 1956 and 1957 productions of *Petrushka* at the Staatsoper, Vienna, and Covent Garden, London.

23.
Petrushka, 1947
Watercolor, ink and pencil,
27.5 × 19 cm
Signed lower left
Framed together with Cat. 24
London, Collection of Nina
and Nikita D. Lobanov-
Rostovsky (R154)

24.
The Ballerina, 1947
Watercolor, gold, ink
and pencil 27.5 × 19 cm
Signed and dated lower left
Framed together with Cat. 23
London, Collection of Nina
and Nikita D. Lobanov-
Rostovsky (R155)

25.
The Moor, 1947
Watercolor, silver paint, ink,
and pencil, 27.5 × 19 cm
Signed lower left in pencil
Identifications in upper margins
Framed together with Cat. 26
London, Collection of Nina
and Nikita D. Lobanov-
Rostovsky (R157)

26.
The Moor with a Sword, 1947
Watercolor, black ink, gold
paint and pencil, 23 × 16 cm
Signed and dated lower right
Framed together with Cat. 25
London, Collection of Nina
and Nikita D. Lobanov-
Rostovsky (R158)

27.
The Second Barrel
Organ Grinder
Watercolor and black ink,
31 × 23 cm
Signed and dated lower right

London, Collection of Nina and
Nikita D. Lobanov-Rostovsky
(R162)

28.
Lady with Her Son
Watercolor, ink
and pencil, 26 × 18 cm
London, Collection of Nina
and Nikita D. Lobanov-
Rostovsky (R187)

29.
Young Girl Disguised
as a Polish Maid, 1956
Watercolor, ink and pencil,
31 × 24 cm
Signed and dated lower left
London, Collection of Nina
and Nikita D. Lobanov-
Rostovsky (R249)

30.
Balloon Vendor
and Boy from the People, 1956
Watercolor and ink,
31 × 23.5 cm
Signed and dated lower left
London, Collection of Nina
and Nikita D. Lobanov-
Rostovsky (R252)

31.
Costume for a Lady, 1911 (?)
Velvet, silk, cloth, braid
and cord with metal thread
and metal buttons
Length of shoulder, 11 cm;
Bosom, 80 cm; Waist, 64 cm;
Length of back, 30.5 cm;
Length of sleeve, 52 cm;
St. Petersburg, State Museum
of Theater and Music
(GIK 18089/3)
Petrushka was one of Benois' favorite spectacles and he made designs for eleven separate productions, the original and most famous being Diaghilev's for the Ballets Russes in 1911. But for Benois *Petrushka* also came to assume a tragic meaning, for it was in June, 1911, that the first serious rift between Benois, Diaghilev, and Bakst occurred – when Diaghilev, unbeknown to Benois, asked Bakst to touch up the portrait of the Showman on the wall of Petrushka's room in Scene 2 (see Cat. 19), a gesture that caused Benois much grief and rancour. Although he collaborated with the Ballets Russes again on the production of *Le Rossignol* in 1914, Benois never

forgave or forgot Diaghilev's apparent iniquity.
Benois continued to repeat, modify and elaborate the basic images that he had invented for the Paris premiere throughout his life (1920, 1930, 1947, 1956 et al.), although he did not always indicate the actual date of execution. Consequently, when a particular set or costume seems to be for an early production, it may, in fact, be a later rendering – a state of affairs that creates a major problem in dating and chronology.[1]

[1] For a comprehensive discussion of the legend of Petrushka in Russian culture, including the ballet *Petrushka*, see J. Douglas Clayton, *Pierrot in Petrograd*, Mc-Gill Queen's University Press, Montreal 1994; and C. Kelly, *Petrushka, the Russian Carnival Puppet Theatre*, Cambridge University Press, Cambridge 1990.

Le Rossignol
Opera in three acts with incidental dances by Igor Stravinsky and Stepan Mitusov based on a tale by Hans Christian Andersen. Produced by Sergei Diaghilev's Ballets Russes at the Théâtre National de l'Opéra, Paris on 26 May 1914, with choreography by Boris Romanov and designs by Alexandre Benois.
The tale is of the Emperor and the nightingale who enchants him with a song, but who is then banished in favor of a mechanical bird. Finally, however, the nightingale is brought back as the Emperor is dying, and she effects his cure by her song.

32.
The Throne Room.
Décor for Act III, 1914
Gouache on paper laid down
on canvas, 99 × 109.5 cm
Signed and dated lower left
San Antonio (Texas), Collection
of Robert Tobin, (R85.39)
Stravinsky and Mitusov began to work on the opera *Le Rossignol* in 1910, if not before,[1] and Benois was captivated immediately by the music. Benois was drawn to the piece since he had long wanted to express his interpretation of the art of the Far East: "At first I

thought of keeping to the style of the *chinoiseries* which were so popular during the eighteenth century. But as I worked on, I became rather irritated by their obvious absurdity, and my own enthusiasm for what was authentically Chinese began to reflect itself in my conception. As for the costumes, colored Chinese broadsheets served as invaluable material (...) Ultimately, I achieved something distant from pedantic precision, something of a crossbreed, but something that fitted Stravinsky's music perfectly".[2]

The decorative effect of the Paris production was impressive. Anatolii Lunacharsky referred to Benois'"fantastic *chinoiserie*"[3] and the critic A. Maslovsky praised the artist for his "knowledge of style and psychological penetration."[4] Even so, Diaghilev staged *Le Rossignol* with Benois' designs only twice in Paris and four times in London, before changing the opera into a one-act ballet and entrusting the designs for this to Matisse (produced in Paris in 1920).

[1] According to Stravinsky (*Dialogi. Vospominaniia. Razmyshleniia. Kommentarii*, Muzyka, Leningrad 1971, p. 379), he began to think about *Le Rossignol* even as early as 1908.
[2] Aleksandrova, *Aleksandr Benua*, Vol. 2, p. 535.
[3] A. Lunacharsky, "Russkie spektakli v Parizhe" in *Sovremennik*, 1914, Book 14-15. Quoted in Etkind, *Aleksandr Nikolaevich Benua*, p. 99.
[4] A. Maslovsky, "Balety S. Diagileva i russkie khudozhniki" in *Teatr*, Berlin 1922, April, No. 9, p. 6.

Queen of Spades

Opera in three acts and seven scenes with music by Peter Tchaikovsky and libretto by Modest Tchaikovsky based on a story by Alexander Pushkin and adapted by Alexandre Benois. Produced by Alexandre Benois and Emile Cooper at the State Theater for Opera and Ballet, Petrograd, on 3 May, 1921 with choreography by Leonid Leontiev and designs by Alexandre Benois.

A fanatical gambler, the officer Herman is in love with Liza, whose grandmother, nicknamed the Queen of Spades, knows the secret of three winning cards. Desirous of learning the secret so that he may marry Liza and ensure her welfare, Herman ponders the riddle of the cards. He sequesters himself in the chambers of the Countess and demands that she reveal the secret, but she dies from shock and Liza accuses Herman of favoring fortune in gambling to fortune in love. Liza then forgives him and the ghost of the Countess discloses the magic sequence – three, seven, ace. But realizing that the pull of the gambling-house is stronger than their love, Liza commits suicide, while Herman now applies the secret, except that the ace turns out to be the Queen of Spades – the mocking face of the Countess. Herman goes mad and kills himself.

33.

Décor for Act III, Scene 2:
On the Quay of the Neva, 1919
Pencil, watercolor and gouache,
37.5 × 61.6 cm
Signed and dated in ink
Lugano, Thyssen-Bornemisza Collection

On several occasions Benois referred to the *Queen of Spades* as being his favorite opera and he came to the tale from a love of Pushkin's writing and of Tchaikovsky's music. Of course, the Petrograd production was certainly not Benois' first exposure to Tchaikovsky's masterpiece, for he remembered attending a production of the opera as a young man in 1890 and in 1903 he assisted with the décor for a Mariinsky production. In any case, for the Petrograd interpretation Benois also drew upon the lessons that he had learned in illustrating the tale for the Golike and Vilborg edition of 1911 (D39; Fig. 33) and, as then, so now, he tried to evoke the image of a Pushkinian St. Petersburg whose outward majesty and order only concealed personal weakness and confusion. Benois' mise-en-scène and designs scored a great success, causing some critics to maintain that this production was the finest "in the history of the Russian operatic theater", an opinion that Benois seemed to share.[1]

[1] Bernardt, *Aleksandr Benua i muzyka*, p. 48. For Benois' own comments on the *Queen of Spades*, including the Petrograd production, see Aleksandrova, *Aleksandr Benua*, Vol. 1, pp. 657-58.

La Princesse Cygne

Ballet in two scenes by Nikolai Rimsky-Korsakov based on his opera *The Story of Tsar Saltan* after a story by Alexander Pushkin. Produced by Les Ballets de Mme. Ida Rubinstein at the Théâtre National de l'Opéra, Paris, on 29 November, 1928, with choreography by Bronislava Nijinska and designs by Alexandre Benois.

A tempest casts the son of Tsar Saltan, Prince Guidon, and his mother upon a foreign shore, where their appearance frightens the dancing mermaids. Suddenly Guidon sees a vulture aloft, carrying a swan in its claws. Guidon kills the bird of prey with his bow and arrow, but the magic swan puts him to sleep and he dreams a fabulous dream. Guidon is crowned king in the town of Ledenets, the swan turns out to be a beautiful princess, and the two are united in marriage.

34.

Décor for Scene 2:
The Miraculous Apparition
of the Town of Ledenets
Pencil, watercolor and gouache,
44 × 61 cm
Signed and inscribed in pencil lower center
Lugano, Thyssen-Bornemisza Collection

Swan Lake

Ballet in two acts by Peter Tchaikovsky with scenario by Marius Petipa and Lev Ivanov with choreography by Margherita Wallmann and costumes by Alexandre Benois. Produced at La Scala, Milan, on 31 December, 1949.

Princess Odette is turned into a swan by the magician Rothbart. At midnight, however, she and her companions regain their human form, and at one such transformation, Prince Siegfried falls in love, swearing to rescue her. Expected to choose his bride one night at a castle ball, Siegfried is bewitched by Odile, daughter of Rothbart, who – as a black swan – looks like Odette. When the latter appears, Siegfried realizes that he has broken his oath, but he is forgiven by Odette. Rothbart then conjures up a tempest and the two lovers are drowned.

35.

Handwritten letter on four pages from Alexandre Benois to Cyril Beaumont dated 29 April, 1947 carrying a watercolor sketch for Tchaikovsky's ballet *Swan Lake*
Watercolor, pencil and ink,
22.5 × 17.5 cm (paper size)
New York, Collection of Alik Rabinovich

Swan Lake was not a favorite ballet of Benois, although during the 1940s he worked on at least three versions, one for Sol Hourok in New York in 1945, and two others for La Scala, Milan, in 1949 and 1954. In spite of his worry that Tchaikovsky's *Swan Lake* in paticular was "partly banal", Benois, nevertheless, defended Tchaikovsky's music in general from contemporary critics who tended to dismiss it all as sweet and superficial.[1]

In this letter Benois thanks Beaumont for having introduced him to the balletomane Peter Williams, because "Je suis surtout sensible à son culte de Tchaikovsky qui reste pour moi, à côté de L. Delibes, le vrai génie de la musique pour ballet". The English ballet critic and bibliophile, Cyril Beaumont (1891-1976), wrote many books and articles on the Russian ballet.[2] While Benois would have made this watercolor simply because Beaumont was an enthusiast of *Swan Lake*, he may have already entered into negotiations with La Scala for the 1949 production and was, therefore, thinking of possible resolutions.

[1] Bernardt, *Aleksandr Benua*, p. 49.
[2] See, for example, his *Bookseller at the Ballet. Memoirs 1891-1929*, Beaumont, London 1975.

Les Deux Tisserands

Comedy sketch in four scenes by Jean-Louis Brousse adapted from the fairy-story by Hans Christian Andersen. Produced by Georges Lampin for the Théâtre Marigny, Paris, on 6 December, 1940, with incidental music by Konstantin Konstantinov.

Based on Hans Christian Andersen's *The Emperor's New Clothes*, the comedy opens with two men telling the King of a wonderful attire which they can weave, but which cannot be seen by fools or by anyone unfit for office.

The Ministers examine the work of the "weavers" who have requested precious silks, brocades, and gold thread in order to weave the costume, although, fearful for their station, the Ministers refuse to admit that they cannot see anything. The "weavers" come to dress the King, who is also full of praise, even though he cannot see anything. The naked King then leads a solemn parade, and all are silent except for a little boy who exclaims: "But the King is bare".

36.

Décor for Scene 1, 1940
Pencil, ink, waterfolor
and gouache, 27.8 × 38.4 cm
Signed and dated lower left
Lugano, Thyssen-Bornemisza
Collection

37.

Décor for Scene 4
Pencil, ink, watercolor
and gouache, 27.8 × 38.4 cm
Signed lower left
Lugano, Thyssen-Bornemisza
Collection

Book Illustrations

A letter of the Russian alphabet designed by Benois for his book *Azbuka v kartinakh A.N. Benua* (The Alphabet in Pictures by Alexandre Benois), Department for the Preparation of State Papers, St. Petersburg 1905 (reprinted as a facsimile edition by Iskusstvo Moscow, 1990).
A copy of the 1905 edition, from the collection of Alik Rabinovich, New York, is included in the exhibition (D7).

38.

The Letter "Kh" for Khan, Khalat (Khan, Dressing-Gown)
Gouache, Indian ink,
bronze paint, watercolor,
36.5 × 30.8 cm
Moscow, State Tretiakov
Gallery (Inv. No. 5501)
Benois began to work on his Russian alphabet, a sentimental journey into his own childhood and into the make-believe world of his three young children, Anna, Elena, and Nikolai, in 1903. Already an experienced stage designer, Benois seems to have approached his assignment as a theater in miniature and we can almost imagine these images as projections by his favorite toy, the "magic lantern",[1] some of which he then repeated in actual ballet productions (the *"Arap" for A* or Moor returning in *Petrushka*, for example). From his original album of sketches in the State Russian Museum, it is clear that Benois made many versions for each letter and entertained various possibilities before deciding on his definitive choices, some of which, incidentally, were dictated by his own children.[2] Curiously enough, in spite of Benois' passionate commitment, he was unhappy with the book when it appeared in August-September, 1905, observing in his "Diary": "I'm not pleased with the Alphabet (...) c'est de l'allemand ordinaire. Bitter taste".[3] Several of Benois' immediate colleagues, including Chekhonin and Dobujinsky, also compiled illustrated editions of the Russian alphabet and Nikolai Cherepnin, composer of *Le Pavillon d'Armide*, composed fourteen miniatures based on Benois' *Azbuka*.

[1] Aleksandrova, *Aleksandr Benua*, Vol. 1, p. 218.
[2] See N. Vasilieva (intr.), *Azbuka A.N. Benua v kartinakh*, Iskusstvo, Moscow 1990, p. 56.
[3] *Ibid.*, p. 65.

39

Eight Postcards on the Theme of Toys, 1904-20s
Each card, 9 × 14.2 cm
i) *The Monastery* (untitled)
ii) *The Country Estate*
Signed lower right

iii) *First Acquaintance*
Signed lower right
iv) *Choir of Wetnurses*
Signed lower right
v) *Poultry Yard*
Signed lower center
vi) *Infantry*
Signed and dated lower right
vii) *From the World of the Fantastic, No. 1*
Signed lower right
viii) *Russian Toys*
Oxford (Ohio), Collection of C. and A.L. de Saint-Rat
Nos. i-vii are seven out of a set of twelve postcards entitled *Russkie natsionalnye igrushki* (Russian National Toys) lithographed by Isaak Kadushin, St. Petersburg, and published by the Society of St. Eugeniia, St. Petersburg, while No. viii was printed in aid of the starving by H. Burg, Paris, 1920s.[1]
Collecting children's toys was a veritable passion among Russian artists and writers of the early 20th century, both of the Symbolist and of the avant-garde generations. Benois himself was interested in common tin soldiers and animals and especially in the traditional wooden toys made at Sergiev Posad near Moscow (Zagorsk) and sold at fairs; he collected toys and even published an appreciation of them in the St. Petersburg art journal *Apollon*.[2] Leonid Brailovsky, Georgii Narbut, Alexei Remizov, and Sergei Sudeikin were among Benois' immediate colleagues who, attracted by the bright colors, crude outlines, and good humor, also collected toys and used them as iconographic or literary sources. The avant-garde, especially the Neo-Primitivists such as David Burliuk, Natalia Goncharova, Alexei Kruchenykh, Nikolai Kulbin, and Mikhail Larionov, also drew upon toys, infantile language, and children's art for inspiration.
The fascination with the culture of the child led to a variety of interesting endeavors – exhibitions of children's drawings, commercial and patriotic posters such as Bakst's for the Philanthropic Bazaar of Dolls in St. Petersburg in 1899[3] and Brailovsky's "Dolls to Benefit War Orphans" (1914),[4] the publication of col-

lections of children's stories and poems, and even Yuliia Slonimskaia-Sazonova's establishment of a puppet theater for adults in 1916 which Benois supported and promoted.[5]
The Society of St. Eugeniia (also called The Red Cross), founded in St. Petersburg in 1882, undertook many publishing ventures, including postcards (1892 onwards) and books [for example, in 1911 it published Benois' guide to the Hermitage Painting Gallery (D10)]. Among the sets of postcards that it issued were reproductions of works by modern Russian artists including Ilia Repin, Dobujinsky and Nicholas Roerich as well as Benois and Bakst: at the end of 1903, for example, the Society published twelve postcards based on Bakst's costumes for *La Fée des Poupées* (Cat. 43).

[1] In composition this postcard is very similar to Benois' image for the letter "I" (*igrushki*) [Toys] in his *Azbuka* (see Fig. 34). For some information on Benois' twelve postcards see Etkind, *A.N. Benua*, p. 101.
[2] A. Benois, "Igrushki" in *Apollon*, St. Petersburg 1912, No. 2, pp. 49-54.
[3] For a reproduction see Pruzhan, *Bakst* (English), p. 47.
[4] For a reproduction see M. Anikst and E. Chernevich, *Russian Graphic Design 1880-1917*, Abbeville, New York 1990, p. 152.
[5] See A. Benois, "Marionetochnyi teatr" in *Rech*, Petrograd 1916, 20 February, p. 3.

*For books, photographs, and archival materials pertaining to the life and work of Benois see "Documentary Section" below.

Léon Bakst

Léon Bakst
Elysium, 1906
Watercolor and gouache
on paper on board, 158 × 140 cm
Moscow, State Tretiakov Gallery
(Cat. 40)

Léon Bakst
*Design for the Costume
for the Gypsy Fortune
Teller*, 1900
Watercolor, 29.5 × 22 cm
New York, Collection
of Alex Rabinovich
(Le Coeur de la Marquise, Cat. 41)

At page 104
Léon Bakst
*Design for the First Costume
for an Elderly Lady of Phaedra's
Court with Variations of Detail
for an Old Lady*
Pencil, watercolor and gold paint,
29 × 21.7 cm
Lugano, Thyssen-Bornemisza
Collection
(Hippolytus, Cat. 42)

At page 105
Léon Bakst
*Design for Alexei Bulgakov's
Costume as Shahriar*, 1910
Pencil, watercolor, gouache,
gold and silver paint (laid down),
35.5 × 22 cm
Lugano, Thyssen-Bornemisza
Collection
(Schéhérazade, Cat. 45)

Léon Bakst
Costume for Vera Trefilova
as the Japanese Doll, 1903
Painted silk
St. Petersburg, State Museum
of Theater and Music
(La Fée des Poupées, Cat. 43)

Léon Bakst
Costume for the Commander,
1904
Wool, braid, appliqué
St. Petersburg, State Museum
of Theater and Music
(Oedipus al Colonus, Cat. 44)

At page 108
Léon Bakst
*Design for Nathalie Trouhanova's
Costume as La Péri*, 1911
Lithograph colored by hand
in watercolor, gold and silver
paint, 59.8 × 43.7 cm
Lugano, Thyssen-Bornemisza
Collection
(La Péri, Cat. 46)

At page 109
Léon Bakst
*Design for the Costume
of a Pilgrim*, 1911
Pencil, watercolor, gouache,
and silver paint (laid down)
28.2 × 22.8 cm
Lugano, Thyssen-Bornemisza
Collection
(Le Dieu Bleu, Cat. 47)

BAKST
19

Léon Bakst
*Design for the Costume
of Four Beggar Women*, 1911
Pencil, watercolor, gouache,
gold and silver paint (laid down),
28.2 × 19.8 cm
Lugano, Thyssen-Bornemisza
Collection
(Le Dieu Bleu, Cat. 48)

Léon Bakst
Drawing of a Bayadère's Costume
Pencil, watercolor, gouache, gold and silver paint, 29.7 × 19 cm
Lugano, Thyssen-Bornemisza Collection
(Le Dieu Bleu, Cat. 49)

At page 112
Léon Bakst
Design for Ida Rubinstein's Costume for Act IV, 1912
Pencil, watercolor and silver paint (laid down), 27 × 19.6 cm
Lugano, Thyssen-Bornemisza Collection
(Hélène de Sparte, Cat. 50)

At page 113
Léon Bakst
Design for the Costume of One of the Chorus in Scene 7: The Shore of Lake Ilmen at Dawn, 1917
Pencil and watercolor on card, 44.9 × 22.4 cm
Lugano, Thyssen-Bornemisza Collection
(Sadko, Cat. 51)

BAKST
1912

BAKST
1917

Léon Bakst
Design for Scene 4:
The Awakening, 1921
Pencil and watercolor,
48 × 66.8 cm
Lugano, Thyssen-Bornemisza
Collection
(The Sleeping Princess, Cat. 52)

Léon Bakst
Design for the Costume
for Cantalbutte, Master
of Ceremonies in Scene 1, 1921
Pencil, watercolor, gouache
and gold and silver paint
28.5 × 22.3 cm
San Antonio (Texas), Collection
of Robert Tobin
(The Sleeping Princess, Cat. 53)

Léon Bakst
*Costume for Cantalbutte,
Master of Ceremonies
Danced by Jean Yazvinsky
in Scene 1*, 1921 (?)
Purple bronze broacade lined
with orange velvet, decorated
with heraldic roses and thorny
branches in gold and silver
San Antonio (Texas),
Collection of Robert Tobin
(The Sleeping Princess, Cat. 54)

Léon Bakst
*Costume for One
of the Queen's Blue Pages
in Scene 1*, 1921 (?)
Dark blue velvet decorated
in silver and lace with deep
violet velvet cuffs and royal
blue silk ribbon
San Antonio (Texas),
Collection of Robert Tobin
(The Sleeping Princess, Cat. 55)

Léon Bakst
*Décor for the Curtain
for the Beginning of Act I*, 1922
Pencil, watercolor, gold
and silver paint, 52.8 × 80 cm
Lugano, Thyssen-Bornemisza
Collection
(Le Martyre de Saint-Sébastien,
Cat. 56)

Léon Bakst
Décor for the Set of Act I:
The First Mansion,
La Cour des Lys
Pencil, watercolor, gouache
and gold paint (laid down),
43.4 × 58 cm
Lugano, Thyssen-Bornemisza
Collection
(Le Martyre de Saint-Sébastien,
Cat. 57)

Léon Bakst
Design for Henri Rollan's,
M. Gabrio's and M. Numès'
Costumes as the Three Generals
in Act II: L'Ile des Bienheureux,
1922
Pencil, watercolor, gouache,
gold and silver paint (on card),
48.8 × 33 cm
Lugano, Thyssen-Bornemisza
Collection
(Judith, Cat. 58)

Léon Bakst
Décor for the Set of Act I:
The First Mansion,
La Cour des Lys

Léon Bakst
Design for Henri Rollan's,
M. Gabrio's and M. Numès'
Costumes as the Three Generals
in Act II: L'Ile des Bienheureux,

Léon Bakst
Design for the Set of Act II:
Les Demeures de Phaedre, 1923
Pencil, watercolor and gouache
(on card), 33.5 × 52.3 cm
Lugano, Thyssen-Bornemisza
Collection
(Phaedre, Cat. 59)

Léon Bakst
Design for Mlle. Sylvie's Costume
as Hipponoé, the Theban Slave,
in Act I: l'Atrium du Palais
de Thésée à Thrézène, 1923
Pencil, watercolor, gold
and silver paint, 29 × 21.2 cm
Lugano, Thyssen-Bornemisza
Collection
(Phaedre, Cat. 60)

Esclave Thébaienne
1er role
(Mlle Sylvine

bakst 1923

121

Léon Bakst
*Design for M. Desjardins'
Costume as Theseus*
Pencil, watercolor, gold
and silver paint (laid down),
30.8 × 22.3 cm
Lugano, Thyssen-Bornemisza
Collection
(Phaedre, Cat. 61)

Léon Bakst
Le Sultan Samarcande, 1922
Pencil, watercolor, gouache,
gold and silver paint,
67.3 × 48.5 cm
Lugano, Thyssen-Bornemisza
Collection
(Cat. 62)

Léon Bakst
Le Sultan Vindicatif, 1922
Pencil, watercolor, gouache
and silver paint, 66.8 × 48.6 cm
Lugano, Thyssen-Bornemisza
Collection
(Cat. 63)

Léon Bakst
*Design for a Masquerade
Costume for Mr. Kharitonenko,*
1914
Watercolor, bronze paint,
and pencil on paper on board,
25.8 × 19.1 cm
Moscow, State Bakhrushin
Theater Museum
(Cat. 66)

At page 126
Léon Bakst
*Fantaisie sur le Costume
Moderne,* 1910
Pencil, watercolor and gouache,
33 × 25.4 cm
New York, The Metropolitan
Museum of Art, Elisha
Whittesley Fund
(Cat. 64)

At page 127
Léon Bakst
*Design for a Decadent Dress
for Mrs. Legar,* ca. 1910
Watercolor, bronze paint,
and Indian ink, on paper
on board, 30.8 × 23.3 cm
Moscow, State Bakhrushin
Theater Museum
(Cat. 65)

Léon Bakst
*Fantasy on Modern Costume:
Atalanta*, 1912
Pencil, watercolor and silver
paint, 45.2 × 28.4 cm
Lugano, Thyssen-Bornemisza
Collection
(Cat. 67)

Léon Bakst
*Evening Jacket (Trois Quarts)
for Ekaterina Geltser*, 1913
Black tulle crêpe embroidery
with black and white beads
Paris, Collection of Alexandre
Vassiliev
(Cat. 68)

Léon Bakst
*Evening Jacket (Trois Quarts)
for Ekaterina Geltser*, 1913
Net tulle with bead flower
pattern embroidery in rose,
magenta, red and green
Paris, Collection of Alexandre
Vassiliev
(Cat. 69)

Léon Bakst
*Fancy Dress Designed
for Alice Garrett,* 1922-23
Tunic to about mid-length
New York, The Metropolitan
Museum of Art ,
The Costume Institute,
Estate of Marcia Sand Fund
(Cat. 70)

Léon Bakst
*Fancy Dress Designed
for Alice Garrett*, 1922-1923
Tunic
New York, The Metropolitan
Museum of Art ,
The Costume Institute,
Estate of Marcia Sand Fund
(Cat. 71)

Designer unknown
(after Léon Bakst), *Table*, 1913
Wood and copper,
Height, 70 cm; Width, 26 × 35 cm
Paris, Collection of Alexandre
Vassiliev
(Cat. 72)

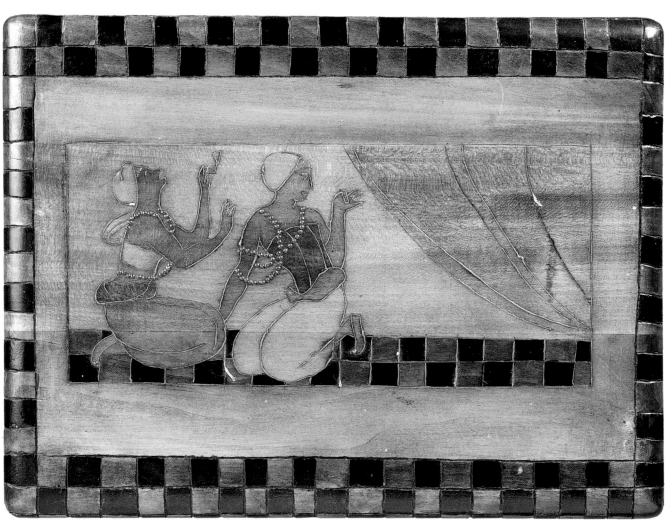

List of Works

Léon Bakst*
(Lev Samoilovich
Rozenberg)

Born 27 April 1866, Grodno; died 27 December 1924, Paris. 1883-87 attended the Academy of Arts, St. Petersburg; 1890 met Alexandre Benois; 1890-93 illustrated magazines such as *Khudozhnik* (Artist) and *Peterburgskaia zhizn* (St. Petersburg Life); from 1890 onwards Bakst was active in book design and illustration, contributing graphic ornaments to diverse publications such as children's books, literary miscellanies, and the Modernist reviews, *Mir iskusstva* (World of Art), *Zolotoe runo* (The Golden Fleece), and *Lukomore* (The Shore); 1891 travelled to Europe, the first of many trips abroad; 1897 contributed to the spring exhibition of the Academy of Arts; 1898 cofounded the World of Art society, assuming technical responsibility for its journal; contributed to Sergei Diaghilev's "Exhibition of Works by Russian and Finnish Artists"; 1901 with Alexandre Benois, Evgenii Lancéray, and others codesigned *Sylvia* which Diaghilev prepared for the Mariinsky Theater (not produced); 1902 made his debut as a stage designer for productions of *Le Coeur de la Marquise* and *Hippolytus* at the Imperial Hermitage Theater, St. Petersburg; published his first article in *Peterburgskaia gazeta* (St. Petersburg Newspaper), the first of many statements on art, fashion and culture that he contributed to newspapers and magazines; 1902-03 collaborated with Sergei Shcherbatov and Vladimir von Meck on the Contemporary Art showrooms in St. Petersburg; 1903 designed the production of *La Fée des Poupées* (*Die Puppenfee*) choreographed by Nikolai and Sergei Legat; thereafter active in numerous drama, opera, and ballet productions; 1903 converted from Judaism to Lutheranism in order to marry Liubov Gritsenko, third daughter of Pavel Tretiakov, but converted back to Judaism after his divorce in 1910;1904 designed productions of *Oedipus at Colonus* and *Antigone;* 1905 helped to organize the underground satirical journal *Zhupel* (Bugbear); 1906 contributed to Diaghilev's Russian section at the "Salon d'Automne", Paris, designing the sculpture garden for it; received the Légion d'Honneur; painted the portrait of Diaghilev and his nurse; 1906-08 taught at Elizaveta Zvantseva's private art school in St. Petersburg; 1907 travelled in Greece with Valentin Serov, investigating the culture of Ancient Greece; 1909 designed *Cléopâtre, Le Festin,* and *Judith* (with Valentin Serov) for the Saison Russe in Paris; thereafter designed or codesigned many productions for Diaghilev, Ida Rubinstein, and other impresarios in Europe and the United States, including: *Le Carnaval, L'Oiseau de Feu, Les Orientales, Schéhérazade* (1910); *Le Martyre de Saint Sébastien, Narcisse, La Péri* (not produced), *Sadko, Le Spectre de la Rose* (1911); *L'Après-midi d'un Faune, Daphnis et Chloé, Le Dieu Bleu, Hélène de Sparte, Papillons, Salomé, Thamar* (1912); *Boris Godunov, Hullo, Tango!, Jeux, La Pisanelle ou la Mort Parfumée, La Tragédie de Salomé* (1913); *Le Légende de Joseph, Midas, Orphée, Papillons* (1914); *The Big Show* (including *The Sleeping Beauty*) (1916); *Les Femmes de Bonne Humeur* (1917); *La Boutique Fantasque* (1917-19); *Aladin ou la Lampe Merveilleuse* (1919); *Mecca* (1920); *The Sleeping Princess* (1921); *Artemis Troublée, Judith, Le Martyre de Saint-Sébastien, Spectacle d'Art Russe* (1922); *La Nuit Ensorcelée, Phaedre* (1923); *Istar* (1924); *The Gods Go A-Begging, Orphée* (1926). 1909-10 published a long article on Classicism and modern art in *Apollon* (Apollo) in St. Petersburg; 1912 denied a St. Petersburg residency permit because of his Jewish status; 1912-14 designed several gowns, costumes and accessories for galas and balls in St. Petersburg; 1914 appointed Academician of the St. Petersburg Academy of Arts, an award that lifted his St. Petersburg residency ban; 1915 lived several months in Switzerland, taking cures; 1915-

22 painted murals on the theme of *The Sleeping Beauty* for James de Rothschild's house in London; 1918 designed the costumes for *La Boutique Fantasque*, but broke with Diaghilev after the latter commissioned André Derain to design the sets; 1922-23 travelled in the United States, working mainly for Alice and John Work Garrett at Evergreen House in Baltimore; 1924 returned to the United States for a lecture tour, also visiting Evergreen again; 1925 first posthumous exhibition at the Galerie Charpentier, Paris.

Selected Bibliography

Much has been written on Bakst, but the following are important sources of information:

A. Alexandre, *The Decorative Art of Léon Bakst*, The Fine Art Society, London 1913.
A. Levinson, *Léon Bakst*, Wasmuth, Berlin 1923.
A. Levinson, *Bakst. The Story of the Artist's Life*, Kogan, Berlin 1923; Bayard, London 1923; reprinted by Blom, New York 1971.
A. Levinson, *The Designs of Léon Bakst for The Sleeping Princess*, Benn, London 1923.
R. Lister, *The Muscovite Peacock. A Study of the Art of Léon Bakst*, Mortlocks, Golden Head Press Cambridge, (Mass.) 1954.
Bakst. Catalog of exhibition at The Fine Art Society, London, December, 1973-January 1974.
I. Pruzhan, *Bakst*, Iskusstvo, Leningrad 1975.
Bakst. Catalog of exhibition at The Fine Art Society, London, September-October, 1976.
N. Borisovskaia, *Lev Bakst*. Iskusstvo, Moscow 1979.
S. Golynets, *L.S. Bakst*, Khudozhnik RSFSR, Leningrad 1981.
Bakst and Benois. Catalog of exhibition at the Marion Koogler McNay Art Museum, San Antonio (Texas), 1985.
I. Pruzhan, *Bakst*, Aurora, Leningrad 1987 (editions in English, French, and German).
A. Schouvaloff, *Bakst*, Sotheby's, London 1991.
On Stage: The Art of Léon Bakst. Catalog of exhibition at the Israel Museum, Jerusalem, 1992.
Léon Bakst. The Sleeping Beauty. Catalog of exhibition at the Tel-Aviv Museum of Art, 1992.
S. Golynets, *Lev Bakst*, Izobrazitelnoe iskusstvo, Moscow 1992.
Léon Bakst. Sensualismens Triumf. Catalog of exhibition at the Dansmuseet, Stockholm, 1993.
C. Spencer, *Bakst and the Ballet Russes*, Academy Editions, London 1995.
E. Bespalova, "Leon Bakst's Textile and Interior Design in America" in *Decorative Arts*, New York 1997, Vol. V, No. 1, pp. 2-28.
For further bibliography, including a list of Bakst's own publications, see Pruzhan, *Bakst* (1987), pp. 239-42; Schouvaloff, *Bakst*, pp. 255-65.
For a comprehensive listing of the stage productions in which Bakst was involved as designer see *Bakst and Benois*, pp. 25-33; Schouvaloff, *Bakst*, pp. 241-48.

Paintings and Drawings

40.
Elysium, 1906
Watercolor and gouache on paper on board,
158 × 140 cm
Moscow, State Tretiakov Gallery (1563)
An enthusiast of Hellenic culture, Bakst painted this fanciful vision of the mythological paradise for the actress and impresario Vera Komissarzhevskaia. In the summer of 1906 Komissarzhevskaia decided to move her Dramatic Theater into a new space on Ofitserskaia Street in St. Petersburg and, a champion of Russian and European Symbolism, she commissioned Bakst to design the tempera on canvas stage curtain (now in the collection of the State Russian Museum, St. Petersburg). In the Classical subject of *Elysium* and in the peculiar bird's eye view, Bakst was both rephrasing earlier compositions such as his illustration to Vasilii Rozanov's article "Stars" of 1901 and anticipating his celebrated panneau *Terror Antiquus* (1908, State Russian Museum, St. Petersburg).
True to his meticulous nature, Bakst not only painted this large preliminary study, but also painted the curtain itself. Vasilii Khvostov, a stage carpenter who worked for the Dramatic Theater, recalled that "up on the scaffolding [Bakst] painted it like a picture. I remember how Bakst prompted such fear and veneration in me. Externally he seemed like a gentleman: dazzling top hat, overcoat flung across his arm – with a silver topped cane in the other hand. But he took his togs off, climbed up the scaffolding, and, with his assistants, for the longest time worked away on his curtain – and this curtain became a real work of art".[1] Actually, *Elysium* was the outside curtain, concealing the second, plush one which, in turn, concealed the stage.
Komissarzhevskaia opened her new Dramatic Theater on 10 October, 1906 with a production of Ibsen's *Hedda Gabler* (directed by Vsevolod Meierkhold) and continued the season with other Symbolist plays such as Maurice Maeterlinck's *Soeur Béatrice* and Alexander Blok's *Fairground Booth*.

[1] V. Khvostov, "Vospominaniia teatralnogo plotnika" in A. Altshuler (ed.), *Vera Fedorovna Komissarzhevskaia*, Iskusstvo, Leningrad-Moscow 1964, p. 256. This book (opposite p. 176) carries a reproduction of the curtain *in situ*.

Stage Designs

Le Coeur de la Marquise
Pantomime in one act with a prologue and epilogue in verse by Frédéric Febvre with music by Ernest Guiraud. Produced by Marius Petipa at the Imperial Hermitage Theater, St. Petersburg, on 22 February, 1902, with designs by Léon Bakst.
Information on the plot of *Le Coeur de la Marquise* has not been forthcoming, although according to the yearbook of the Imperial Theaters, the *dramatis personae* included the Marquise, her companion Lisette, the Fortune-Teller, young ladies, Doctor Pierrot, the Vicomte, a street singer, officers and a servant girl. The yearbook also gives G. Guiraud as the composer which, presumably, is a misprint for Ernest Guiraud.[1]

41.
Design for the Costume for the Gypsy Fortune Teller, 1900
Watercolor, 29.5 × 22 cm
Signed and dated lower right
New York, Collection of Alik Rabinovich
The Imperial Hermitage Theater produced plays and ballets of a lighter quality for the Court, Benois, for example, designing Alexander Taneev's opera *Cupid's Revenge* there also in 1902 and Bakst creating the costumes for Josef Bayer's *La Fée des Poupées* the following year. According to Prince Peter Lieven, *Le Coeur de la Marquise*, Bakst's first professional theater engagement, demonstrated that his "gift for theatrical costume was at once apparent. The production was brilliant, the costumes entrancing. Unfortunately, the play was given once only, for a Court gala performance".[2] Among the dancers were Olga Preobrazhenskaia, Marius Petipa, and the Legat brothers. Bakst and his World of Art colleagues Alexander Golovin and Konstantin Somov were also responsible for the designs of the accompanying programs (Fig. 53). The date of 1900 on this sketch would indicate that Bakst had been commissioned to prepare designs well before the actual production.

[1] See L. Gelmersen (ed.), *Ezhegodnik Imperatorskikh teatrov. Sezon 1901-1902*, Imperial Theaters, St. Petersburg 1902. Supplement for the Imperial Hermitage Theater, p. 14.
[2] P. Lieven, *The Birth of the Ballets-Russes*, Unwin, London 1956, p. 425.

Hippolytus
Tragedy by Euripides, translated and edited by Dmitrii Merezhkovsky, with music by E. Overbeck. Produced by Yurii Ozarovsky at the Alexandrinsky Theater, St. Petersburg, on 14 October, 1902, with designs by Léon Bakst.
Hippolytus is the son of Theseus, King of Athens. Phaedra, Theseus's Queen, is in love with Hippolytus – which is the doing of Aphrodite whom Hippolytus

has slighted, preferring a life honoring the chaste and athletic Artemis. When Phaedra's passion is revealed to Hippolytus, he reacts so violently that Phaedra fears his anger and kills herself. Because of an oath not to admit the real course of events, Hippolytus cannot tell the truth to Theseus. Theseus, therefore, banishes him. As Hippolytus is riding away, a bull of unnatural size appears from the sea and frightens his horses who stampede, and Hippolytus is dragged to his death. Artemis then appears to tell the truth to Theseus, but not in time to save Hippolytus who dies in the arms of his father.

42.
Design for the First Costume for an Elderly Lady of Phaedra's Court with Variations of Detail for an Old Lady
Pencil, watercolor, and gold paint, 29 × 21.7 cm
Inscribed with directions for the dressmaker
(For full transcription see TBC, pp. 30-31)
Lugano, Thyssen-Bornemisza Collection
Hippolytus was the first of Bakst's professional designs for a play set in antiquity and perhaps his relative inexperience contributed to the less than satisfactory result. He had a difficult task explaining his conception of Ancient Greece to Merezhkovsky and Ozarovsky, for, as he wrote to Vladimir Teliakovsky, he feared that "a mutual misunderstanding between the writer [translator] and the artist will ensue, the former demands from the latter things that contradict the style and conditions of the scene".[1] Indeed, Bakst's designs did not win universal support and after the dress rehearsal, Konstantin Korovin was asked to "improve" the clouds in the décor. Still, the production did receive some positive reviews, for, as the critic Yurii Beliaev wrote: "These were not the usual Greeks on stage in a *style empire* or, worse, Greeks from an operetta; these were Greeks from Etruscan vases, from sepulchral bas reliefs (...) The costumes were beautiful, new..."[2] Andrei Bely, the Symbolist poet and philoso-

pher who knew Bakst from his sittings for several portraits, also emphasized the authenticity of Bakst's reincarnation of Hellas in his essay of 1906, asserting that these "drawings from the life of antiquity constitute almost a scientific tract".[3]

[1] Letter from Bakst to Vladimir Teliakovsky dated 11 January 1902. Quoted in Pruzhan, *Bakst* (1975), p. 60.
[2] Yu. Beliaev, "Ippolit" in *Novoe vremia*, 1902, 16 October. Quoted in *ibid*.
[3] A. Lavrov and S. Grechishkin: "Neizdannaia statia Andreia Belogo 'Bakst'" in I. Andronikov et al. (eds.), *Pamiatniki kultury. Novye otkrytiia. Ezhegodnik 1978*, Nauka, Leningrad 1979, p. 97.

La Fée des Poupées (Die Puppenfee)
Ballet divertissement in one act by Josef Bayer. Produced by Nikolai and Sergei Legat at the Imperial Hermitage Theater, St. Petersburg, on 7 February, 1903, and then at the Mariinsky Theater, St. Petersburg, on 16 February, 1903, with choreography by Nikolai and Sergei Legat, musical additions by Peter Tchaikovsky, Riccardo Drigo, Anatolii Liadov, Anton Rubinstein, and Louis Moreau Gottschalk, and designs by Léon Bakst.
A toy shop on Nevsky Prospect in St. Petersburg boasts an enormous selection of toys and dolls that impersonate the owner, the mailman, and the many passersby such as a Spanish lady, a French lady, etc. The most important of the dolls is the Fairy Queen who animates her charges, so that the entire toy shop comes to life as the dolls march, dance negro dances, waltz, etc.

43.
Costume for Vera Trefilova as the Japanese Doll, 1903
Painted silk,
Length of shoulder, 12.5 cm;
Bosom, 84 cm; Length of back, 55 cm; Length of sleeve, 16 cm;
Skirt, Waist, 54 cm;
Common Length, 56 cm
St. Petersburg, State Museum of Theater and Music
(GIK 17796/25)

La Fée des Poupées marked Bakst's second appearance as a ballet designer after *Le Coeur de la Marquise* and his company was an auspicious one with Vera Trefilova as the Japanese Doll, Anna Pavlova as the Spanish Doll, Matilda Kchessinskaya as the Fairy Doll, and Olga Preobrazhenskaia as the Baby, all watched by the Imperial Family. Bakst's sets and costumes expressed playfulness, ingenuity, and "geographical accuracy", but not the brilliant sensuality for which he is now remembered and his decors here were received simply as "a faithful copy"[1] of the Gostinyi dvor (shopping arcade) on Nevsky Prospect in St. Petersburg in the 1850s. To some extent, Bakst and the Legats were appealing to a fashion for the naive and unassuming artifact, especially for the art of the toy which interested the World of Art artists in particular (see Cat. 39). At the end of 1903, the St. Eugeniia Society in St. Petersburg produced twelve postcards based on Bakst's costumes, including the Japanese Doll, which, according to Benois, had been inspired by his own collection of toys.[2]

[1] Newspaper report of the time. Quoted in V. Krasovskaia, *Russkii baletnyi teatr nachala XX veka*, Iskusstvo, Leningrad 1971, p. 69, where neither author, nor source is given.
[2] Benois, *Reminiscences*, p. 230. For a one page reproduction of the set of twelve postcards see LRC, pp. 32-34.

Oedipus at Colonus
Tragedy by Sophocles translated by Dmitrii Merezhkovsky. Produced by Yurii Ozarovsky at the Alexandrinsky Theater, St. Petersburg on 9 January, 1904, with designs by Léon Bakst.
Oedipus of Thebes has realized that, unknowingly, he has killed his father Laius, has married his mother Jocasta, and has fathered four children by her. In his horror, he has blinded himself and asked to be banished from his land. The aged Oedipus in exile now appears with his daughter Antigone. He travels as far as Athens (Colonus) and there is

discovered by his elder daughter Ismene. Ismene has left Thebes where her brothers are fighting for the throne. One of Oedipus' sons, Polynices, who has been overthrown by his younger brother Eteocles and seeks Oedipus' support in bringing down Thebes and his younger brother, now appears in Athens. Oedipus rejects his plea for help, curses both sons, and asks King Theseus to help him die in secret. The latter escorts Oedipus to an unknown destination and returns to tell of Oedipus' death, but he refuses to disclose the manner of death or the location of the grave.

44.
Costume for the Commander, 1904
Wool, braid, appliqué,
Length of shoulder, 13.5 cm;
Bosom, 96 cm;
Common length, 102 cm;
Length of sleeve, 16 cm
St. Petersburg, State Museum of Theater and Music
(GIK 18069/2)
Bakst's designs for *Oedipus at Colonus*, especially the costumes, had much in common with those for *Hippolytus* and demonstrated both an archaeological understanding of Ancient Greece and a vivid artistic imagination. As Ida Rubinstein, a fellow enthusiast for the Classical epoch, remarked of Bakst: "From the depths of time he summoned the artistic coarseness, the nakedness of that era when Oedipus cried out and Antigone wept."[1] It is of interest to compare Bakst's resolutions of the sets and costumes for both tragedies with his designs for Gabriele d'Annunzio's *Phaedre* of 1923 (Cat. 59-61) and with those of Alexander Vesnin, Konstantin Medunetsky, and the Stenberg brothers for Alexander Tairov's productions of Racine's *Phèdre* in 1922 and 1923.

[1] "Ida Rubinshtein o sebe" in *Solntse Rossii*, St, Petersburg 1913, No. 25, p. 12.

Schéhérazade
Choreographic drama in one act. Music by Nikolai Rimsky-

Korsakov, book by Léon Bakst and Alexandre Benois, choreography by Michel Fokine. Produced by Sergei Diaghilev at the Théâtre National de l'Opéra, Paris on 4 June 1910, with designs by Léon Bakst.

The Shah Shahriar, suspecting his favorite wife, Zobeida, of being unfaithful, pretends to go out hunting. As soon as he leaves, the ladies of the harem persuade the Great Eunuch to let in the black slaves. An orgy ensues, led by Zobeida and her favorite negro. The Shah suddenly returns and orders the transgressors to be executed. Seeing that he hesitates to punish her, Zobeida stabs herself and dies at the feet of her master.

45.
Design for Alexei Bulgakov's Costume as Shahriar, 1910
Pencil, watercolor, gouache, gold and silver paint (laid down)
35.5 × 22 cm
Signed and dated lower right
Lugano, Thyssen-Bornemisza Collection
A gesture to the fashion for heady mixtures of Oriental sex and violence, *Schéhérazade*, with its theme from the prologue of *1001 Nights*, was much in keeping with Bakst's and Fokine's own esthetic preferences at this time. Moreover, *Schéhérazade* attracted a Parisian public nurtured on the poetical and artistic fantasies of the European Symbolists such as Charles Baudelaire, Aubrey Beardsley, and Gabriele D'Annunzio and coincided with a bourgeoning fashion for the "East" on stage, something demonstrated by the popularity of parallel spectacles such as *Islamey* (1912), *Le Roi de Lahore* (1924), *Aziade* (1926) and, of course, Bakst's other spectacular explorations such as *Cléopâtre* (1909), *La Péri* (1911; Cat. 46) and *Le Dieu Bleu* (1912; see Cat. 47-49).
Given this context, we can understand why the appeal of Bakst's female costumes for *Schéhérazade* has tended to be stronger than that of his male interpretations. His excited enchantresses tease and seduce with their "long, viscid, and terrifying *sharovary* symbolizing volup-

tuousness, cruel as the sting of a wasp."[1] But, of course, when we examine the lavish costume for the Schahriar, we also understand that for Bakst lust and sensuality were no less "male" than "female". Even the cautious Benois was captivated by Bakst's exotic "universe of sensations, inspiring you to read the Arabian tales".[2]

[1] Ya. Tugendkhold, "Russkii balet v Parizhe" in *Apollon*, St. Petersburg 1910, No. 8, p. 70.
[2] A. Benois, "Russkie spektakli v Parizhe ('Shekherazade')" in *Rech*, 12 July, 1910. Quoted in Pruzhan, *Bakst* (1975), p. 222.

La Péri

One-act ballet based on a Persian fairy-tale with music by Paul Dukas and costumes by Léon Bakst. Rehearsed by Sergei Diaghilev's Ballets Russes in Paris in 1911, but not produced. Iskendar searches for the flower of Immortality and finds it – as an emerald talisman in the form of a lotus – in the hands of Péri, a Persian fairy. Iskendar steals it, but falls in love with Péri. She awakens and sees the Flower, now purple with desire, in Iskendar's right hand. In order to regain her property, she proceeds to dance. The Flower turns white and gold and Iskendar is forever fused with it.

46.
Design for Nathalie Trouhanova's Costume as La Péri, 1911
Lithograph colored by hand in watercolor, gold and silver paint, 59.8 × 43.7 cm
Signed and dated lower right in the stone
No. 26 from an edition of 100
Lugano, Thyssen-Bornemisza Collection
(The original gouache and pencil drawing for this lithograph is in the collection of Nina and Nikita Lobanov-Rostovsky. For reproduction and commentary see LRC, Entry R498)
It is generally assumed that, because of an argument between Diaghilev and Dukas concerning the dancer Nathalie Trouhanova, who, according to Dukas, should have danced the title role, and

because of Bakst's alleged procrastinations, Diaghilev cancelled the ballet. However, Trouhanova's own account of the events is rather different. According to her memoirs, she had a small company of French dancers that used to put on annual Concerts de Danse de N. Trouhanova in Paris. In 1911 her companion Dukas played her the score for his new opus, *La Péri*, which he wanted her to dance – however, Trouhanova was not impressed by the music: "This is a *danse des vaches* from the mountains", she exclaimed, "but La Péri is not a mountain cow, she is a flower!".[1] So Dukas changed the music and she agreed to dance it. As she explained later, *La Péri* was not an easy ballet, because it relied on only two characters and, unless danced well, it could become tedious. Consequently, in order to make her character representation as authentic as possible, she spent several months studying oriental art in London.
One day, Diaghilev and Nijinsky dropped by her Paris studio and invited her to stage and dance La Péri for the Ballets Russes – with choreography by Michel Fokine and designs by Bakst. Flattered by Diaghilev's attentions, Trouhanova agreed, but she soon discovered that Diaghilev's company had taken an instant dislike to her – Fokine never showed up, and Nijinsky expressed no interest in being her partner. When, a few days before the scheduled premiere, Adolf Bolm replaced Nijinsky as Iskendar, Trouhanova threw a fit, walked out, and left the Diaghilev company. However, she continued to work on her version of *La Péri* and, with choreography by Ivan Clustine and designs by René Piot, *La Péri* was produced by her own company in June, 1912. The production was well received, prompting her exaggerated claim that it was "the very best French choreographical and musical work of the entire early 20th century".[2]

[1] Trukhanova, "Ogni rampy", l. 169. For more information on Trouhanova and *La Péri*, see L. Garafola: "Soloists Abroad: The

Pre-War Careers of Natalia Trouhanova and Ida Rubinstein" in *Experiment*, Los Angeles 1996, No. 2, pp. 7-39
[2] Trukhanova, "Ogni rampy", l. 199.

Le Dieu Bleu

A Hindu legend in one act by Jean Cocteau and Frédéric de Madrazo with music by Reynaldo Hahn. Produced by Sergei Diaghilev at the Théâtre du Châtelet on 13 May 1912 with choreography by Michel Fokine and designs by Léon Bakst.
At a Hindu ceremony, a young man is about to enter the priesthood, but the maiden who loves him tries to stop this. The High Priest condemns her action and gives her over to the monsters of the temple. However, the maiden invokes the Goddess and the Blue God who deliver her from this fate. They retire gracefully as the two lovers are reunited.

47.
Design for the Costume of a Pilgrim, 1911
Pencil, watercolor, gouache, and silver paint (laid down)
28.2 × 22.8 cm
Signed and dated lower right
Lugano, Thyssen-Bornemisza Collection

48.
Design for the Costume of Four Beggar Women, 1911
Pencil, watercolor, gouache, gold and silver paint (laid down)
28.2 × 19.8 cm
Signed and dated lower right
Lugano, Thyssen-Bornemisza Collection

49.
Drawing of a Bayadère's Costume
Pencil, watercolor, gouache, gold and silver paint,
29.7 × 19 cm
Signed lower right
Lugano, Thyssen-Bornemisza Collection
In 1900 Bakst and Fokine had attended one or more performances by the Ballet Troupe of the Royal Siamese Court in St. Petersburg. They had been profoundly impressed both by the "distinctive choreographic de-

sign" of the dancing[1] and by the peculiar costumes of the dancers, and later on Bakst transferred the short skirts and tapered headdresses to his costumes for *Les Orientales* (1910), *La Péri*, and *Le Dieu Bleu*.

Full of enthusiasm, Fokine then suggested that Diaghilev undertake a ballet related to the culture of Southeast Asia. Diaghilev liked the idea and he commissioned Bakst to design the sets and costumes for *Le Dieu Bleu* which Diaghilev scheduled for 1911 and then postponed until the following year. Bakst's set representing the Hindu temple surrounded by gigantic cliffs and lush, tropical foliage was among his most exotic. The costumes also extended Bakst's fertile imagination: he made a generous application of the pearls, pendants and scarves that he loved so much and even had Nijinsky (the Blue God) painted blue (Fig. 54). Still, despite such splendor and the dancing by Tamara Karsavina (the maiden), Lidiia Nelidova (the Goddess) and Nijinsky, *Le Dieu Bleu* was not an overall success, at least from the choreographic standpoint, and many observers found the result both tedious and pretentious. On the other hand, Cyril Beaumont was rather struck by the spectacle, at least by its premiere in London in February, 1913, because "Bakst proved that while he could evoke all the cruelty and voluptuousness of the East, as in his setting for *Schéhérazade*, he could also, by a different combination of color and design, conjure up the mystery and sense of awe produced by the East in a mood of religious exaltation".[2] The costume design for the Blue God can be seen in the background of Emil Hoppé's 1916 photograph of Bakst (D56).

[1] N. (=V.) Svetlov, "Siamskii balet" in Gelmersen (ed.), *Ezhegodnik Imperatorskikh teatrov. Sezon 1900-1901*, p. 294. For further information on the Siamese ballet in St. Petersburg and Bakst's response see Bowlt, "Theater of Reason, Theater of Desire", Note 78.
[2] C. Beaumont, *The Diaghilev Ballet in London*, Putnam, London 1940, p. 58.

Hélène de Sparte

Tragedy in four acts by Emile Verhaeren with incidental music by Déodat de Séverac. Directed by Alexandre Sanine for the Ida Rubinstein Company at the Théâtre du Châtelet, Paris, on 4 May, 1912, with designs by Léon Bakst.

Helen dreams of peace and prosperity with her husband Menalus, now that Troy has fallen. But fate decrees otherwise, for, victim of an incestuous love for Helen, her brother, Castor, kills Menalus, whereupon the vengeful niece, Electra, kills Castor. Unheedful of the counsel of Castor's twin brother, Pollux, Helen retires to the countryside where she is feted by fauns, nymphs and satyrs. Her father, Zeus, then summons her to his celestial abode and she is granted immortality.

50.
Design for Ida Rubinstein's Costume for Act IV, 1912
Pencil, watercolor and silver paint (laid down), 27 × 19.6 cm
Signed and dated lower right
Lugano, Thyssen-Bornemisza Collection

Sadko

Opera in four acts and seven scenes by Nikolai Rimsky-Korsakov with libretto by the composer Vladimir Belsky. The Théâtre National de l'Opéra, Paris, planned a production in 1917 with designs by Léon Bakst, but it was not realized.

As the merchants of Novgorod rejoice, Sadko, a local singer arrives and entertains them with his song. The scene then changes to the shores of Lake Ilmen where Sadko's singing attracts a group of swans who turn into beautiful maidens, including Volkhova, the Sea Princess. Volkhova confesses her love for Sadko, but then returns to her father, the King of the Ocean, announcing that Sadko will presently catch three golden fish and travel in foreign lands. Sadko does, indeed, catch the fish, embarks on a voyage in the merchants' ships, and finds trea-

sure. But Sadko becomes marooned on a plank of wood at sea and plunges to the ocean floor and the Underwater Kingdom. Sadko then wakes up to find himself at the edge of Lake Ilmen and to witness the arrival of his ships laden with treasure.

51.
Design for the Costume of One of the Chorus in Scene 7: The Shore of Lake Ilmen at Dawn, 1917
Pencil and watercolor on card 44.9 × 22.4 cm
Signed and dated lower right
Lugano, Thyssen-Bornemisza Collection

Although the costumes that Bakst designed for this project are informed by a fanciful elaboration of ethnographical detail and, as Alexander Schouvaloff affirms, still suggest individual personalities, they are less scintillating, less sumptuous than his concurrent designs for *Les Femmes de Bonne Humeur* (produced in Rome in April, 1917). Indeed, other lavish productions of *Sadko* (e.g. Diaghilev's at the Théâtre du Châtelet in 1911 with designs by Boris Anisfeld) must have constituted a formidable precedent, especially with the "tumbling tresses of aquatic vegetation and horizons of blue, luminous and fairy-like waves"[1] plus an "entire trunk of live crabs."[2]

As a matter of fact, the previous year had seen Diaghilev's revival of the opera-ballet for the American season, although he replaced the Anisfeld designs with new ones by Natalia Goncharova. Benois, on the other hand, came to *Sadko* in 1930 with his designs for a production by the Opéra Russe at the Théâtre des Champs-Elysées, which critics praised for its vitality, imagination – and practicality.

[1] Review in *Le Gaulois*, Paris 1911, 7 June. Quoted in R. Buckle, *Diaghilev*, Weidenfeld and Nicolson, London 1979, p. 109.
[2] Fokin, *Protiv techeniia*, p. 470.

The Sleeping Princess

Ballet in a prologue and three acts based on a fairy tale by

Charles Perrault, *The Sleeping Beauty*; original music by Peter Tchaikovsky and original choreography by Marius Petipa and Ivan Vsevolozhsky. Produced by Sergei Diaghilev at the Alhambra Theatre, London, on 2 November, 1921, with choreography by Nicholas Sergeyev and additional choreography by Bronislava Nijinska, partial reorchestration by Igor Stravinsky, and designs by Léon Bakst.

The Princess Aurora receives gifts from the Fairy of the Lilacs, the Fairy of the Crystal Fountain, and the other Fairies in celebration of her christening. But the Master of Ceremonies has forgotten to invite the Wicked Fairy, Carabosse, who, in revenge, casts an evil spell, plunging the Princess, her parents, her attendants, and her Castle into an everlasting slumber. However, one hundred years later, guided by the Lilac Fairy, Prince Charming happens upon the scene and awakens the Princess with a kiss, thereby arousing everyone else from the deep slumber. The happy couple marry amidst general jubilation.

52.
Design for Scene 4: The Awakening, 1921
Pencil and watercolor, 48 × 66.8 cm
Signed and dated lower left
Lugano, Thyssen-Bornemisza Collection

53.
Design for the Costume for Cantalbutte, Master of Ceremonies in Scene 1, 1921
Pencil, watercolor, gouache and gold and silver paint
28.5 × 22.3 cm
Signed and dated lower right
San Antonio (Texas), Collection of Robert Tobin (R81.53)

54.
Costume for Cantalbutte, Master of Ceremonies Danced by Jean Yazvinsky in Scene 1, 1921 (?)
Purple bronze broCade lined with orange velvet, decorated with heraldic roses and thorny branches in gold and silver
Length from shoulder to bottom edge, 195 cm

San Antonio (Texas), Collection of Robert Tobin (RP35)

55.
Costume for One of the Queen's Blue Pages in Scene 1, 1921 (?)
Dark blue velvet decorated in silver and lace with deep violet velvet cuffs and royal blue silk ribbon; Jacket from shoulder to bottom edge, 86 cm; Pants from waist to knee, 67 cm
San Antonio (Texas), Collection of Robert Tobin (RP200)
For his 1921 production of *The Sleeping Princess*, Diaghilev had hoped to draw upon Alexandre Benois' talents at historical restoration, but Benois was in Russia so Diaghilev invited Bakst to design the ballet instead. True to his nature, Bakst invented a rhetorical and ambitious scheme of décors and costumes, mixing many styles and evoking his decorative experiences of *La Légende de Joseph* (1914) and *Les Dames de Bonne Humeur* (1917). His stage directions even specified that all the people and animals in the Castle should remain still until the Prince awakened the Princess, but the dogs, cats, and birds refused to cooperate. The sumptuous décors and costumes drained Diaghilev's financial resources and, as a result, Sir Oswald Stoll, who managed the Alhambra production, confiscated them and this led to the final rupture between Diaghilev and Bakst. However, Diaghilev did reuse part of *The Sleeping Princess* in Paris on 18 May 1922 (as *Le Mariage d'Aurore*), but with sets and costumes by Alexandre Benois and Natalia Goncharova.[1]

[1] For more detailed discussion see Beaumont, *The Diaghilev Ballet in London*, pp. 191-214.

Le Martyre de Saint-Sébastien
Mystery play in five acts by Gabriele D'Annunzio with musical interludes by Claude Debussy and choreography by Michel Fokine. Produced on 22 May 1911 by Ida Rubinstein at the Théâtre du Châtelet, Paris, with designs by Léon Bakst, and revived minus Act II for the Théâtre du Châtelet, on 17 June, 1922.

Sébastien, leader of the archers of Emesus, is seized with a holy delirium. He calls upon Heaven for a sign, shoots an arrow that does not fall, and dances on live embers which for him have the coolness of lilies (the first ordeal). The Emperor Diocletian orders Sébastien to sing, but he breaks the lyre and enacts the Divine Passion, for which the Emperor gives him the Orb of Victory. But Sébastien destroys the emblem and, as punishment, he is suffocated on the lyre beneath garlands and flowers (second ordeal). Sébastien is then bound to the trunk of a laurel tree, for he is to die from the arrows of his own archers. They shoot, but his body bears no trace of the arrows (last ordeal) and his soul ascends to Paradise.[1]

56.
Décor for the Curtain for the Beginning of Act I, 1922
Pencil, watercolor, gold and silver paint, 52.8 × 80 cm
Signed and dated lower right
Lugano, Thyssen-Bornemisza Collection

57.
Décor for the Set of Act I: The First Mansion, La Cour des Lys
Pencil, watercolor, gouache and gold paint (laid down)
43.4 × 58 cm
Signed lower right
Lugano, Thyssen-Bornemisza Collection
Le Martyre de Saint-Sébastien, one of the several collaborations between Ida Rubinstein and Bakst, enabled the former to make her first independent appearance on the Paris stage in the role of St. Sébastien. Not all reviewers of the time, however, were impressed, Anatolii Lunacharsky dismissing the designs as an "anachronistic mixing of styles."[2] Bakst made the two décors above for Rubinstein's revival of the play (minus Act II) that premiered at the Théâtre National de l'Opéra, Paris, on 17 June, 1922. The play itself, this "pastiche, vexing from all points of view," was now greeted with derision,[3] although, as some recompense, Bakst's designs were acknowledged as a "triumph of painted décor".[4]

[1] Based on the synopsis by A. Schouvaloff. See TBC, p. 89.
[2] A. Lunacharsky, "Parizhskie pisma. Misteriia o muchenichestve sv. Sebastiana" in *Teatr i iskusstvo*, St. Petersburg 1911, 10 July, p. 544.
[3] Critique by François de Nion. Quoted in TBC, p. 93
[4] Critique by Georges le Ferre. Quoted in *ibid*.

Judith
Dramatic comedy in three acts by Henry Bernstein with music by Eugène Cinda Grassi. Produced by André Antoine for the Théâtre du Gymnase, Paris, on 13 October, 1922, with set by Serge Soudeikine and costumes by Léon Bakst.
The Jewish city of Bethulia is besieged by the army of Holophernes, the general of Nebuchadnezzar, who longs for a true and lasting love. Judith, a chaste Jewish widow, enters the enemy camp and seduces the willing Holophernes. While he is slumbering, rather the worse for drink, Judith cuts off his head and, in triumph, returns to Bethulia. Encouraged by this, the Jews make a sortie and put the enemy to flight.

58.
Design for Henri Rollan's, M. Gabrio's and M. Numès' Costumes as the Three Generals in Act II: L'Ile des Bienheureux, 1922
Pencil, watercolor, gouache, gold and silver paint on card
48.8 × 33 cm
Signed and dated lower right
Lugano, Thyssen-Bornemisza Collection
Bakst came to the basic plot of *Judith* with rich experience inasmuch he had designed, together with Valentin Serov, Diaghilev's production of Alexander Glazunov's opera of the same name at the Théâtre du Châtelet in 1909. That momentous presentation had been distinguished not only by the rich sets and costumes, but also by the singing of Feodor Chaliapin (as Holophernes) and Felia Litvin (as Judith). Bakst's renderings for this 1922 drama on the same theme were more rushed, but less energetic, for he was weary, overcommitted, and

anxious about his American engagements. Still, the visual impression was positive, one French critic asserting that "Le spectacle était habilement presenté dans des décors de Soudeikine et de costumes de Bakst d'un equilibre parfait, dans des harmonies tantôt violentes et tantôt sourdes, toujours soumises au chef d'orchestre électricien".[1]

[1] *Comoedia Illustré*, November, 1922. Quoted in TBC, p. 100.

Phaedre
Tragedy in three acts by Gabriele d'Annunzio, translated from the Italian by André Doderet and with music by Ildebando Pizzetti. Produced by Armand Bour for the Ida Rubinstein Company at the Théâtre de l'Opéra, Paris, on 7 June, 1923, with designs by Léon Bakst.
The plot is similar to that of Hippolytus, except that D'Annunzio gives Hippolytus the three gifts of a horse, a silver vase and a Theban slave whom Phaedre kills, has her kiss the pure Hippolytus and Theseus summon Poseidon who kills Hippolytus, and finally has Eurythos tell the truth to Theseus whereupon Artemis kills Phaedre by her arrows.

59.
Design for the Set of Act II: Les Demeures de Phaedre, 1923
Pencil, watercolor and gouache on card, 33.5 × 52.3 cm (image size)
(48.5 × 67.3 cm paper size)
Signed and dated lower right
Lugano, Thyssen-Bornemisza Collection

60.
Design for Mlle. Sylvie's Costume as Hipponoé, the Theban Slave, in Act I: l'Atrium du Palais de Thésée à Thrézène, 1923
Pencil, watercolor, gold and silver paint, 29 × 21.2 cm
Signed and dated lower right
Lugano, Thyssen-Bornemisza Collection

61.
Design for M. Desjardins' Costume as Theseus
Pencil, watercolor, gold and silver paint (laid down),

30.8 × 22.3 cm
Signed lower center
Lugano, Thyssen-Bornemisza
Collection
Bakst had travelled in Greece
with his friend Valentin Serov in
1907, but published his impressions in the form of a book, *Serov
i ya v Gretsii*, only in 1923, the
year he was working on *Phaedre*.
Acquaintance with these impressions helps us to understand
Bakst's special vision of Hellas
and his perpetual amazement at
the "secrets of the Greek past".[1]
The translated excerpts in the
*Selected Writings by Alexandre
Benois and Léon Bakst* below
demonstrate the intensity of
Bakst's passion for the Greek is-
lands, especially Crete.

[1] Letter from Bakst to Liubov
Bakst dated 20 May, 1907.
Quoted in Zilbershtein, Samkov,
Valentin Serov, Vol. 1, p. 604.
For further commentary on
Phaedre see TBC, pp. 109-19.

**Costume Designs
not created for specific
productions**

62.
Le Sultan Samarcande, 1922
Pencil, watercolor, gouache,
gold and silver paint,
67.3 × 48.5 cm
Signed and dated lower right
Lugano, Thyssen-Bornemisza
Collection
In addition to the detailed commentary in TBC (pp. 102-05), A.
Schouvaloff writes that this work
"is based on an earlier drawing
which Bakst made in 1919 for
the revue *Aladin ou la lampe merveilleuse*".[1]

[1] Letter from Schouvaloff to John
Bowlt dated 12 February, 1998.

63.
Le Sultan Vindicatif, 1922
Pencil, watercolor, gouache and
silver paint, 66.8 × 48.6 cm
Signed and dated upper left
Lugano, Thyssen-Bornemisza
Collection

Dress Designs

64.
*Fantaisie sur le Costume
Moderne*, 1910

Pencil, watercolor and gouache,
33 × 25.4 cm
New York, The Metropolitan
Museum of Art, Elisha
Whittesley Fund (61.557.5)

65.
*Design for a Decadent Dress
for Mrs. Legar*, ca. 1910
Watercolor, bronze paint,
and Indian ink, on paper
on board, 30.8 × 23.3 cm
Moscow, State Bakhrushin
Theater Museum (214644)

66.
*Design for a Masquerade Costume
for Mr. Kharitonenko*, 1914
Watercolor, bronze paint,
and pencil on paper on board
25.8 × 19.1 cm
Moscow, State Bakhrushin
Theater Museum (193502)
This costume was for one of the
several masked and costume balls
that were organized in St.
Petersburg in the winter and
spring of 1914, the most famous
of which was the Ball of Colored
Wigs sponsored by Princess
Elizaveta Shuvalova. The precise
identity of this particular "Mr.
Kharitonenko" is not known, although he could have been the
wealthy Kharkhov businessman,
Pavel Ivanovich Kharitonenko
(1852-1914), or his son, a dandy
and playboy. A relative (?) of
Kharitonenko was Princess
Natalia Gorchakova (née Kharitonenko) who attended one of
Countess Mariia Kleinmikhel's
fancy-dress balls also in a Bakst
ensemble (D47; Figs. 68-70; and
see *Selected Writings by Alexandre
Benois and Léon Bakst*, Note 18).

67.
*Fantasy on Modern Costume:
Atalanta*, 1912
Pencil, watercolor and silver
paint, 45.2 × 28.4 cm
Signed and dated lower right
Lugano, Thyssen-Bornemisza
Collection
Atalanta was one of a group of
"fantasies on modern dress" that
Bakst undertook in 1912-14.
Other fantasies included *Aglaia*,
Alcyone, *Deauville*, *Dryad*,
Iolanta, *Isis*, *Nike*, and *Philomela*.
For Bakst's own commentary see
"Dressing the Woman of the
Future. (A Conversation)" in
Selected Writings below.

68.
*Evening Jacket (Trois Quarts)
for Ekaterina Geltser*, 1913
Black tulle crêpe embroidery
with black and white beads,
Height, 95 cm; Length, 70 cm
Paris, Collection of Alexandre
Vassiliev
The ballerina Ekaterina
Vasilievna Geltser (1876-1962)
danced for several companies, in-
cluding the Mariinsky Theater,
St. Petersburg, and was prima
ballerina at the Bolshoi Theater,
Moscow. She also starred with
Sergei Diaghilev's Ballets Russes
in Paris in 1910. This jacket, de-
signed by Bakst, was made in the
atelier of Nadezhda Petrovna
Lamanova (1861-1941).

69.
*Evening Jacket (Trois Quarts)
for Ekaterina Geltser*, 1913
Net tulle with bead flower
pattern embroidery in rose,
magenta, red and green,
Height, 105 cm; Length, 70 cm
Paris, Collection of Alexandre
Vassiliev (See Cat. 68)

70.
*Fancy Dress Designed
for Alice Garrett*, 1922-1923
Tunic to about mid-length,
length from shoulder,
110 cm; trousers ankle length,
89 cm; Headdress diameter
about 42.4 cm;
Shoes, length 29 cm;
height of heel 18 cm
Tunic with camisole bodice
of moir patterned silver lame,
embroidered with rhinestones,
gold and turquoise beads
in geometric pattern. Boned
skirt of blue/gold lame with
appliqué medallions, pailletted
embroidery in jade green, pink
and magenta, folded back
in front to expose lower skirt
embroidered to match bodice.
Jodphur style trousers of white
satin trimmed with ropes
of pearls. Headdress of gold
lame and deep blue, overlaid
with white gauze and black
net studded with pearls. Wired
pearls extend upward from
either side and stringed pearls
hang downward forming chin
strap. Bright pink satin shoes.
New York, The Metropolitan
Museum of Art, The Costume
Institute, Estate of Marcia

Sand Fund (1978.184.9a-L)
Alice Warder Garrett (1877-
1952), wife of the diplomat John
Work Garrett, lived in France
during the 1910s, before returning to the United States. In 1921
they moved into the family mansion in Baltimore, Evergreen
House, where Mrs. Garrett in-
stalled her own private theater.
Evergreen became an axis of social and cultural life – guests including Léon Bakst who designed some of her dresses and
part of the interior.[1]

[1] For a comprehensive discussion
of Bakst's activities at Evergreen
see Bespalova.

71.
*Fancy Dress Designed for Alice
Garrett*, 1922-23
Tunic, Midlength at CB,
77 cm; trousers 96 cm;
belt length, 82 cm
Black velvet tunic with full
gathered skirt lined in white
satin. Long draping sleeves
slit on top to reveal emerald
satin lining. Vest of emerald
green satin banded with gold
tissue and embroidered with
pearls, edge-to-edge closing
with large oval crystal surrounded by rhinestones.
Jodphur style trousers of blue-
grey silk with dull gold paisley
motifs, trimmed with self-fabric
bows and swags of pearl strands
and beaded tassels. Belt of
matching fabric embroidered
with gold, silver, tinsel, pearl
and rhinestones.
New York, The Metropolitan
Museum of Art, The Costume
Institute, Estate of Marcia Sand
Fund (1978.184. 4a-c)
(See Cat. 70)

72.
Designer unknown
(after Léon Bakst), *Table*, 1913
Wood and copper, height, 70
cm; width, 26 × 35 cm
Paris, Collection of Alexandre
Vassiliev
The table, made in Paris, carries
a design after a scene from
Schéhérazade.

*For books, photographs, and
archival materials pertaining to
the life and work of Bakst see
Documents below.

Documents

71. Léon Bakst,
Logo for the journal *Lukomore*
(The Shore), Petrograd 1917,
6 July, No. 21, back outside cover.
See D33

Books, catalogs, photographs relevant to Alexandre Benois and Léon Bakst (D1-D92).
Note: Unless indicated otherwise, all items are from the collection of the Institute of Modern Russian Culture, Los Angeles, United States

D1.
Académie nationale
de musique, Théatre de l'Opéra,
Cinq concerts historiques Russes
Moreau Frères, Paris 1907
28 × 23 × 1.5 cm
Program of Sergei Diaghilev's first historic season of Russian concerts and performances in Paris carrying reproductions of Léon Bakst's portraits of the composers Milii Balakirev and Sergei Liapunov.

D2.
Apollon (Apollo)
St. Petersburg 1909-1910
26 × 21 × 2 cm
Naples, Collection of the
Istituto Universitario Orientale
Léon Bakst designed the frontispiece for *Apollon* and No. 2-3 carried his article, "Puti klassitsizma v iskusstve" (The Paths of Classicism in Art).

D3.
Léon Bakst, *Dioné*
Unbound illustration
for *Journal des dames et des modes*
Paris 1913, 1 May, No. 34,
p. 73
15 × 9 cm
Los Angeles, County Museum

of Art, Doris Stein Research and Design Center for Costumes and Textiles

D4.
Léon Bakst,
Serov i ya v Gretsii.
Dorozhnye zapiski
(Serov and I in Greece.
Travel Notes)
Slovo, Berlin 1923
22 × 15.5 × 0.5 cm

D5.
Alexandre Benois, *Istoriia zhivopisi v XIX veke.*
Russkaia zhivopis
(The History of Painting in the XIX Century. Russian Painting)
Evdokimov, St. Petersburg 1901
26.5 × 19 × 2 cm
Cover designed by Léon Bakst.
Benois published this as a supplement to Muther's survey of 19th century painting (see D37).

D6.
Alexandre Benois,
Russkaia shkola zhivopisi
(The Russian School
of Painting)
Golike and Vilborg,
St. Petersburg 1904
42 × 35 × 4 cm
New York, Collection
of Alik Rabinovich

D7.
Alexandre Benois,
Azbuka v kartinakh
Alexandra Benua
(The Alphabet in Pictures
by Alexandre Benois)

Department for the Preparation of State Papers, St. Petersburg 1905
32.6 × 26 × 3 cm
New York, Collection
of Alik Rabinovich

D8.
Alexandre Benois (text)
Léon Bakst (cover),
Russkii muzei Aleksandra III
Knebel, Moscow 1906
53 × 41 × 5.3 cm
Los Angeles, Getty Research Institute, Special Collections
Cover design after Léon Bakst
Alexandre Benois

D9.
Alexandre Benois
Tsarskoe Selo v tsarstvovanie Imperatritsy Elizavety Petrovny
(Tsarskoe Selo in the Reign of Empress Elizaveta Petrovna)
Golike and Vilborg,
St. Petersburg 1910
33 × 27 × 5.5 cm

D10.
Alexandre Benois,
Putevoditel po kartinnoi galeree Imperatorskago Ermitazha
(Guide to the Painting Gallery of the Imperial Hermitage)
Society of St. Eugenia,
St. Petersburg 1911
15.5 × 12 × 3 cm

D11.
Alexandre Benois,
Istoriia zhivopisi vsekh vremen i narodov
(The History of Painting

of All Times and of All Peoples)
Shipovnik, St. Petersburg 1912,
Vol. 1
29 × 24 × 6 cm

D12.
Alexandre Benois,
*Istoriia zhivopisi vsekh
vremen i narodov*
(The History of Painting
of All Times and of All Peoples),
Shipovnik, St. Petersburg 1912,
Vol. 1
6 × 5 × 0.25 cm
Promotional brochure.

D13.
Alexandre Benois,
The Russian School of Painting,
Knopf, New York 1916
(trans. Abraham Yarmolinsky)
28 × 22 × 2.5 cm

D14.
Alexandre Benois,
Versal (Versailles),
Akvilon, Petrograd 1922
33.5 × 24.5 × 1 cm

D15.
Alexandre Benois,
Vozniknovenie Mira iskusstva
(The Emergence of the World
of Art), Committee for the
Popularization of Artistic
Editions at the State Academy
of Material Culture,
Leningrad 1928
20 × 15 × 3 cm
Cover by Viktor Dmitrievich
Zamirailo (1868-1939).

D16.
Alexandre Benois,
*Reminiscences of the Russian
Ballet*, Putnam, London 1941
(trans. Mary Britnieva)
22.5 × 15 × 4 cm

D17.
P. Choumoff (P.I. Shumov),
Photograph of Léon Bakst
in his Paris studio at 112,
Bd. Malesherbes, ca. 1920
22.5 × 16.4 cm;
framed 32 × 23. 9 cm
London, Collection
of Alexander Schouvaloff
Bakst is holding a Chinese porcelain figure.

D18.
P. Choumoff (P.I. Shumov),
Photograph of Léon Bakst,
ca. 1920

16.4 × 22.1 cm; framed
22.9 × 31.5 cm
London, Collection
of Alexander Schouvaloff

D19.
*Comoedia Illustré: Journal
Parisien Théâtral,
Artistique et Littéraire,*
Paris 1909, 1 June, No. 11,
pp. 308-309
31 × 24 × 2.5 cm

D20.
*Comoedia Illustré: Journal
Parisien Théâtral, Artistique
et Littéraire,* Paris, 1910, 15
June, Special Supplement
to No. 18, Les Ballets Russes,
pp. 516-517
31 × 24 × 2.5 cm
Cover designed by Bakst.

D21.
*Comoedia Illustré: Journal
Parisien Théâtral, Artistique
et Littéraire,* Paris 1913, 5 June,
Special Supplement to No. 17,
Huitième Saison des Ballets
Russes
31 × 24 × 2.5 cm

D22.
*Comoedia Illustré: Journal
Parisien Théâtral, Artistique
et Littéraire,* Paris 1913,
20 June, No. 18, pp. 868-69
31 × 24 × 1 cm

D23.
Sergei Diaghilev (ed.),
*Ezhegodnik Imperatorskikh
teatrov. No. 9-10.
Sezon na 1899-1900*
(Yearbook of the Imperial
Theater, No. 9-10. 1899-1900
Season), St. Petersburg 1901
28 × 23.5 × 4 cm
New York, Collection
of Alik Rabinovich
Cover by Léon Bakst, decora-
tions by Konstantin Somov, note
by Alexandre Benois on the
Alexandrinsky Theater.

D24.
Sergei Diaghilev,
*Russkaia zhivopis v XVIII veke.
D.G. Levitsky, 1735-1822*
(Russian Painting in the18th
Century. D.G. Levitsky,
1735-1822), Evdokimov,
St. Petersburg 1902, Vol. 1
33 × 29 × 4 cm
Frontispiece by Léon Bakst.

D25.
Sergei Diaghilev (comp.),
*Katalog Vystavki russkikh
portretov*
(Catalog of the Exhibition
of Russian Portraits)
St. Petersburg Department
for the Preparation of State
Papers, 1905, Vol. 1
24 × 17 × 4.5 cm
The handwritten emendations
are by Alexandre Benois.

D26.
Sergei Ernst,
Aleksandr Benua,
Committee for the
Popularization of Artistic
Editions at the Russian
Academy of Material Culture,
St. Petersburg 1921
21 × 16 × 1.25 cm
This was the first published
monograph on Alexandre
Benois.

D27.
Liudvig Gelmerson (ed.),
*Ezhegodnik Imperatorskikh
teatrov. Sezon 1901-1902*
(Yearbook of the Imperial
Theaters, 1901-02 Season),
Imperial Theaters,
St. Petersburg 1902
28 × 23.5 × 4 cm
Cover designed by Léon Bakst.

D28.
(Ekaterina Geltser)
Photograph of the ballerina
Ekaterina Vasilievna Geltser
(1876-1962) wearing
a beaded dress, ca. 1913
(photographer unknown)
Paris, Collection
of Alexandre Vassiliev.

D29.
Arnold L. Haskell (ed.),
*Memorial Exhibition
of Russian Ballet. Illustrated
Catalogue*
Hunt, Barnard, London 1930
22 × 15 × 1.5 cm
Cover by Alexandre Benois.

D30 a, b.
Nikolai Kutepov,
*Velikokniazheskaia i tsarskaia
okhota na Rusi, s X po XVI vek;
Tsarskaia okhota na Rusi tsarei
Mikhaila Feodorovicha
i Alekseieia Mikhailovicha;
Tsarskaia i imperatorskaia okhota
na Rusi, konets XVII i XVIII vek;*

*Imperatorskaia okhota na Rusi,
konets XVIII i XIX vek:
istoricheskii ocherk Nikolaia
Kutepova*
(Hunting in Russia by the Great
Princes and the Tsars from
the 10th through the 16th
Centuries; The Tsar's Hunting
in Russia at the Time of Tsars
Mikhail Fedorovich and Alexei
Mikhailovich; The Tsar's
and Imperial Hunting in Russia,
Late 17th and 18th Centuries;
Imperial Hunting in Russia,
Late 18th and 19th Centuries;
A Historical Account
by Nikolai Kutepov)
Department for the Preparation
of State Papers, St. Petersburg
1896-1911 (four volumes)
(a) Volume 3 (1902)
36.8 × 27 × 6 cm
(b) Volume 4 (1911)
36.8 × 27 × 5.6 cm
Illustrations and decorations
by Léon Bakst, Alexandre
Benois, Evgenii Lancéray,
Klavdii Lebedev, Leonid
Pasternak, Ilia Repin,
Andrei Riabushkin, Frants
Rubo, Nikolai Samokish,
Valentin Serov, Alexei
Stepanov, Vasilii Surikov,
and Viktor Vasnetsov
Los Angeles, University
of Southern California,
Special Collections,
Doheny Library
Volume a contains illustrations
by Alexandre Benois and Léon
Bakst.
Volume b contains illustrations
by Alexandre Benois.

D31.
André Levinson,
*The Designs of Leon Bakst
for The Sleeping Princess.*
Benn Brothers Limited,
London 1923
39.5 × 30.5 × 3.5 cm
Los Angeles, Special
Collections, Doheny Library,
University of Southern
California.

D32.
Prince Peter Lievenn,
The Birth of the Ballets-Russes,
Allen & Unwin, London 1956
(trans. Leonide Zarine)
22.5 × 15 × 3.5 cm
Left frontispiece by Alexandre
Benois, right frontispiece by
Léon Bakst.

D33.
Lukomore (The Shore)
St. Petersburg 1917,
6 July, No. 21.
33 × 25 × 0.3 cm
Header and back cover illustration by Léon Bakst.

D34.
Mir iskusstva (World of Art)
St. Petersburg 1904,
Nos. 1-2, p. 2
32 × 26 × 1.5 cm
This issue carries Alexandre Benois' essay on Arkhangelskoe with frontispiece by Léon Bakst.

D35.
Mir iskusstva. (World of Art)
St. Petersburg, 1904,
No. 5, p. 161
32 × 26 × 1.5 cm

D36.
Mir iskusstva (World of Art)
Promotional Brochure
Commercial Press
St. Petersburg 1903
24.5 × 16 × 0.25 cm
Front and back covers carry logos by Léon Bakst.

D37.
Richard Muther,
Istoriia zhivopisi v XIX veke
(History of Painting
in the XIX Century)
Rudometov, St. Petersburg 1899
(trans. from German into
Russian Zinaida Vengerova)
27.5 × 19.5 × 3 cm
Cover designed by Léon Bakst.
Benois published his book on
19th century Russian painting as
a supplement to Muther's survey
(see D5).

D38.
Alexander Pushkin,
Mednyi vsadnik (Bronze
Horseman)
Orchis, Munich 1923
24.8 × 16.5 cm
Illustrations by Alexandre
Benois.

D39.
Alexander Pushkin,
Pikovaia dama
(Queen of Spades),
Golik and Vilborg,
St. Petersburg 1911, p. 67
30.5 24 × 2.5 cm
Illustrations by Alexandre
Benois.

D40.
Alexei Remizov, *Tsar Dodon*,
Great and Free Chamber
of Monkeys, Petrograd 1921
21 × 13.5 × 0.5 cm
Oxford (Ohio), Collection
of C. and A.L. de Saint-Rat,
Cover and illustrations by Bakst.

D41.
*Salon d'Automne. Exposition
de l'Art Russe*, Moderne
Imprimerie, Paris 1906
17.5 × 13.5 × 1.5 cm
Catalog of the exhibition with
cover design by Ivan Bilibin and
texts by Sergei Diaghilev and
Alexandre Benois

D42.
Alexander Shashkovsky (ed.),
*Ves Peterburg na 1913 god.
Adresnaia i spravochnaia kniga
g. S.-Peterburga*
(All St. Petersburg in 1913.
St. Petersburg Address Book
and Directory)
Suvorin, St. Petersburg 1913,
pp. 34-35
30.5 × 23.5 × 7.5 cm
Page 35 of Section III
("Alphabetical Index of the
Inhabitants of St. Petersburg")
shows Bakst's address, i.e. 5a,
Nadezhdinskaia St.; page 49
shows Benois' address and telephone number, i.e. 31,
Admiralty Canal, tel. 48572.

D43.
*Souvenir Program for the Russian
Opera and Ballet at the Royal
Theatre, Drury Lane*
(London season), 1914,
Brunoff, Paris 1914
31.5 × 25 × 0.5 cm
Oxford, (Ohio) Collection
of C. and A.L. de Saint-Rat
With set and costume designs by
Léon Bakst.

D44.
*Souvenir Program for Serge
de Diaghileff's Ballet Russe*
(New York season),
Morris Gest, New York 1916
31.5 × 23.5 × 0.5 cm
Oxford, (Ohio) Collection
of C. and A.L. de Saint-Rat
With set and costume designs by
Léon Bakst.

D45.
*Souvenir Program
for "The Sleeping Princess",*

Alhambra Theatre, London
Brunoff, Paris 1921
31.5 × 25 × 0.5 cm
Oxford (Ohio), Collection
of C. and A.L. de Saint-Rat.
With set and costume designs by
Léon Bakst.

D46.
Starye gody
(Bygone Years)
St. Petersburg 1907,
July-September, Vol. 2,
27 × 20 × 4 cm
Coedited by Alexandre Benois.
This issue contains Benois' essay
on the history of the Elizabeth
Palace in Tsarskoe Selo.

D47.
*Stolitsa i usadba: Zhurnal
krasivoi zhizni*
(Town and Country:
A Journal of Beautiful Living)
St. Petersburg 1914, 20 April,
No. 8, pp 18-19
36 × 26 × 0.4 cm
Page 18 carries Léon Bakst's article, "On the Art of Today",
while page 19 carries a reproduction of his design for the Oriental
Costume that Princess Natalia
Gorchakova wore at Countess
Mariia Kleinmikhel's Costume
Ball in St. Petersburg.

D48.
*Stolitsa i usadba: Zhurnal
krasivoi zhizni*
(Town and Country:
A Journal of Beautiful Living)
St. Petersburg 1916, 1 July,
No. 60-61
36 × 26 × 0.4 cm
The cover carries a reproduction
of one of Alexandre Benois' designs for *Petrushka* (first reproduced in Valeriian Svetlov's book
on the ballet (see D50).

D49.
*Stolitsa i usadba: Zhurnal
krasivoi zhizni*
(Town and Country:
A Journal of Beautiful Living),
Petrograd, 1917, 30 April,
No. 80
36 × 26 × 0.4 cm
The cover incorporates a reproduction of Léon Bakst's painting,
Supper (formerly in the collection of Alexander Korovin and
now in the collection of the State
Russian Museum, St. Petersburg).

D50.
Valeriian Svetlov,
Sovremennyi balet
(Contemporary Ballet)
Golike and Vilborg,
St. Petersburg 1911
31 × 22 × 4 cm
Silk cover and frontispiece by
Léon Bakst; many illustrations of
works by Bakst and Benois.

D51.
Vasilii Vereshchagin,
*Russkii knizhnyi znak/
L'ex-libris russe*
(Russian Bookplates)
Golike, St. Petersburg 1902
30 × 21 × 3 cm
Frontispiece designed by Léon
Bakst. Binding by Alexander
Shnel after a design by Léon
Bakst. This copy belonged to the
private library of Nicholas II.

D52.
*Vesenniaia vystavka kartin
v zalakh Imperatorskoi
Akademii khudozhestv*
(Catalog of the Spring
Exhibition of Paintings
in the Halls of the Imperial
Academy of Arts)
Imperial Academy of Arts,
St. Petersburg 1897
22.5 × 15.5 × 1 cm
Both Benois and Bakst were represented at this exhibition.

D53.
A. Zamiatina, *Muzei
izobrazitelnykh iskusstv
im. A.S. Pushkina. Izbrannye
proizvedeniia Kartinnoi gallerei*
(Pushkin Museum of Fine Arts:
Selected Works from the
Painting Gallery)
Pushkin Museum of Fine Arts,
Moscow 1948
31 × 23.5 × 7.5 cm
The pencil emendations are in
Alexandre Benois' hand: "A pathetic attempt to justify the incompetence of this book..."

D54.
Zhar-ptitsa (Firebird)
Berlin 1922, No. 9
32 × 25 × 6 cm
Zhar-ptitsa carried many reproductions of works by Alexandre
Benois and Léon Bakst. The
journal is open at Andrei
Levinson's article on Bakst, i.e.
"Vozvrashchenie Baksta" (The
Return of Bakst).

D55.
Zolotoe runo
(Golden Fleece)
Moscow, 1906, No. 2, p. 31
35.5 × 32 × 1.5 cm
This issue contains Alexandre Benois' article "Artistic Heresies" and several reproductions of Léon Bakst's work, including his portrait of Konstantin Somov.

D56-D81 are photographic portraits by E.O. Hoppé (1878-1972) from the Collection of Curatorial Assistance, Pasadena, California.
Dates refer to photographic sessions, not to ballet productions.

D56.
Léon Bakst, 1916
5 × 7 cm
02204-B
Bakst's costume design for the *Blue God* (*Le Dieu Bleu*) can be seen in the background.

D57.
Adolph Bolm
in *Prince Igor,* 1912
5 × 7 cm
01520-D

D58.
Tamara Karsavina
and Adolph Bolm in *Thamar,*
1911
5 × 7 cm
01515-D

D59.
Adolph Bolm (the Prince)
and Tamara Karsavina (Thamar)
in *Thamar,* 1912
Handcolored gravure print
(handcolored in 1914)
9 × 11 cm
01515-D-II

D60.
Michel Fokine and Vera Fokina,
ca. 1914
5 × 7 cm
02475-A

D61.
Michel Fokine and Vera Fokina
in *Schéhérazade,* ca. 1914
5 × 7 cm
02475-F

D62.
Vera Fokina, ca. 1914
5 × 7cm
02475-P

D63.
Vera Fokina, ca. 1914
4 × 6 cm
02475-Q-I

D64.
Tamara Karsavina, 1911
5 × 7 cm
01515-H

D65.
Tamara Karsavina, 1912
5 × 7 cm
01515-I

D66.
Tamara Karsavina
in *Schéhérezade,* 1911
5 × 7 cm
01515-C

D67.
Tamara Karsavina
in *Schéhérezade,* 1912
4 × 6 cm
01515-0027

D68.
Tamara Karsavina
in *Le Spectre de la Rose,*
1912
5 × 7 cm
01515-0014

D69.
Tamara Karsavina
in *Pulcinella,* 1912
6 × 6 cm
01515-0029

D70.
Tamara Karsavina
as Pimpinella in *Pulcinella,* 1912
8 × 10 cm
01515-0033

D71.
Tamara Karsavina
as Pimpinella in *Pulcinella,*
1912
6 × 7 cm
01515-E

D72.
Tamara Karsavina
in *Firebird,* 1912
5 × 7 cm
01515-Q

D73.
Tamara Karsavina
in *Carnaval,*
1912
8 × 10 cm
01515-T

D74.
Tamara Karsavina
as the Nymph in *Midas,* 1912
8 × 10 cm
01515-L

D75.
Tamara Karsavina
and Adolph Bolm in *Firebird,*
1912
8 × 10 cm
01515-J

D76.
Tamara Karsavina and Adolph
Bolm in *Le Pavillon d'Armide,*
1912
8 × 10 cm
01515-P-II

D77.
Vaslav Nijinsky in *Le Spectre
de la Rose,* ca. 1911
Handcolored print
(handcolored in 1914)
9 × 11 cm
02382-C-I

D78.
Anna Pavlova in Japanese
costume, 1912
8 × 10 cm
01501-0011

D79.
Olga Spessiva (Spesivtseva),
1921
5 × 7 cm
15481-B

D80.
Olga Spessiva (Spesivtseva)
in *Sleeping Beauty,* 1921
5 × 8 cm
15481-C

D81.
Olga Spessiva (Spesivtseva)
15481-D-I

D82-D92 are original postcards of Russian ballet dancers from the collection of Alexandre Vassiliev, Paris.

D82.
Michel Fokine, ca. 1907

D83.
Michel Fokine in *Le Pavillon
d'Armide,* 1907

D84.
Michel Fokine in *Carnaval,*
1910

D85.
Michel and Vera Fokine
in *Daphnis et Chloé,* 1912

D86.
Tamara Karsavina in *Carnaval,*
1910

D87.
Tamara Karsavina, 1911

D88.
Tamara Karsavina, 1916

D89.
Matilda Kchessinskaya, 1913

D90.
Vaslav Nijinsky, ca. 1907

D91.
Vaslav Nijinsky in *Le Pavillon
d'Armide,* 1907

D92.
Anna Pavlova in *Le Pavillon
d'Armide,* 1907

Selected Writings by Alexandre Benois
and Léon Bakst

*Introduced and translated
by John E. Bowlt
and Elizabeth Durst*

This selection of writings by Alexandre Benois (Fig. 72) and Léon Bakst pays homage to the literary talents of the two artists. None of the texts has appeared in English nor Italian translation before.

Benois, in particular, was not only a painter and designer of universal acclaim, but also a prolific writer of scholarly books, essays and catalog entries, of informed attributions, of letters, diaries and memoirs, and the extracts below constitute only a fraction of his vast critical and epistolatory heritage – his actual publications, for example, number over eight hundred (Fig. 73). Obviously, the passages here can scarcely provide an adequate impression of the broad diapason of disciplines, ideas and individuals that Benois examined and assessed, for, although he had much to say about his favorite themes of Versailles and St. Petersburg, his interests encompassed the Italian Renaissance, the Dutch and Flemish masters, the *fin de siècle,* folk culture, the printing arts, industrial design, scenography, the European academies, and many other subjects.

Curiously enough, there still does not exist an adequate anthology of Benois' writings even in Russian, although in the 1960s the late Ilia Zilbershtein did much to focus attention on Benois the writer through his editorship of the post-Revolutionary writings;[1] later on Natalia Aleksandrova assumed much of the responsibility for editing and annotating the Russian memoirs,[2] and Igor Khabarov has just republished Benois' Parisian critiques of 1930-1936.[3] Of course, many of Benois' key statements can be found in the numerous articles and reviews that he published in the leading Russian newspapers such as *Birzhevye vedo-mosti* and *Rech,* but even so, many other unpublished writings are scattered among archives in Moscow, St. Petersburg, France, Italy, and the United States, and they still await collation, annotation, and publication. In this respect, the extracts from Benois' 1916-18 "Diary", published here for the first time, are of particular interest: written in ink in a tight, almost cryptographic style, the five hundred and fifteen pages record impressions of family and friends, cultural institutions, the city of Petrograd, the February and October revolutions, the Great War, and general philosophies of life. What is especially surprising is the sobriety, clarity, and often sardonic humor that accompany these descriptions – surprising when we remember the disorientation and confusion at that crucial moment in the destiny of Russia.

With Bakst the problem of selection is less acute, since he was not a professional critic and historian in the way that Benois was and he published only occasionally. In any case, his concerns were more specific and topical and his several articles and interviews in St. Petersburg and Paris newspapers and journals were somewhat repetitive; Bakst also tended to use language in order to describe and pronounce rather than to analyze. A case in point is the account of his 1907 trip with Valentin Serov to Greece (D4), excerpted here, which contains an abundance of private and often witty comments on local types and customs, but surprisingly little on esthetic and historical aspects. Bakst's correspondence, too, even with his wife, Liubov Pavlovna, is impressionistic and temperamental, although the intensity of his schedule – his "workoholism" – betrays a nervousness that must have contributed to the mercurial mood changes and increasing bouts of depression that he experienced towards the end of his life. Still, one of Bakst's constant endeavors was to accommodate the "low" manifestations of a dominant esthetic, such as fashion and interior design, within discussions of "high" art. For example, he made every effort to defend fashion, arguing that the style of a given fashion was an important indicator of prevailing artistic attitudes. Bakst sought to expand the repertoire of the contemporary artist and his own experiments in fashion design can be regarded as part of this noble aspiration.

In "The Paths of Classicism in Art" Bakst asserts that the art of the immediate future will draw its strength from more simplified forms, while still relying upon the refined art of the Classical tradition. He identifies this tendency in the Hellenic elegance of Isadora Duncan, whose interpretive dance and transparent tunic inspired Bakst and fashion designers alike. The cult of the body and its nakedness, as described by Bakst in the anthology *Nagota na stsene* (Nudity on the Stage), was part of a significant cultural shift that was occurring in the theater and also in contemporary fashion. The popular Parisian *couturier*, Paul Poiret,[4] who in ca. 1908 was adhering to the slim, Neo-Classical line of the *style empire,* now began to liberalize the female figure, emphasizing gauze-like tunics, not without the influence of the Ballets Russes. But although Bakst referred to Poiret on several occasions, the extent of the their esthetic interaction is still difficult to define (cf. Figs. 74, 75).

Bakst joined the league of professional fashion designers in the early 1910s (Cat. 64-71; Figs. 76-79). Graceful lines, sumptuous fabrics, and innovative decorative elements characterize many of his designs for Jeanne Paquin's fashion house of late 1912.[5] By this time Parisian fashion had been swept up in the tide of the exotic, with turbans, minarets, tunics and wrapped skirts dominating the "look" – and in his statements on fashion Bakst interprets these trends as being indebted to his work for the Ballets Russes: Parisiennes, he argues, are uninhibited in their imitation of the theater and even go so far as to darken their skin to achieve the look of the exotic and the Eastern. The influence of *Schéhérazade* and other of Bakst's resolutions was felt in the United States and throughout Europe, including Russia, and St. Petersburg witnessed lavish parties designed by the celebrated artist who,

until the outbreak of the First World War, made regular visits to his homeland. Early 1914 saw at least two balls which were inspired, if not actually created, by Bakst. His dress that Princess Natalia Gorchakova wore at Countess Mariia Kleinmikhel's ball (Fig. 69) anticipates many subsequent designs, while a photograph of the party published in *Stolitsa i usadba* (Town and Country), a Russian counterpart to *Country Life,* (Fig. 68) shows a host of men and women outfitted very much *à la Bakst*. Princess Elizaveta Shuvalova's and Anastasia Leonard's concurrent balls featured the much discussed colored wigs, (Fig. 70) to which Bakst also contributed – explaining that the true source for this vogue was none other than the blue wig that Ida Rubinstein wore in *Cléopâtre* in 1909.

Like the fashion editors of the 1910s, Bakst contended that exotic fantasy and femininity characterized evening wear, while movement, sports, and athletics shaped the dress of the new everyday. In their daytime fashions, therefore, the contemporary woman and man had much in common and, indeed, the popular tailleur style with its snappy simplicity and sobriety of color and tone can be regarded as a response to the feminine desire for greater mobility. But the cult of movement also pervaded evening wear, for the dance mania, especially the tango, necessitated high slits in women's skirts. In any case, for Bakst the feminine ideal was a union of two elements that both emancipated the figure and heightened sexuality through the lavish elements of her evening incarnation. "Fashion is a queen", Bakst writes, and, certainly, he was her faithful servant.

Alexandre Benois

"The Russian School of Painting" (1904)[6]
(...) Individualism, which has helped us escape from the fetters of *peredvizhnik* tendentiousness[7] and from the academic routine – is right now at the point of its most extreme development and most extreme conclusion. So many artists, so many directions, so many schools, and not just in Russia, but everywhere in European art, too (...)
However, such a state of affairs cannot last for ever. As a protest, individualism is a beautiful thing, but as a seasoned, vital, and esthetic system it is useless, even terrifying. Specifically in art, individualism leads to a total barbarity of form, to a debility of work, to an impoverishment and absurdity of conception. For all our adoration of the individual human soul, we

72. Yurii Annenkov (1889-1974), *Portrait of Alexandre Benois,* 1921. Reproduced from Yurii Annenkov, *Portrety,* Petropolis, Petrograd 1922, p. 21

73. Alexandre Benois, *Mednyi vsadnik* (Bronze Horseman), Orchis, Munich 1922. Illustrations, including frontispiece, by Alexandre Benois. See D38.

regard it as almost insignificant when compared to the "psychic organism" of several souls together. Only unity with a single and whole organism, only the aggregate of individualities possesses genuine strength and helps to create – via these same private individualities – essential works of true beauty and power. A haughty alienation leads to impotence, emptiness, and non-existence (...)

"Artistic Heresies" (1906)[8]

(...) If you take a look at the contemporary state of art everywhere, well, you see, on the one hand, the proclamation and cult of the lovely principle of extreme freedom of personality and, on the other, all the dismal consequences that derive from the application of this principle, and fatally so. Artists have crawled into their own corners, they seek consolation in their own self-delight, fight shy of mutual influences and try to be "themselves", whatever the cost. Chaos reigns, something turbid, having hardly any value and, strangest of all, any physiognomy (...)

In its logical conclusion, then, individualism is heresy, because it distracts creativity both from freedom and from light. By "light" I mean everything that invests creativity with meaning and enchantment: the search for, and divination of, beauty, insight into the secret meaning of things, the revelation of what is generally known as poetry. Without these principles artistic creativity is reduced to a mechanical adjustment, to a scientific investigation and, finally, to a chaotic dilettantism (...) In the old days the artist lived in concert with the whole of society and was the brightest representative of the ideals of his time. But, inevitably, the artist of today remains a dilettante, afraid to maintain his aloofness from others, while presenting pathetic crumbs of what he considers to be "his own" – but which, his own consciousness notwithstanding, is still the reflection of surrounding influences, but one weakened and bedimmed...

"Artists and Their Participation in the Theater" (1909)[9]

(...) It would seem quite obvious that artists should be close to the theater and that the theater cannot do without them – something so vital that a fusion of the arts should occur here and now; evidently, we ought to be discerning something grand and beautiful in that artists have come over to the theater and have now begun to involve themselves in the theater. Surely, all these things are beyond question.

However, something quite the reverse has happened. A kind of feud has broken out between actors and visual artists, a need for speeches by "prosecutors and defense lawyers" has been deemed essential and the result is a kind of sedition and with no end in sight. The theater has now reached a stage in its evolution which looks very much like a crisis, and mutual reproaches are flying about. Actors are wailing that they have been quite overshadowed by artists and have been turned into marionettes, while artists are angry at not finding a sufficient elasticity in actors so as to implement their fancies.

It would seem that in these arguments one aspect of the theater should remain to the side – the ballet. After all, it is in the ballet that the fusion of the arts is in the very nature of things: ballet is nothing but plasticity that has come alive to the music. However, misunderstanding is spreading throughout ballet, too, and you can hear more and more moans and groans about the degeneration of the ballet thanks, precisely, to the too rapid a development of the decorative art.

We should note that this dispute is a purely Russian phenomenon and a very recent one, too. In the West, where everything is just as it used to be, i.e. where Wagner is produced with astounding vulgarity, where, in general, "real" artists are barred from the stage at arm's length – there, apparently, people could not even imagine that one could also enjoy beautiful colors and beautiful painting as well as listen to wise words and beautiful singing or see pretty women and fashionable costumes.

If nothing else, this significant and meritorious step forward or, at least, these new and interesting researches belong to the Russian theater. Russia has not only read Wagner's *Gesamtkunstwerk,* but has also desired to attain this ideal – and in all her sincerity (and *naïveté*). Finding no satisfaction in the vulgar routine of professional painters, Russia has turned to "genuine" artists and has resolved upon these bold innovations – of which not a single prominent stage in Europe had ventured to dream.

It all began with Savva Mamontov's opera company[10] (...) A subsequent, more consistent and more lavish application of the new principle occurred on the official stage under Prince Volkonsky and especially V.A. Teliakovsky[11] (...) [But] neither for Mamontov, nor for Teliakovsky was the theater their life. Both approached the theater as dilettantes, interested in conducting certain experiments with the stage. The main thing is that neither the former, nor the latter possessed that "comprehensive sensibility" which the theatrical reformer needs. They introduced new décors, new colors, new, simpliflied and very artistic devices to the *mise-en-scène,* but, even so, they were indifferent to the content of the works for which they did all this.

Mamontov's productions were curiosities, they were engaging and occasionally beautiful, but in all the operas that he put on I cannot remember a single aspect that was born out in the mood demanded by the action or that was convincing as spectacle. Teliakovsky enabled Golovin's magical and colorful talent to unfold in all its brightness, but even here I would be hard put to name a single dramatic, choreographic or musical work that assumed an integral, unifying and clarifying illustration – except for a few successful, but isolated, fragments in *Ruslan, Pskovitianka,* and *Carmen.* When Bakst undertook experiments in this kind of rational illustration, the [theater] directors simply did not understand them, having no inkling of their meaning (...)

On the one hand, the infinite number of such experiments, and, on the the other, the constant egging on of actors to become "leading producers" has led to total confusion, in spite of the superb principle, and at the moment is even eliciting a kind of animosity. Producers yell out to actors: "You must obey artists in the name of beauty and do so unquestioningly". But, instinctively, actors are sensing that they would be selling themselves and their authors if they were to submit to these demands. Artists, however, dream only of seeing their fantasies implemented on a vast scale, are absorbed by their own specific tasks and have no desire to reckon with actors or authors. The result is not a *Gesamtkunstwerk,* but a kind of bedlam that is terrifying audiences, that is demoralizing performers and gradually is trampling under foot any school or specific technique. Indeed, you couldn't perform any worse than young Russian actors are doing.

Naturally, the fact that artists are being attracted to the stage is to be welcomed. But the question as to which artists should be invited is not easy to decide. Just seeing a successful and colorful study, a dexterous sketch or a piquant illustration at some exhibition is not enough to decide that such and such an artist would be of benefit to the theater.

As with the theater, the actor and the producer, the designer must have a particular talent, a particular vocation and a particular sensibility (...)

It's not a case of who has to "submit" to whom, the artist to the actor or the actor to the artist: both must be subordinate to the gods of the stage. The most important thing in the theater is the playwright's idea which should reveal itself in striking and concrete form. This is the main thing and anyone who finds this tiresome or who intends to paint autonomous pictures on stage should not be in the theater, whether he be Rembrandt, Velasquez or Millet.

Just a couple more words on the "style" of our productions. Goodness, how that words buzzes in my ear, how it has been ravaged and vulgarized. Some people understand style to mean a true rendering of this or that era (and that's a naive concept), others understand style to be a certain integrated unity of forms wherein the dramatic work should manifest itself. Some see salvation in some kind of "style in general", while others come up with this or that "stylish stunt", trying to subordinate every tiny detail of the production (...)

All the talk about "style" and all these attempts to "nurture a style" make for a very sad phenomenon, one that exposes a crucial and radical misunderstanding whence there is no way out. Whatever the business on hand, it's not those who are talking, dreaming or arguing that have real significance, but those who "can get it done", who are born to do their own thing. In the theater the only person who creates something original and valuable (beyond the tedious questions of what's old and new – in fact, nothing is ever repeated and *everything is always new*) is he who has the capacity of "foreseeing" – with total clarity – the embodiment of his reveries and who possesses the gift of confronting this embodiment head on.

Such people "say" little, but they *know* what they are doing and they get it done.

A shining example of a born theater person is Stanislavsky.[12] You can criticize him however much you want (specifically, the decorative aspect of the Moscow Art Theater leaves a lot to be desired), but you have to face the fact that it is precisely this man of deed rather than of word who has succeeded in creating a grandiose and lasting whole, a real monument with real style – and right now, in our time of total dislocation (...)

"The Tasks of the Graphic Arts" (1910)[13]
(...) Thanks mainly to Diaghilev's World of Art enterprise, we are now witnessing a flowering of the "graphic arts" and can name many leading artists who are dedicating their energies

to the printing arts: K. Somov, E. Lancéray, I. Bilibin, S. Yaremich, V. Zamirailo, M. Dobujinsky[14] ... and many others. We contemporaries now take delight in the Russian book of the first decade of the 20th century and, undoubtedly, it will continue to bring joy to bibliophiles of the future – something that cannot be said of books published twenty or thirty years ago.

The graphic arts (...) constitute a sphere of art that allows for, and even demands, maximum restraint, maximum subordination, maximum appreciation. The liberties allowed in the paintings and drawings that we produce at our own risk and "independently", the liberties that are even desirable in a self-sufficient kind of creativity are disallowed in book illustration and book design in general. This is because the artist is now dependent upon another kind of art; and even if he may be obliged to submit to this wholeheartedly, he must never forget how essential it is to combine his own task with the task to which he has been summoned (...) One does not have to submit, but then one must harmonize ones independence with the spirit of the assignment. Just like muralists, decorators or studio painters assisting architects: it's precisely because extreme individualism has destroyed the harmony between painting and architecture that mural painting has perished

The artist who is resolved to make his own statement on the stage is a poor collaborator of the person who has built that stage, a poor collaborator of the person who has built that wall (what I have in mind is the beautiful cohesion of the entire building).

(...) It is original and independent artists such as Rops and Beardsley who came to the book with the unwieldiness and cumbersomeness of their powerful personalities that have produced the most worthless specimens of graphic art.

(...) In the tiny building that any book represents we should not forget the "walls", the primary goal or the distinctive laws of this particular idiom.

The graphic arts can be regarded in two ways: either as an illustration or as a decoration. But, certainly, both should *serve* the cause of the book and not play independent roles (...) It is important that the graphic illustrator examine whether deep down he has something vital and valuable to say about the work being illustrated, whether he understands it; and, if it transpires that he does not and cannot "see" it explicated in clear and definite images, then he should refuse the project.

(...) Even when the artist has been called upon just to decorate a book, he should always remember its integrity, that his role is a subordinate one and that the book can become beautiful only if he succeeds in creating something of beauty within this subordination and this harmony.

(...) Some almost cross the confines of good taste in striving to express the basic idea of this or that book via ornament. Others compose beautiful vignettes, tail-pieces and illuminations which would be just as appropriate to a "history of such and such a ministry" or to a collection of erotic poetry.

(...) We must not forget the architecture of the book.

(...) First and foremost, the artist working on a book should pay attention(...) to the basic exigencies of the beauty in that book: the elaboration of the format, the quality, surface and color of the paper, how the text appears on the page, the distribution and interrelationship of full and empty spaces, the typeface, pagination, how the pages have been cut and collated, etc. (...)

"What the Academy of Arts Could Be Today" (1912) [15]

My departure-point is of a purely negative character. At the moment the Academy serves neither art in general, nor the art of the state in particular. Standing at this lectern, I do not wish to renew the assaults on the Academy which we all know by heart and of which we are all so weary (...)

So the question is: wherein lies the cardinal sin? Does it lie in the several inadequacies of the statutes, in an absence of talent, in the general state of affairs or perhaps in the venerable age of the current personnel in charge of the Academy itself? None of these, I think (...) I feel (and I am profoundly convinced of this) that for many years the Academy has been trying to live an *alien* life. The burdensome impression that its activity produces derives from a feeling of deep disharmony between its inner nature and what *it is trying to appear* to be. By nature the Academy is a state or *official* institution which possesses its own psychology; and this is a psychology germane in equal measure to the entire world of bureaucrats, i.e. of people who are subservient, who are outwardly interdependent and who are dutibound to *serve* not the train of their free thought and their free impulse, but what is called *prescription and structure* (...)

Ladies and gentlemen, I repeat that the real sin lies not in deficiencies in the statutes and so on, but in the fact that the Academy *is not living the life* that it should be – and not just here, but in the West, too. Once upon a time the Academy was a kind of Parnassus. The best artists were invited to join and their duty was to observe so called good taste in all its purity within the *state.* Institutions were formed within the Academies so as to nurture this good taste in young people and to provide the *state* with the same kind of servants – the priests of good taste. Such was our Academy, too. But then culture in general underwent a crisis upsetting even the "aristocratic" idea of good taste and the very notion that it should be observed (...)

It is time, ladies and gentlemen, to realize that this tragic comedy must draw to a close. There is nothing worse than someone living at loggerheads with himself. But it is precisely this kind of divided existence that the Academy represents and it cannot go on like that. So there are two choices: either it should cease to exist or it should find its own foundations. A state institution should serve the state and *only the state. Ladies and gentlemen, let us forget the idea of a free Academy* (...) Free creativity has no need of this and will always find its own revelatory path.

People will tell me (and are already telling me) that in promoting an Academy whose purpose would be to act as a vast state studio providing the entire nation with state art I am undermining the very essence of contemporary art – individualism or, if you like, personal initiative. No way. I would advise you *not to worry* about individualism (...)

I must confess that I have simply grown weary of individualism, of this disunited creativity and artistic chaos. Recently, the anonymous, academic art of the *fin de siècle* seemed tedious, indeed, but I would say that there is nothing more tedious than the creativity of today with its unlimited variegation and countless private, but trivial revelations. Anyway, let this continue to exist, let people seek and find, let them inspire each other to make ever new discoveries. *However, this is not the Academy's business* (...)

It's all a case of [the right] *people. And don't let anyone give me that irksome remark*: "We don't have the right people". That's what we used to hear when S.P. Diaghilev was establishing *our* journal, *Mir iskusstva* [World of Art] – yet the journal became a reality, lived and played an exclusive role in the history of contemporary art – *because the right people came forward.* We heard the same words when Prince Sergei Mikhailovich Volkonsky, who's here with us, wished to reform the Russian theater, but they

did not stop him or his colleagues, and now we see the Russian theater at the zenith of public opinion worldwide – *because the right people came forward.* I heard these words just recently when we were dreaming of creating a Russian science of art (there was no such thing until the 1900s), but now we have an entire library and an entire regiment of prominent scholars – *because the right people have come forward* (...) Do not leave the Academy cut off from everything, from life, even from "official" life, for an era will come to pass when, once again, splendors will be created, ones worthy of the most glorious pages of the past – and then our streets, our squares, our temples and our palaces will shine with great beauty (...)

"The Last Futurist Exhibition" (1916)[16]

My friends are insisting that I express my opinion about the "last Futurist exhibition", but, quite frankly, I do not have any real approaches that would let me judge its artistic creativity. I feel that it would be in bad faith just to get off the hook by using words such as "charlatans, affectation, madness", etc. In fact, a lot of people have invested a lot of hard work in this and have spent a lot of time doing it, and without much profit. You just wouldn't turn out such trash for years (trash from our viewpoint) if you weren't convinced of something, although what that conviction consists in, I don't know. Or maybe I'm just not capable of catching the bug: it is absolutely alien to me.

(...) First off – there's no denying that many [of these artists] and many in the exhibition have talent. I am familiar with Tatlin's theatrical designs which charm by their very distinctive colors and extraordinary, if precarious, balance of lines. Maybe this is *just* a juggling trick, but juggling is also an art and requires talent. The other Futurists – and they're almost all the same band – also possess strength and brilliance of color. Moreover, and their deliberate crudeness of device notwithstanding, they *know how* to paint. On a purely technical level their paintings are not only very curious, but also instructive for the specialist. Finally, what their mentors are saying is often very clever and, in essence, is worthy of debate. It's not simply rubbish, but has been thought through and more or less "constructed". Nevertheless, they lack the principal feature of art – they do not "tempt", do not "infect", do not enchant, and, no doubt, that explains the tedium, the oppressive tedium (...)

No, this is certainly not rubbish, it's not just ranting and raving, but is something very serious. It is a sign of the time and what is even more serious is the fact that we are not regarding it seriously. In truth, all of us, all the earth's inhabitants at the moment, are genuine decadents, degenerates just like the Romans who, placing their trust in the foundations of an everyday life that their ancestors had established, "missed" the assault of the Barbarians, their own decomposition, and the appearance of the new and vital force of Christianity. To us it's all peanuts: the most monstrous blasphemy, the vilest mockery of things held sacred – we tolerate it, because we're so used to thinking that we ooze strength, health, and life, whereas [in fact] we are feeble, wracked by diseased and lack the essential force of life. It is precisely because of this absence of the essential force of life that the whole world has grown cold and that intelligent, educated and nice people are falling on each other with gas and cannon – and why the art market speaks of Madonnas, Venuses, Michelangelo's David and nooks and crooks of nature as if they were boots or cabbage pies (...)

Mr. Malevich speaks quite simply about how the conscious habit of seeing depictions in paintings has disappeared. But do you know what that means? Well, it's just like appealing for the disappearance of love, in other words, of the heartfelt principle without which we would all be doomed to freeze to death (...)

(...) Unnumbered, high up in the corner, right next to the ceailing in the holy place hangs a "work" which, undoubtedly, is by this same Malevich – depicting a black square framed in white. No doubt, this is the same "icon" that the Futurists are offering us instead of the Madonnas and shameless Venuses. Quite logically, this is the "domination over the forms of nature" to which not just Futurist art is leading us with its hodge-podge and scrap-heap of "objects", with its crafty, but insensitive and rational experiments, but also the whole of our "new culture" with its media of destruction, with its even more horrifying means of mechanical "restoration", with its cult of the machine and its "americanism" (...)

So of course, the Futurists' exhibition is tedious because the whole of their creativity and all their activity is a total rejection of love, a total affirmation of the cult of emptiness, of gloom, of the "nothing" of the black square in the white frame (...)

"Diary", 1916-18[17]

Wednesday, 16 November (29 November) 1916
(...) We are dining at the Gorchakovs[18] togeth-er with the "young" Felix Yusupov.[19] Extremely upset, he spent the whole evening arguing about Rasputin. He feels that Rasputin is the first to blame for why "everything is going to hell". We were especially struck by his story about one of Rasputin's admirers who always follows the elder around wearing dresses bedecked with little bells on brightly colored ribbons. One day this young weirdo suddenly turned up at a luncheon at Tsarskoe Selo. "Filka" (that's what Gorchakov calls him) is convinced that the situation *can* still be saved if Rasputin can be removed. Akitsa,[20] who was sitting next to Yusupov, ventured to doubt whether such a hero could be found, while I, in a somewhat masked fashion, expressed my usual opinion: it is not the symptoms of the disease that must be cured, but the very source of the disease itself.

Thursday, 17 November (30 November) 1916
In the evening we went to hear *The Golden Cockerel* at the People's House.[21] It was Nabokov who organized this *partie de plaisir*,[22] even finding the tickets for us, although for some reason he himself didn't turn up. The production is terrifyingly vulgar – the Russian "cockerel" kind of taste (not without Bilibin's mastery). This opera (certainly, one of my favorites) requires a completely different approach. I would use the 18th century Russian *lubok* as a foundation.[23] All the music points to this, especially the gallant soldiers' march, so typical, which has nothing in common with the boyars and *streltsy*[24] (...)

Wednesday, 30 November (13 December) 1916
(...) We are doomed because all sections of society, the intelligentsia and the government, are bound together and confused by an absurd "national pride"; and all sections are equally mendacious and incapable of reckoning with the actual situation and the reality of our conditions. Christian Russia has forgotten Christ and has become entangled in some kind of vainglorious "national grudge" (...)

Saturday, 31 December, 1916
(13 January, 1917)
(...) This time we observed New Year's Eve with extraordinary pomp, not without the help of the artists Jakovleff (Sasha Yasha) and Shukhaev (Shukh),[25] our own children and their friends, and S.S. Prokofiev ("Prokoshka") – our pride and joy (...) Especially effective and even frightening was the appearance of the colossal figure of the Old Year in a work or alle-

151

gorical play composed of Sasha Yasha sitting on Shukh's shoulders. Both were draped in sheets and Jakovleff had stuck a white beard to his chin, while the gigantic cardboard palms and soles stuck on hands and feet produced the total illusion that a real giant was standing before us. Furthermore, Prokofiev conducted a brief, but monstrously sounding "symphony", which was executed on copper kitchen saucepans by an orchestra made up of our youngsters. There were also several impromptus (charades not especially distinguished by their wit) and finally (or maybe it was at the beginning) Sasha Yasha, Lelia and Koka[26] came on as instant portrait virtuosi, coproducing caricatures of all present, one after the other. So Kostia Somov – for some reason – was represented in a colonial helmet among the palms and pyramids of Egypt. An abundant supper topped the party (with boiled chicken – and Atechka was quite amazed by Prokoshka's gluttony). With the coming of the New Year all our desires came to one – for peace very soon! Indeed, this is what Akitsa and I desire above all (...)

[Tuesday], 28 February (13 March) 1917
(...) Well, if you like, this is REVOLUTION! Now I'm very anxious, too, and it's an anxiety (which at all costs tries to conceal itself) that manifests itself in a certain disorderliness (...) Just as I write this, I can hear a truck driving past, droning and booming in the clear frosty air, and the shouts of "Hurrah!" Obviously, one of the innumerable detachments of soldiers and workers armed with rifles and bare sabers is again rushing past our house. In most cases, they bowl along at full speed towards the Tuchkov Bridge (...) It's very *comme il faut* for a couple of younger soldiers to lie on the mudguards of the trucks and adopt a take aim pose. Very picturesque like that and looks much more devil-may-care. The people greet each vehicle by taking off their hats and shouting "Hurrah!"(...)

Monday, 6 March (19 March) 1917
(...) Dr. Kulbin suddenly passed away yesterday.[27] Friends want me to write an obituary, but what can I say about this very curious, although essentially rather absurd, personage? As an artist, he is simply without talent, an amateur, a typical innovator "at all costs", something like a "professional innovator". Quite a few of them have sprung up nowadays. In addition, I didn't know him well enough to judge him and his theories adequately (...)

Sunday, 12 March (25 March) 1917
(...) Meierkhold has also joined up with the leftist bosses, going around in his turn-down collars *à l'empereur* (or *à la Danton*), something between a young poet and a Jacobin of 1793.[28] He came down hard on *me* in particular (a vendetta for my malevolent feuilletons). Even though he did not refer to me by name, it was obvious that he had me in mind – as being "power snatcher" No. 1 and it was precisely these "snatchers" against whom he fulminated in his speech, alluding to certain "tributes of loyalty" (evidently, Meierkhold does admit that, even though I produced [the book] *Tsarskoe Selo,* I did *not* present it to the Emperor) and to the fact that someone had been receiving St. Vladimir medals for all kinds of hobnobbing (recently I did receive a St. Vladimir Cross for my contribution to the Red Cross Publishing-House), etc. (...)

April-May 1917[29]
(...) At this time (April-May) the same ladies, led by my Akitsa, were in raptures over Kerensky,[30] regarding him virtually as an angel descended upon earth, i.e. an angel of peace. Our ladies in the kitchen also shared this enthusiasm. I remember how Dunia, Masha, Katia, and the cook herself, Vera Grigorievna, would ask half-jokingly "Who is our saviour?" and their unanimous response would be, "Kerensky!"

25 October (7 November)1917
(...) During the very day of the insurrection I had been going about my business [as usual]. I remember passing by the Winter Palace as I was coming home in the streetcar. It was about three o'clock. It was already getting dark and I could not quite make out whether something was happening on the Square or not. I could sense that some kind of dark mass was moving amidst the mountains of piled up firewood, although I just could not make out what it was exactly. I had no idea that "it was all happening right now" and that we were living the final hours of the "bourgeois régime".

[Thursday, 27 October (9 November) 1917]
(...) Attended the first session of our convocation in the Winter Palace.[31] Lunacharsky gave the welcoming speech and promised that Lenin himself would be coming. He concluded with the words: "Vladimir Ilich [Lenin] aspires to make your acquaintance, Alexander Nikolaevich, and he will be asking you to accept the portfolio of the Ministry of Art"

(which, however, did not yet exist and was not even in the planning stage). Seeing this man who so intrigued us at close range and hearing him talk peeked our interest (especially mine), but his "portfolio proposal" terrified me – literally – and I refused right away. In spite of Lunacharsky's promise, Lenin did not turn up either that day or the next, so he and I never established a personal contact (...)

From the very first day, a certain comrade Ignatev was appointed to our convocation as a kind of "governmental eye", although I have retained only the vaguest memory of him. I feel that he was rather alarmed by such an unexpected appointment and he rather kept himself to himself. Still, I remember that it was with him that I made a comprehensive survey of the Palace, inspecting the whole second floor (what the French call the "premier" and the Italian the "piano nobile"). But we did not go up to the third floor because of lack of time and the gathering darkness. The papers that Kerensky had left to the mercy of fate were already being put in order here, although the department called The Alexander III Chambers proved to be in a really chaotic state: closets and drawers had been broken open, the floor was a thick carpet of papers, many of which were important state documents (...)

Friday, 10 November (23 November) 1917
(...) [Lunacharsky] is *terrified of terror* (just as I was of certain measures that Sergei [Diaghilev] regarded as essential, for example, replacing (1910) Cherepnin's *Fire-Bird* with Stravinsky's!). Still, it is very doubtful that [Lunacharsky] would have the courage or skill to *react* to terror. If the Bolshevik usurpation is what Diaghilev used to call a "symptom", then, in fact, we can predict how it's all going to end. A lot of pomp and fireworks, but maybe it's just theater (after all, fireworks need fire) and hardly anything of permanence will emerge. Surely, it will be sober common sense and the incomparably harsher reality of every day that will triumph – along the lines of what reigned before the insurrection.
Oh, as long as Rembrandt's *Danae*, Van Eyck's *Annunciation*, Poussin's *Polyphemus*, Raphael's *Stanze*, the Chartres Cathedral, etc. don't perish in the imminent turmoil (...)

Sunday, 12 November (25 November) 1917
(...) I experienced a measure of sadness this evening at the [Mariinsky] Theater (...) The auditorium of the Mariinsky Theater, usually a delight to behold, today seemed despondent and sad. The luxurious Imperial boxes are empty. The audience is totally different, not a single old habitué –as if we're not in St. Petersburg, but in a quite different city.

Sunday 7 January (20 January) 1918
(...) In my heart I have never believed that Meierkhold and Golovin would ever let me go near the St. Petersburg stage and that *Petrushka* would ever be performed.[32] If I have created a new production of *Petrushka* and spent three months doing so, then I've done so simply to keep myself busy in this difficult time. Even today I am not loath to continue the design for the Blackamoor's room that I had started (my daughter, Anna, gave me a very subtle and new idea) (...)

Sunday, 14 January (27 January) 1918
(...) I have finished *l'Education Sentimentale.* After half way through volume two I just couldn't put it down. Many thanks to Flaubert! Much could be criticized (the very idea of the book and the way in which it goes forward are often strained), but, in general, it is a wonderful work and for me the "smell of Paris" is especially sweet. But why, in rereading so much, do I now imagine the same places differently than when I first read the novel in the early 1890s? (...)

"An Exhibition of V.V. Kandinsky" (1936)[33]

This very curious exhibition is in a gallery that occupies a villa in the Boulevard Montparnasse, one rather unfamiliar to the general public (No. 9-terre), next to the bus stop on the Rue de Sèvres. The appearance in Paris of an artist who, virtually before anyone else did, discovered a whole new field of "abstract art", could be regarded as a kind of sensation. All of Kandinsky's appearances in Germany, where he gained wide recognition for both his paintings and his graphic works, were also sensations. There's a lot of the latter at this show which, taken altogether, provides a fairly full impression of the artist.
Personally, however, I must confess to not comprehending very much of all this. Moreover, this kind of art gives me an almost agonizing sensation, although perhaps the reason for this is a lack of understanding, an organic defect on my part. In theory and in principle I am quite ready to allow that an art that "doesn't depict anything" or "doesn't signify anything" has a right to exist. This may well be a *genuine* art like, say, "pure" music.

But it is not for me to apprehend and enjoy this kind of art and without the moment of enjoyment (albeit enjoyment of the tragic or of horror) I simply cannot understand or accept this art. So as to feel the special tremor for which "it's worth living" I (like any "materialist") need something comprehensible, if not to my reason, then to my consciousness or subconscience. But I cannot find anything at all "comprehensible" in Kandinsky.

I wouldn't be surprised if, looking into the future, I were to see only this kind of abstracted art. What can hinder art from embarking in that direction? Indeed, the whole of our culture is displacing our [focus of] attention! I would add only that, while the reality of such a shift would not surprise me, it would vex me to the *quick* (...)

Be that as it may, at least the Kandinsky exhibition is a significant phenomenon as is anything created on the basis of a profound belief in a certain truth and with extraordinary endurance. Seeing this is a *must,* at least so as to convince oneself that this is an impasse – or is a *path* that might lead somewhere.

Léon Bakst

"The Paths of Classicism in Art" (1909-1910)[34]

(...) As for the future direction of art, the spring of the 20th century has brought us to a total impasse. Much has thawed under the burning rays; much has been destroyed. The hazy air is balmy, teeming with new creatures and their brilliant, delicate little wings (...)

Let us look at painting of the 19th century not through the dense forest of petty movements which, like branches, are growing from various trunks. Let us try to apprehend the common, broader physiognomy of artistic production in the previous century. We will note that an ancient battle, the irreconcilable discord between the Classicists and Romantics, can be traced throughout the entire 19th century(...)

It would be a grave mistake to limit the strivings of the Classical school of the mid-19th century to the ideals of [Jacques Louis] David. The fundamental flaw in his understanding of the progress of Classical art has long ago been recognized. No longer does anyone pursue the canons of that beauty – the absolutely beautiful leg of Apollo. Only David recognized such a beautiful leg in a painting (...)

I realize that if I pronounce the name of the great [Jean François] Millet in this context, whom it is customary to consider an enemy of

Classicism, I will cause bewilderment insofar as the classification of Millet's work (...) is now firm and definitive, and a new point of view regarding his artistic ideal is unthinkable.

But to begin, let us explore the new ideals of perfect form, which, while changing and almost always evolving from Classical ideals, have been embodied in a vibrant and enagaging form for half of the 19th century (...)

The hollowness and apparent insincerity of David's inspiration was not to Millet's liking. He contrasted the turbulent episodes of the creator of *The Sabines* with the majestic, hardened poses of his shepherds and with the rhythmical bas-relief compositions of his *Gleaners* (...)

The ultimate and most menacing enemy of art in general and of any school of painting in particular is, of course, individualism, which a quarter of a century ago solemnly proclaimed that the very existence of the artist was the key to artistic legitimacy.

For the last twenty-five years that fatal principle of painting has been travelling a course opposite to that of all the great schools. Let me explain: the principle of all the great schools of art – Egyptian, Khaldian, Assyrian, Greek, and the Renaissance – was the need for the artist to approach a certain type or the ideal which was then privy to the imagination (...)

Let us look for other, powerful signs that indicate that we are advancing towards the birth of a new and great art and not toward degeneration.

Let us first turn to Fashion. I write Fashion with a capital letter. It's time we established that a movement which accurately reflects the tastes of the cultured part of humanity and which in all seriousness we call fashion is of profound conceptual importance. Essentially, it is one of our most significant indicators of the oscillations of artistic ideas.

Fashion is queen.

Yes. Wherever there is art, there is fashion.

An artist conceives of a painting and, while still imagining it, paints in one tone or another. Suddenly he stops at delicate light-blue, at that same color which our mothers hated for its "unfashionableness".

For our artist, however, this nuance is the most enchanting, the most unexpected, and the most impressive.

But within a few months, to his astonishment, he meets swarms of fashionable women dressed in outfits of that same shade of light blue which had triumphantly established itself in his imagination and which he, after all, had discovered! (...)

74. Léon Bakst, *Modern Dress*, 1910 Watercolor, 32.5 × 29 cm Private collection.

75. Edward Steichen (1879-1973), Photograph of Two Women Modelling Dresses Designed by Paul Poiret, 1911. Reproduced in *Art et Décoration,* Paris 1911, January-June, No. XXIX, p. 105

77. Anonymous caricature captioned, "Shut up, you stupid, vulgar, disgusting, low blockhead!!! Don't you understand that such torture allows her to put on a dress after Léon Bakst's latest design!!" Reproduced in *Novyi satirikon*, St. Petersburg 1913, No. 5, p. 9

—[Молчите, глупый, грубый, гадкій, низкій, тупица!!! Поймите же, что эта пытка позволяетъ ей надѣть костюмъ по послѣднему рисунку Леона Бакста!!..

76. Photograph of Mme. Germaine Bailac wearing a dress and hat designed by Léon Bakst and made by Jeanne Paquin, 1913. Reproduced in *Comoedia Illustré*, Paris, 1913, 5 June, No. 17, p. 811

What we have noticed in terms of tone, repeats itself in form.

At any moment a favorite array of angles and combinations of lines, which find their expression in the finest paintings, the best architecture, or the decoration of fashionable attire, attests to a genuine transition of artistic thought (...) from an overly popular, ubiquitous combination of form. The artist precedes the couturier, but ahead of him is his predecessor, the innovator (...)

Slowly but surely, our taste, fashion (...) is leading us back to the art of antiquity! (...)

And so, future art is moving towards a new and more simplified form (...)

Let us speak of another source of inspiration of the new painting (...)

What attracts, what fascinates, and I will say further, what moves us in children's drawing?

We can identify three qualities that exist in the art of virtually any child who is not completely lacking in talent: sincerity, movement, and the pure, bright color of paint (...)

The art of the future will return to the cult of the individual, to his nakedness. Artists will seek inspiration in the forms of the naked body and, like the Periclean Greeks, we will return to their view of beauty in nature.

"Nudity on Stage" (1911)[35]

It would be quite incorrect and myopic to identify the reasons for this development [nudity on stage] as being a loss of shame, i.e., as simply salaciousness or pornography.

Quite the contrary, although at first glance this may seem strange! (...)[36]

Generally speaking, new tastes are determined by new movements in art, and more specifical-ly, by those in the theater. "Reacting" against the previous generation of feeble, neurasthenic bureaucrats and office-workers, the contemporary young generation has turned to sport, gymnastics, physical labor and dance, in a word, to the style of movement, just as someone weary of sitting around all the time yearns to run and make his pulse beat faster! (...)

Here we have the "cult of the healthy body full of life and movement" in contrast to the cult of yesterday with its piquant poison of the half-naked body.

Artists, actors, writers and, out in front, young people, all in unison are seeking and advocating this "new course" (even though they may not be aware of this).

If this is pornographic, then, of course, [so are] the ladies and gentlemen showing off their underwear and nighties on stage in our "farces" night after night.

Quite certainly, Isadora Duncan is beautiful and pure and her "barefootedness" is one more testimony to the fact that, with our nakedness, with our bodies, we are aspiring towards a Graecian cult, towards the beautiful, the strong and the pure!

"Dressing the Woman of the Future. (A Conversation)" (1913)[37]

Surely the way people dress has interested other artists, too? Leonardo da Vinci, for example. Although I do not mean to compare myself to him, I do feel that such a thing as a person's everyday dress should be important to those who love art (...)

It follows that a man or woman (...) should be dressed in a manner consistent with the general tonal harmony of their environment.

Shouldn't an artist be obliged to express the ideas of his era in dress? My efforts are devoted precisely to this task.

I arrived at these thoughts while creating drawings for the new ballet *Jeux*.[38] The music for this ballet tries to articulate concepts of the future in sound (the action takes place in 1925).

Seeking to implement my ideas, I offered my art to Mme. Paquin's fashion house and created dresses that would suit the contemporary woman. The results of this endeavor can be seen on exhibit. What are the most characteristic qualities of our century? I asked myself that question before I began designing these dresses and came to the conclusion that the qualities are playfulness, an interest in sport and the beautiful movements associated with this, in a word, "sportiness."

No doubt, you have noticed a remarkable revival in our time – the trend towards physical exercise and every kind of sport. Similarly, my designs are inseparably linked to the modern woman's aspiration towards uninhibited movement.

Primarily, my dresses are intended for women who are strong and healthy in body and spirit (...) I wanted to create a joyful spring on earth. If, in my drawings, one detects elements referring back to Classicism, to the period where the human race was at its most beautiful and the level of culture was at its highest, they are motivated by a desire to express precisely these conditions of human life. In my drawings you will find a simplicity and also a transparency of color that is seeking harmony with the transparent simplicity and invigorating wonder of springtime. At least, this is what I have attempted to express.

(...) I have torn myself from my own past and have turned away from the Persian style. I must confess that I am quite weary of it all. The moment I introduced this style into the Russian ballet, it began to catch on everywhere. Even women have begun to use black powder so as to lend their faces the coloring of the Orient (...)

I have chosen a range of intense, sensual colors to match the intensity of freedom and light. I have opened the window on to the garden to see spring enjoying the healthy celebration of radiant wonder. The artificial scent of distilled roses had overpowered the invigorating scent of the rebirth of nature, of the blossoms and the modest spring flowers. Still, I must say first and foremost that my drawings should not be considered finished or as having completed their entire course of evolution. We live in a time of transition (...)

(...) The general look of the costume remains the same whether one sees it up close or from a distance, an effect that, in my opinion, requires sincerity in art. My costumes for the ballet *Le Dieu Bleu* at Covent Garden can be seen as a transition from the Persian style to an Indian style. The dresses that I have created for Paquin are the "next step along this new path."

From the journalist interviewing Bakst:

Bakst's dresses have individual titles: *Atalanta* is made from black crêpe de chine but in a new Greek style; *Iolanta,* with its original simplicity could harken from the Middle Ages; *Isis* is a beautiful gesture to Egypt; *Aglae* is made from white satin; *Deauville* has a black satin jacket and a skirt of fine silk. But these are merely names. The dresses themselves make a tremendous impression with their strong and stern beauty. They are intended for a healthy nation that loves fresh air.

In Bakst's words, we are approaching a time when there will be little distinction between men's and women's dress. "When exactly that will be," according to the artist, "is still impossible to determine. But the tailleur style is already a step in that direction. Our great grandmothers would faint at the sight of what they would consider unfeminine clothing. The distinctive feature of the new woman – the woman of the future – will be an unusual femininity and grace of movement. Her dress will come close to men's clothing, but there will be a few finer distinctions such as a [special] kind of ribbon, lace, and so on."

Such will be the dress of the woman of the future.

"L. S. Bakst on Contemporary Fashions" (1914)[39]

Parisiennes are born with the understanding that whatever strikes them in the theater will find its vital reflection in fashion. This is the only way I can explain why my productions have had such continued influence on the transformation of women's dress, right up to the colored wigs. The perpetual thirst for novelty compels the Parisienne to search for new elements of dress in the most varied epochs and in the most unexpected sources (...)

Dark blue, green and gold hair find their origin in the ballet *Cléopâtre* and Gabriele D'Annunzio's tragedy *La Pisanella*, both of which were produced last year at the Paris Théâtre du Châtelet with Ida Rubinstein in the lead roles. Ida Rubinstein first wore a colored wig (dark blue) in *Cléopatre*. Eventually, after having travelled the globe and asserting

78. Léon Bakst, *Dioné*.
Design for a dress made
by Jeanne Paquin in the series
Costumes Parisiens, 1913.
Plate from *Journal des Dames
et des Modes*, Paris 1913, vol. 1,
No. 34, 1 May, p. 73. See D3

79. Deni (pseudonym of Viktor
Nikolaevich Denisov 1893-1946),
Woman according to Bakst, 1914.
Reproduced in *Lukomore*
(The Shore), 1914, No. 2, p. 15

its rights to full citizenship, the fashion for colored turbans and Eastern costumes evolved out of the extraordinary success of *Schéhérazade* and what appeared to have been made exclusively for the stage such as the dark, southern make-up which I applied to every actor and actress in *Schéhérazade* infected contemporary Paris. Nowadays Parisiennes stroll around with faces painted in saffron, brown, or yellow even during the daytime (...)

We can still remember the scandals on the streets of Paris, Berlin, London and St. Petersburg when women appeared in *sharovary* pants. In any event, the skirt of the contemporary female dress is close to pantaloons.

If we look carefully, we see one pant leg, in which both legs are covered. The slit continues to creep up, the legs separate and here we have pantaloons. In general, women's dress of today requires a distinction between day and evening wear. By day women incline towards the suffragette, that is, they aspire towards the freedom of movement and simplicity of clothing that men have. But by night, acutely conscious of her rights as ruler of the world, she dresses up. She tries to keep her pantaloons, but they are not the pants of an athlete or businessman, running around the City of London from early morning on, but the wide *sharovary* of the odalisque (...) Colored wigs, decorated arms, exotic make-up and a tendency to wear *sharovary* have already attracted attention at certain high society balls.

"Fashion" (1914)[40]

I have been reading about the "sad sensation" – the "high society ball" at which "women appeared in blue, green, orange and pink hair." Even greater is our sorrow and surprise when we read that "no one had anticipated such a spectacular victory of Futurism within a circle that claims to be an oasis of taste and good form." (...)

Don't people in Russia realize that the colored wig is merely the latest stage in a gradual revolution that for six years has steadily changed the female figure, women's dress, the line and color of the female silhouette and the nature of decoration, creating a style peculiar to the 20th century? (...)

Paradoxically speaking, the elegant woman of today, while following fashion closely and extending it in the lines and colors of her fabrics, hairstyle, jewelry and in her manner of walking and wearing shoes, is the embodiment of prevailing ideas in plastic form (...)

The fight for equal rights for men and women has created daytime styles for women that are strikingly similar to men's clothing. This *tailleur* style of dress is sporty for the woman who strolls about in patent leather shoes just as a man would [because] in such a dress a woman can easily leap onto a tram or an automobile – and with such simplified clothing you don't have to worry about dust getting in everywhere.

Yet evening wear is the apotheosis (...) of everything that is contradictory or alien to men's fashion. It is where the Eternal Feminine reigns over the masculine "principle". Here, in the evening, the range of *bright colors* (by day, modest sandy, gray, brown, and black), the soft, boldly constructed pleat, and the sensual transparency of the trim are raised to a cult-like status. There have been marvelous discoveries regarding the hidden influence of color on our moods and (...) the male psychology. Contemporary evening wear I would compare to war, a decisive battle waged by the "evening" woman with the man, a war in which she retakes the entire arsenal of lines and colors for the inevitable future victory of the daytime emancipated woman (...)

Given the power of the law of complimentary colors, neither face, nor hair can escape the vivid beauty of the pure colors that have spread throughout contemporary women's dress and are intoxicating both sexes from head to toe (...) Naturally, with such a sumptuous array of pure and vivid colors, the woman of today is also obliged to apply color to her face and hair, enabling them to compete with the main colors of the dress.

Today's Parisienne is considered a paragon only if she is supplemented by a final, but magnificent and harmonious touch of color, a fantastic bright flower or a poisonous, beguiling plant. Perhaps this is the next Eve.

The harsh dawn of the first half of the 20th century shows us the new look of our contemporary female friend – the emancipated androgen.

"On the Art of Today" (1914)[41]

There are two dominant movements in art at the moment. One is slavishly retrospective and the other, hostile to the former, is futuristic, with its sights set far ahead (...) The former movement pulls us back to our predecessors, to the art of the deceased, to their illuminated canons, while the latter destroys everything old and builds the foundation for the art of the future that will be judged by our great grandchildren. But where is our own art, where is the new art, where are the contemporary joy and delight in an art that really expresses our life and not that of our grandfathers or our great grandchildren?

When will we break this ruinous habit of disdaining, disregarding, and, above all, of *not noticing* the present moment? (...)

Look at what's going on. We live in buildings built in the last century, with antique furniture upholstered in shabby material, among priceless paintings, now beyellowed or heavy in patina. Through charming stains and rust spots we look into dim and faded mirrors, in which we can hardly make out our contemporary, but shameful figure, dressed in clothing made from ancient pieces of material. Indeed, it would seem that our zealous "passéists" would be eager to trade even perfect English hygiene for what they assure us are the wonderful *chaises percées* which possess so much charm of bygone centuries (...)

But now take a look at another camp, that of the notorious Futurists, who are the enemy of the passéists. Everything is charted on the map according to an anticipated future evaluation. But their disdain for the current moment is identical to that of the passéists (...) .

Who has the courage to admit that both the past and the future are superfluous, that they have little value for contemporary life, and hardly add to the scale of human happiness? (...)

"Serov and I in Greece. Travel Notes" (1923)[42]

We're anchored for four hours outside Canea. It's a sunny morning in spring. Our overcrowded steamer comes up quietly and smoothly. The sway of the ship is barely noticeable; what a blessed feeling of relief – the end of seasickness.

I run along the deck, brushing against the warm resinous ropes, and stare excitedly at the majestic, if unfamiliar, island. How unexpected Greece is! Rows of sandy-red cliffs cut by the dark yellow lines of the fortresses, where, toy-like at a distance, tiny soldiers march in columns. Above is a scattered herd of sandy-gray olive groves and even higher there are more bare cliffs, wild, classical, and dotted like a leopard's skin with uneven dark-brown spots. The silver sky of morning effuses a bold and blinding light, which caresses the sensuous cupolas of the Turkish houses, but beats down painfully on my neck, boots and hands.

Putting my hands in my pockets, I'm amazed to find the erotic photographs which a filthy old Greek had forced upon me on the deck yesterday as we sailed from Pyres. I throw the photographs in the water – pitiful, nocturnal aphrodisiacs – ridiculous in this environment, so bracing and invigorating (...)

The road to the museum is hidden among the sandy-yellow ruins in which the whole of Olympia abounds...The perfidious cool of the marble vestibule seems like paradise to us. But in the halls where parts of a pediment from a temple of Zeus have been set up the windows are wide open (...) Within an hour my neck was aching, because with the pediment placed so high up, my head was always thrown back.

I had a crazy idea.

"Valentin [Serov], we're alone...Let's climb up on to the platform of the pediment. I want terribly to run my hand over the marble, to find out what Niobe's shoulders are like, what her breasts are like. Everyone does that. Rodin "tests himself like that in real life"', is how I justified myself.

Where are we off to now? To the bazaar, of course. There are the cafés and under the dim arcades, you can smell the currants, dried herbs, roots and olive oil.

We head towards a scarcely audible melodic noise.

Coming closer, we hear that it is the polyphonous wail of an Arabian song, accompanied by a tambourine. People are singing in concert outside some of the boui-bouis (Arabian cafés) (...)

Contemporary Athens seems to be a pretentious and provincial little town, a comically monkeyfied Paris, a center for Greek swindlers, cheats, and lovers of cabaret songs, addicted to the boulevard chic of Paris (...)

Schematic bibliographies of Benois and Bakst are included in the List of Works. Abbreviated references in the footnotes below are to this source

[1] Zilbershtein prompted a new Soviet view of Benois by publishing his obituary to Benois (albeit anonymously) under the title "Pamiati Aleksandru Nikolaevichu Benua" in *Iskusstvo*, 1960, No. 5, pp. 70-71. This preceded his publication of the first collection of Benois' essays, coedited with Alexander Savinov, i.e., *Aleksandr Benua razmyshliaet (...)*
[2] Aleksandrova, *Aleksandr Benua: Moi vospominaniia.*
[3] Khabarov, *Aleksandr Benua. Khudozhestvennye pisma 1930 Parizh 1936.*
[4] The Parisian fashion designer, Paul Poiret (1879-1944), included St. Petersburg and Moscow in the European tour that he made with his parade of models in 1912.
[5] The famous Paris fashion house, popular with actresses and celebrities, was owned by Jeanne Paquin. Mme. Paquin accepted a number of dress designs from Bakst in late 1912 and realized them in March 1913.
[6] A. Benois, *Russkaia shkola zhivopisi,* Golike and Vilborg, St. Petersburg 1904, p. 86.

[7] A reference to the didactic painting of the Russian Realists such as Ilia Repin, many of whom were members of the Society of Travelling Exhibitions (*peredvizhniki*) in the 1870s-90s.

[8] A. Benois, "Khudozhestvennye eresi" in *Zolotoe runo,* Moscow 1906, No. 2, 80-88.

[9] A. Benois, "Uchastie khudozhnikov v teatre" in *Rech,* St. Petersburg 1909, 25 February, p. 3.

[10] A reference to the Opera Company that the railroad tycoon, Savva Ivanovich Mamontov (1841-1918), founded in 1885, The Company attracted many important singers and artists such as Fedor Chaliapin, Konstantin Korovin and Mikhail Vrubel.

[11] Sergei Mikhailovich Volkonsky (1860-1937) was director of the Imperial Theaters in 1899-1901; Vladimir Arkadievich Teliakovsky (1861-1924) in 1901-17. The latter played a major role in charging Alexander Yakovlevich Golovin (1863-1930) with important design commissions for the Alexandrinsky and Mariinsky Theaters.

[12] Konstantin Sergeevich Stanislavsky (1863-1938) invited Benois to work for the Moscow Art Theater in 1909 shortly after the appearance of "Artists and Their Participation in the Theater". Benois' first designs there were for a cycle of Molière plays produced in 1912-13.

[13] A. Benois, "Zadachi grafiki" in *Iskusstvo i pechatnoe delo,* Kiev 1910, No. 2-3, pp. 41-48.

[14] Konstantin Andreevich Somov (1869-1939), Evgenii Evgenievich Lancéray (1875-1946), Ivan Yakovlevich Bilibin (1876-1942), Stepan Petrovich Yaremich (1869-1939), Viktor Dmitrievich Zamirailo (1868-1939) and Mstislav Valerianovich Dobujinsky (1875-1957) were all members of the World of Art.

[15] A. Benois, "Chem mogla-by byt Akademiia khudozhestv v nastoiashchee vremia" in I. Repin et al., *Trudy Vserossiiskogo sezda khudozhnikov,* Golike and Vilborg, Petrograd, 1914, Vol. 3, pp. 92-98. Benois gave this as a lecture to the All-Russian Congress of Artists, St. Petersburg on 3 January, 1912.

[16] A. Benois, "Posledniaia futuristicheskaia vystavka" in *Rech,* 1916, 9 January, p. 3. Benois was reviewing the exhibition, "O. 10. The Last Futurist Exhibition" held between 19 December, 1915 and 19 January, 1916 at the Dobychina Bureau, Petrograd. Kazimir Malevich, Vladimir Tatlin, and many other radical artists contributed works, including Malevich's *Black Square.*

[17] These extracts are from the "Diary" that Benois kept between Wednesday, 14 September (27 September), 1916, and Tuesday, 23 January (5 February), 1918. The manuscript of the "Diary", entitled *Dnevnik 1916-1918* [Diary 1916-1918], was donated to the Institute of Modern Russian Culture, Los Angeles, by Benois' elder daughter, Anna Alexandrovna Benois-Tcherkessoff (1895-1984). Editorial impositions are contained within brackets and omissions are indicated by ellipses. We would like to thank Lia Barshchevsky for helping us decipher Benois' difficult calligraphy.

[18] Princess Natalia Pavlovna Gorchakova (née Kharitonenko) (see Cat. 66) and her husband Prince Mikhail Konstantinovich Gorchakov were ardent collectors of painting, and their St. Petersburg house contained superb examples of Canaletto, Borovikovsky, Rokotov, etc.

[19] The wealthy playboy Prince Felix Felixovich Yusupov (Sumarokov-Elston,1887-1967) is now remembered for his primary role in the murder of the priest Grigorii Efimovich Rasputin (1872-1916). See the first volume of Yusupov's memoirs, i.e. F. Youssoupoff, *Avant l'Exil 1887-1919,* Plon, Paris 1952. His wife, Irina Alexandrovna (1895-1970), was the niece of Nicholas II.

[20] "Akitsa" or "Atia/Atechka" was Benois' term of endearment for his wife, (Anna Karlovna, née Kind, 1869-1952), also an artist.

[21] Benois published a review of the production, i.e., "O 'Zolotom petushke' N.A. Rimskogo-Korsakova v Narodnom dome" in the Petrograd newspaper *Rech* for 25 November, 1916.

[22] Vladimir Dmitrievich Nabokov (1869-1922) was editor of the newspaper, *Rech,* to which Benois was a regular contributor of art reviews.

[23] The *lubok* was a cheap, handcolored print, often with a satirical and jocular narrative.

[24] The *streltsy* were members of the special military corps founded by Ivan the Terrible.

[25] The artists Alexandre Evgenievich Jacovleff (1887-1938) and Vasilii Ivanovich Shukhaev (1887-1973) were both members of the World of Art society.

[26] Lelia, i.e., Elena (1898-1972), was Benois' younger daughter, Anna (1895-1984) being the elder; Koka (Nikolai 1901-88) was his son.

[27] Nikolai Ivanovich Kulbin (1868-1917), the "Doctor of Russian Futurism", was a radical artist of eclectic disposition. See Cat. 10.

[28] Benois and the theater director, Vsevolod Emilievich Meierkhold (1874-1940), were both members of the Commission for the Preservation of Artistic Values that Maxim Gorky established in March, 1917. Very different in their esthetic and ideological attitudes, Benois and Meierkhold were at constant loggerheads. See, for example, Meierkhold's remarks on Benois in his article, "Benois-rezhisser" in *Liubov k trem apelsinam,* Petrograd, 1915, No. 1-3, pp. 95-126. Benois made a sketch which he captioned "Meierkhold insulting me at the meeting on 12 March, 1917, in the Mikhailov Theater" (reproduced in Etkind, *A.N. Benua,* p. 285). With the uncertain fate awaiting Russia's palaces and antiquities during this time of war and civic unrest, the Commission discussed issues of preservation, inventorization, and the project for a Ministry of Fine Arts. For further information on the Commission (the session for 12 March took place in the Mikhailov Theater) see Etkind, *ibid.,* pp. 281-86.

[29] Shortly before this point, as Benois himself writes (p. 179), the text ceases to be a diary kept day by day and becomes more of a historical reconstruction based on later memories rather than on contemporary notes. The actual "Diary" then returns several pages later.

[30] Alexander Fedorovich Kerensky (1881-1970) was the leader of the Provisional Government.

[31] The People's Commissariat of Enlightenment, headed by Anatolii Vasilievich Lunacharsky (1875-1933), invited Benois to assume various positions in this apparatus. Lunacharsky mandated Benois' directorship of the Painting Gallery at the Hermitage in November, 1918.

[32] Meierkhold and his leading designer in the late 1910s, i.e., Golovin, dominated the St. Petersburg stage, forming an alliance that many resented. Benois started to make designs for a new *Petrushka* in 1917, although the production (by Leonid Leontiev) took place at the Mariinsky only in 1920.

[33] A. Benois; "Vystavka V.V. Kandinskogo" in *Poslednie novosti,* Paris 1936, 13 December. Reprinted in Khabarov, *Aleksandr Benua,* p. 373.

[34] L. Bakst, "Puti klassitsizma v iskusstve,"*Apollon,* St. Petersburg, 1909-10, No. 2, pp. 63-77; No. 3, 46-61.

[35] L. Bakst, [Untitled statement] in N. Evreinov, ed., *Nagota na stsene,* Morskoe ministerstvo, St. Petersburg 1911, pp. 10-11.

[36] The ellipses in this section repeat those in the original text.

[37] L. Bakst, "Kostium zhenshchiny budushchego

(Beseda)" in *Birzhevye vedomost i vedomosti* (Evening edition), St. Petersburg 1913, 23 March, No. 13463, p. 5.

[38] *Jeux* was produced by Sergei Diaghilev in Paris in 1913 with music by Debussy and designs by Bakst. The story of a flirtation between two girls and a young man during a game of tennis, *Jeux* was a gesture to the "new young things" of the mechanical, urban age and was set in the year 1925. For *Jeux* Bakst designed simple undecorated sports clothes that, in some ways, anticipated the *prozodezhda* [industrial clothing] of the Soviet Constructivists.

[39] (M. Ch.), "L. S. Bakst o sovremennykh modakh" in *Utro Rossii,* Moscow, 1914, 9 February, No. 33, p. 6.

[40] L. Bakst, "Moda" in *Peterburgskaia gazeta*, St. Petersburg 1914, 20 Feburary 20, No. 49, p. 3.

[41] L. Bakst, "Ob iskusstve segodniashnego dnia" in *Stolitsa i usadba,* St. Petersburg 1914, No. 8, pp. 18-19.

[42] L. Bakst, *Serov i ya v Gretsii. Dorozhnye zapisi*, Slovo, Berlin 1923, pp. 9, 25, 26, 33, 34 See. D4. Bakst and Serov travelled in Greece in May, 1907.